THE COVENANT OF GRACE IN PURITAN THOUGHT

ℛ

American Academy of Religion
Studies in Religion

Editors
Charley Hardwick
James O. Duke

Number 45
THE COVENANT OF GRACE
IN PURITAN THOUGHT
by
John von Rohr

THE COVENANT OF GRACE
IN PURITAN THOUGHT

by

John von Rohr

Scholars Press
Atlanta, Georgia

THE COVENANT OF GRACE IN PURITAN THOUGHT

by

John von Rohr

©1986
The American Academy of Religion

Von Rohr, John.
  The covenant of grace in Puritan thought.

  (AAR studies in religion ; 45)
  1. Covenants (Theology) -- History of doctrines.
2. Puritans. I. Title. II. Series: Studies in religion (American
Academy of Religion) ; 45.
BT155.V56   1986   231.7'6   86-13935
ISBN 1-55540-037-X (alk. paper)
ISBN 1-55540-038-8 (pbk. : alk. paper)

Printed in the United States of America
on acid-free paper

To
Harland E. Hogue
and
Douglas G. Adams

colleagues in teaching
and
fellow students of the Puritan way

TABLE OF CONTENTS

PREFACE

This study of covenant theology focuses on the views of Puritan divines in the period dated approximately 1585 to 1660. These years witnessed the emergence and blossoming in England of Puritan covenant thought, as well as its transplantation to the American scene and early expression there. Major attention is accorded to the English writers, inasmuch as their work was prolific and spanned the entire era under consideration, though the emigration of several to New England in the 1630s produced an important first generation of American divines whose contributions to this pattern of thinking are likewise included.

Three further words of preliminary explanation might also be added: (1) Although "covenant theology" or "federal theology" became a predominant mode of theological interpretation among Puritans during these seventy five years, use of the covenant idea was stronger among some than among others. Focus in this study has therefore been primarily on the former. (2) The study has sought to examine not only the idea of covenant as such, but also the broader theological content incorporated into the covenant understanding. Thus it is in fact an examination of major themes in Puritan theology seen, however, through the lens of the "covenant of grace." And (3) in so presenting Puritan ideas, it seeks to identify and portray the general mainstream Puritan point of view as related to these matters. Though occasionally variations within this broad based Puritan outlook are examined, the chief task is to describe its common features. Comparison is frequently made, however, between these views of the main body of Puritan divines and those of others at each of the outer edges of the Puritan movement, the Arminians on the left and the Antinomians on the right.

I wish to thank Pacific School of Religion for sabbatical freedom that on more than one occasion, before my retirement, made possible study at the British Museum and the Dr. Williams's Library in London, as well as writing time in other places. I also wish to thank my wife, Helen, for patience over a long period that has surely been an expression, if not actually a covenant, of grace.

Chapter 1
COVENANT THEOLOGY IN PURITANISM

Puritan thought in the last years of the sixteenth century and the early half of the seventeenth, first in England and then in New England, utilized increasingly the concept of "covenant" as a means of comprehending the human relationship with God. Although this idea, with its characteristic stress upon the bonding of parties in shared commitment, was likewise employed in some church and political circles for the structuring of social relationships, its broader usage appeared in the theological realm. God's dealing with humanity, so it was affirmed, is by way of covenant.

For Puritan divines to make this observation was not, however, to introduce something novel. Biblical thought itself had utilized the covenant theme in both the Old and New Testaments. And though the idea largely disappeared from active usage in the long succeeding period extending through the Middle Ages, it experienced significant revival in the early sixteenth century, especially in the Swiss-German Reformed outlook at the beginning of Protestant history. So Puritan theologians drew upon both an ancient and a much more recent past in developing their covenant theology.

They also drew, however, upon matters deep within the emerging nature of Puritanism itself for the larger elaboration and employment of covenant thought. Theologically Puritanism faced essentially in two directions. On the one hand, as heir of the implicit, if not always explicit, voluntarism inherent in Protestantism's call for faith and obedience as the believer's response to God's proclaimed Word, it affirmed boldly the role of human responsibility and the element of contingency in the divine-human relationship. And on the other hand, as heir of early Protestantism's somewhat more fully explicit emphasis upon God's sovereignty in relation to human affairs, it saw ultimate human destiny as divinely and unconditionally determined by God's eternal decree. This tension, of course, had been present intermittently throughout the long stretch of Christian history and indeed had been prefigured in the biblical record itself. But in the Puritanism of the sixteenth and seventeenth centuries it came somewhat more pronouncedly and self-consciously to the fore. Puritan divines resolutely affirmed this duality of understanding. And it will be a thesis of this study that their theological employment of the covenant theme, especially in its central figure, the covenant of grace, became a means of drawing together into fruitful and structured interrelationship these conflicting perspectives on the way of salvation. Nor was that employment simply for theological purpose. The covenant, in combining divine decree and human decision, also served pastoral purpose, and thus it will likewise be affirmed that the often anguished Puritan search for personal assurance of salvation found substantial assuagement in covenant certainty.

The Puritan Paradox

Standing firmly in the continental Reformed tradition, Puritan thinkers spoke unhesitatingly of God's sovereignty, the eternal decrees, and divine predestination. In their study of the movement's early representatives, especially Huldreich Zwingli, Heinrich Bullinger, Martin Bucer, and John Calvin, and then on through their reading of its later interpreters, Theodore Beza, Peter Martyr Vermigli, Franciscus Junius, Jerome Zanchius, Caspar Olevianus, Zacharius Ursinus, and others, they found these themes to have assumed large, and even commanding, importance. Though the source of all religious knowledge was the biblical revelation, the Bible itself was tenaciously viewed as disclosing these doctrines and sustaining these convictions. So a common thread in Reformed thought was that of God's sovereign control of human life and history and thus God's eternal election for all time and eternity. God's wisdom and power are supreme, and therefore not only the progress of events, but also the ultimate disposition of destinies, is unqualifiedly in God's hands. Various means may be employed to accomplish these ends, but they are still ends planned, decreed, and executed by God.

Somewhat differing emphases, it is true, prevailed within this Reformed tradition, and variations in tone were known. One point of differentiation concerned the extent to which reprobation itself, along with election to eternal life, was affirmed to be a consequence of God's predestining selection and act. Earlier expressions tended in general to be more restrained on this matter and later expressions more explicit. Bullinger, for example, advanced a "single predestination" position, God's election of some to salvation, avoiding identification of rejection with God's sovereign choice, an emphasis likewise found, at least implicitly, in some of the early Reformed confessions.[1] With the passage of time, however, a doctrine specifically enunciating "double predestination" came to the fore. In it God's predestining act is identified as ultimate cause of both election and reprobation. On the whole it was this latter view that became dominant in sixteenth and seventeenth century Reformed theology.[2]

---

[1]Wallace, "Doctrine of Predestination," p. 211, n. 54.

[2]In Lutheran thought, on the contrary, the opposite prevailed. The Formula of Concord, 1576, expressly rejected in Article XI the idea of predestination as the cause of reprobation, attributing this entirely to human sin, and defined predestination itself as solely election to eternal life. See Schaff, *Creeds of Christendom*, 3:168–69.

Yet even within this prevailing pattern a further significant difference emerged, probably more important for the basic tone of predestinarian thought than the distinction between a predestination single or double. It had to do with the place of the doctrine of predestination itself within the larger whole of a theological system, and the nature of the difference may especially be seen by contrasting the thought of Calvin on this matter with that of those of his followers who over the succeeding decades developed a "Calvinist" scholasticism.

Although Calvin affirmed a doctrine of double predestination in the final edition of the *Institutes*, he nevertheless was reluctant to develop a theological system based on the decrees. Rather, his handling of the doctrine placed it within the framework of his discussion of justification, stressing it as ground for assurance that God's saving grace is truly sovereign and cannot ultimately be resisted by human will and sin. Such election, moreover, is in Christ, not simply in abstraction, and Calvin's whole theology was thus firmly tied to the Gospel proclamation, with its promises of mercy and its requirements for faith and obedience. For Calvin, therefore, the doctrine of predestination existed within a soteriological context, rather than a metaphysically speculative one; it was seen in connection with God's work of salvation. From the practical point of view this meant for Calvin avoidance of speculative probing of God's decree concerning one's destiny, for if anyone, he wrote, "breaks into this place, he will not succeed in satisfying his curiosity and will enter a labyrinth from which he can find no exit."[3] Rather, he added, "If we seek God's fatherly mercy and kindly heart, we should turn our eyes to Christ, on whom alone God's Spirit rests. . . . Christ, then, is the mirror wherein we must, and without self-deception may, contemplate our own election."[4] Thus even within a doctrine of double predestination Calvin spoke a language more reminiscent of that of his moderate predecessors than anticipatory of developments soon to come. It was only later that the major change in the Reformed doctrine of predestination took place. This occurred in the late sixteenth and early seventeenth centuries when, as Dewey D. Wallace notes, "predestination was increasingly divorced from its original soteriological moorings in Reformed theology and made the organizing principle in scholastic theological systems built around the divine decrees."[5]

Hence Calvin himself was not a good "Calvinist," if the term be used to refer to that subsequent development in Reformed scholasticism that came also to bear his name. A truer representative of this Calvinism, for example, would be Zanchius of Heidelberg who along with Calvin was well studied by Puritan divines. Before his conversion to Protestant faith Zanchius had

[3]Calvin, *Institutes*, 2:922–23.
[4]Ibid., 2:970.
[5]Wallace, "Doctrine of Predestination," p. 215.

developed scholastic theological interest under the influence of Thomism and the further Aristotelianism of the Italian school at Padua. This led, in his Reformed writing, to the presentation of a metaphysical system, the beginning point of which is the development of God's own being and the elaboration of which portrays God as both efficient and final cause of all events. Then predestination itself becomes an essential part of this divine activity and is placed with due logicality within the doctrine of God. The result is clearly a more speculative doctrine than that of Calvin, and one that also lacks his Christological emphasis. This is likewise seen in the treating of the order of the decrees, a matter on which Calvin did not speculate, for Zanchius affirmed explicitly a supralapsarianism, maintaining God's particular election of some to salvation and others to damnation as occurring not in consequence of the race's sinfulness, an infralapsarian view, but prior to the fall itself. In enunciating this pattern of thought Zanchius was probably the most thoroughgoing and influential of the Reformed scholastics. But he was also joined by many others in the exposition of this type of system in which double predestination became the centerpiece and indeed the organizing principle.

The explication of such predestinarian views was sharpened by the early seventeenth century controversy in Holland with Jacob Arminius and his followers. Arminianism had likewise spoken of God's decrees, though in such manner as to include at a critical point the conditional element, the element of human responsibility. Four decrees were identified in Arminius' *Declaration of Sentiments* of 1608. First there is the decree of God to appoint Christ as Savior who would by his obedience obtain the salvation that had been lost and then become the agent of its communication. Here, as in Calvin, is a Christological starting point for an understanding of salvation and of predestination. The second decree extends this salvation more explicitly to those who repent and believe in Christ and who persevere in that faith. The third decree is for God's provision of sufficient grace to all so that they might believe. Finally the fourth decree turns to the election of particular individuals and appoints the salvation of those whom God foreknew to believe and persevere, and the reprobation of those foreseen as falling away.

The critical matter here is the basing of predestination upon foreknowledge, and therein lies the vast difference between the Arminian viewpoint and all forms of Calvinism. Although God predestines, and likewise gives grace sufficient for the achieving of faith, the final ground for Arminius was still the human choice. Some avail themselves of the grace and some do not, and God's eternal predestination rests upon a foreseeing of those human acts. Such a challenge to divine sovereignty was unacceptable to the majority of Reformed theologians, and at the Synod of Dort in 1619 Calvinism prevailed, with unconditional predestination being therefore declared a central dogma of Reformed faith. So here is one part of the Puritan theological heritage. Although the mode of interpretation was not uniform, Arminianism was emphatically rejected and God's unconditional predestination steadfastly affirmed.

Puritan thought was also significantly shaped by a second characteristic and heritage. This was the emphasis upon personal religion and individual participation generated by the Protestant Reformation, as it reintensified the biblical Gospel's call for vital faith and active obedience. Although the Middle Ages had not been a complete stranger to the idea of justification by faith, the new religious movement of the sixteenth century lifted the tenet to a point of central importance with implications not only for theology but also for the personal participation of believers. And although the Middle Ages had been even less a stranger to the idea of good works, Protestantism from its beginning both deepened and broadened the understanding of their nature through its stress upon the inwardly sanctified and outwardly active life. Then in the interweaving of the two, Luther's "by faith alone" and Calvin's "covenant law," one finds finds joined together the elements that were to emerge in fuller integration in subsequent Protestant expressions, not the least of which was English and American Puritanism.

Exploring this matter, one can note that the Puritan movement, contrary to its classic stereotype as simply a rigid dogmatism or an oppressive legalism, is more and more being seen as embodying a "profound experientialism"[6] and indeed as an early expression of what later came to be designated "pietism." In the nineteenth century Heinrich Heppe wrote about "the puritan pietism of England" and, with the later continental movement in mind, even named early Puritan theologian William Perkins the "father of pietism."[7] Similarly, in more recent discussion of this matter, F. Ernest Stoeffler has affirmed that "essential differences between continental Pietism and what we have called Pietistic Puritanism cannot be established because they are non-existent," adding further that "the pressure toward a certain pattern of piety within the Calvinist tradition (regarded broadly), whether in England, the Low Countries, the Rhineland, or elsewhere was basically the same."[8] Other modern scholars, likewise seeing this trend in the Puritan movement, have identified it as an "evangelical Calvinism."[9]

[6]Stoever, 'A Faire and Easie Way', p. 18.

[7]Heppe, Geschichte des Pietismus, p. 24.

[8]Stoeffler, Rise of Evangelical Pietism, p. 29. In the light of this broad Calvinist pattern, essentially the early sixteenth century Reformed tradition, Stoeffler questions Leonard Trinterud's finding a major source for English Puritan piety in a specifically English medieval mysticism, writing that this mystical piety was not limited to England and that "when the pietistic Puritans quoted older books of devotion they usually referred to continental authors" (Ibid., p. 30). For the latter's view see Trinterud, "Origins of Puritanism," p. 50.

[9]Eusden, "Introduction" to Ames, Marrow, p. 19. See also Hall, "Understanding the Puritans," p. 34.

This Puritan piety urged a good deal of human effort and participation in the pursuit of the evangelical goals. William Haller has described the Puritan path as involving "wayfaring and warfaring,"[10] and these characterizations reflect both the pilgrimage and the battle in which the soul must be engaged. The task of guiding such struggles was largely in the hands of the preachers, those "physicians of the soul" whose diagnoses and prescriptions were constantly relied upon in the search for spiritual health. As Haller put it, Puritan sermons "were chiefly concerned with charting in infinite detail and tireless reiteration the course of the godly soul out of hardness and indifference to the consciousness of its lost condition, and so out of despair and repentance to faith in God, to active perseverance and confident expectations of victory and glory."[11]

Although the Christian story was presented in full splendor as the cosmic drama of salvation, each Christian was called upon to participate in a personal "pilgrim's progress" toward appropriation of that triumph. The saga must be made one's own—and to that end the battle must be joined and the forces of evil overcome through faith and obedience. Urging the importance of the spiritual struggle, Perkins wrote, "As the beggar is alwaies mending and peecing his garment, where he finds a breech: so the penitent and beleeving heart must alwaies be exercised in repairing it selfe where it finds a want."[12] Perkins' successor, Paul Baynes, expressed it in these terms:

> No Christian must stand in the state he is in, without laboring to further perfection. . . . The life of the Christian is the running of race, not a sitting or standing still. . . . Men in the world may come to such confirmed estates, that they may give over trading, and live commodiously on things already gotten; but it is not thus with the soule, which, where it ceaseth to profit, waxeth worse.[13]

In its inward dimension this struggle was primarily for such faith as could lay hold of and receive God's promises of grace. The Gospel proclamation of forgiveness of sin and the gift of new life was ever central for these Puritan divines, and its communication by voice and pen laid heavy claim for a receptive trust on the part of those who would seek to know its benefits. Dogmatic treatises, as well as published sermons, reflected this mood, and the persistent evangelical appeal was for the forsaking of reliance on the self's efforts toward righteousness in favor of a "pitching" of the self upon Christ and his reconciling righteousness before God. Without diminution or cessation the urgency of this act was stressed. The Christian believer must

---

[10]Haller, *Rise of Puritanism*, p. 142.
[11]Ibid., p. 141.
[12]Perkins, "Estate of Damnation," *Works*, 1:419.
[13]Baynes, *Commentarie upon Colossians*, 2:202.

indeed believe—and belief in this context was most centrally the casting of oneself in faith upon God's infinite mercy.

Of no less urgency for the Christian believer was the struggle in its somewhat more outward dimension, the struggle for that "godliness" which represented the ethical fruits of evangelical faith and experience. Affirming the immense scope of such moral obligation, Perkins wrote:

> The outward token of adoption is New-obedience, whereby a man indeavours to obey God's commandments in his life and conversation. . . . First of al, it must not be done unto some few of God's commandments, but unto them all without exception. . . . Secondly, this obedience must extend itselfe to the whole course of a man's life after his conversion and repentance. . . . Thirdly, in outward obedience is required that it proceed from the whole man, as the regeneration which is the cause of it, is through the whole man in body, soule and spirit.[14]

Samuel Bolton put it succinctly by saying, "It is no infringement to our Libertie in Christ to be tyed to the performance of dutie. . . . Christ redeemed us from sinne, but to service."[15] And John Downame, in a treatise entitled *Guide to Godlynesse*, urged emphatically, while offering practical instruction for Christian living, that the believer "must not be lazie and luskish, idle and slothfull; but exceeding industrious, painfull, and diligent."[16] So there are duties to be accepted, strictures to be observed, disciplines to be undertaken. John Preston noted that forgiveness of sin does not "open a doore of libertie to make men more loose."[17] Rather, he said, "a man lives by keeping the Commandements of God, that is, this spiritual life, this life of grace, it is maintained by doing the Commandements."[18] Thus throughout the Puritan literature, from its earliest to its latest, concern abounded for dedicated and disciplined Christian behavior. The Christian believer is called to assume personal responsibility and to participate in the process leading to salvation.

If Puritan emphasis upon God's unconditional predestination was protested by Arminians, its stress upon the necessity of human involvement in the saving process was equally protested by those identified with the outlook of Antinomianism. Under the leadership of such men as John Saltmarsh, Tobias Crisp, and John Eaton, especially toward the middle of the seventeenth century, this movement came to emphasize primarily the role of God's overwhelming grace and the working of the divine Spirit in life's transformation from the old to the new. Salvation is entirely by God's act, and

---

[14]Perkins, "Exposition of the Creed," *Works*, 1:286.

[15]S. Bolton, *True Bounds of Christian Freedome*, p. 196.

[16]J. Downame, *Guide to Godlynesse*, p. 23.

[17]Preston, *New Covenant*, 1:115.

[18]Preston, *Sermons: New Life*, p. 53. Quoted in Kevan, *Grace of Law*, p. 61.

thus there is no place for human effort, or even for human participation. The Law and its demands have no proper part in all of this, either before or after the coming of God's captivating Spirit; even faith itself is solely a divine creation. Renewed by grace, the Christian is lifted above the sordidness of struggle with evil and indeed at times can further be transported into the sublime experience of ecstacy. But, facing this contention, Puritans continued to affirm that further part of their Reformation heritage. Although it is grace that saves, that grace must be received by one's faith and responded to by one's faithfulness. The Christian, as a human person and not a "block or stock," is called upon to act responsibly in trust and obedience.

Thus Puritan thought faced in two directions in response to the claims of predestination and of piety, the conjunction of the two providing Puritanism with its central paradox. Although it might appear that these differences were essentially between declarations of doctrine and proddings from the pulpit, they are not to be identified simply as tensions between the theologian and the preacher. Theologians were preachers, and preachers were theologians. Preaching, moreover, often urged one's confidence in predestination as a ground for assurance,[19] and theology fully included the practical concerns crucial to the life of godliness.[20] Both were part of Puritan exhortation as well as belief. Indeed, even carrying in combination both emphases to the extreme was once at least half seriously recommended when, from a pastoral perspective, Thomas Blake declared, "Ministers should perswade, and people improve endeavours as though they were Pelagians, and no help of grace afforded. They should pray and beleeve, and rest on grace as though they were Antinomians, nothing of endeavour to be looked after." Then, he said, all will come out in neat balance, as "the injury that the Pelagian doth to grace, and the Antinomian to our endeavours, will be on both hands avoided."[21] One must go beneath this level, however, to explore the more profound character of the differences posed by predestination and piety. In the deeper sense they constitute divergences within Puritan theology itself. Confronting one another in Puritanism's central paradox, these emphases represent differing theological perspectives on the nature of God's working and thus also on the manner of the relationship between the human and the divine.

The basic antinomy is that of divine sovereignty and human freedom. If predestination affirms the ultimacy and final efficiency of God's choice, piety urges at least some effective free participation on the part of the human subject. Richard Sibbes wrote, "Though God's grace do all, yet we must give

[19]Dewey D. Wallace writes, "The centrality of preaching the gospel included the preaching of the doctrine of predestination, a teaching that was important in establishing that salvation was entirely the gift of God's grace" (Wallace, *Puritans and Predestination*, p. 44).
[20]William Ames defined theology itself as "the doctrine of living to God" (Ames, *Marrow*, p. 1).
[21]Blake, *Vindiciae Foederis*, p. 115.

our consent."[22] And, somewhat more formally stated, Robert Jenison declared, "The certainty of Gods decree doth not abolish the consent of mans will. . . . Mans actions may bee free, though otherwise in respect of Gods will they be of unchangeable necessity."[23] Such statements presented the matter with all directness and exposed for Puritan reflection this issue which, indeed, had long standing in the history of Christian thought. Yet such a central antinomy also took other forms in its application to the Christian message, or at least further types of theological tension came to light in the attendant discussion. If there is unconditional election, it is of particular persons, but the principle of free consent urges the Gospel be given to all. If only some are chosen, then Christ's atonement is limited, but if the offer is unlimited, then Christ's saving work must have universal application. If salvation is by sovereign election, then God's grace is irresistible, but does not human freedom necessitate a grace that can be rejected? If God saves only those secretly elected but sends Christ and creates the church for public proclamation of the Gospel promises, does not this suggest two wills in God, one hidden and one revealed? Still more, if God's revealed will is ultimately subordinate to that which is secret, does this not make decree more important than event and cause the acts of eternity to invalidate any real meaning for history? And, indeed, might not such a duality of wills point in the last analysis even to an ultimate irreconcilability of God's majesty and God's mercy?

THE ROLE OF COVENANT THEOLOGY

It is in the face of these questions and conflicting factors that covenant theology took hold and flourished in the Puritanism of England and America in the last years of the sixteenth century and the first half of the seventeenth. As earlier noted, covenant thought was not created by Puritan theologians as a novel construct to deal with these issues. It had its own antecedents, both biblical and more recent, and already as it touched the Puritan movement possessed a developed sixteenth century history.[24] But it was readily appropriated by Puritan theologians and then refined more fully for their own particular purposes, for basically it provided a pattern of thinking in which the concerns of predestination and piety could be advanced and at the same time the conflicts they created be in some measure contained. It commended itself as a tool for drawing together the doctrinal and the experiential, as well as an instrument for structuring more clearly the doctrinal questions themselves. And especially in its central concept, the covenant of grace, it served as a comprehensive connective bringing into

[22]Sibbes, "Faithful Covenanter," *Works*, 6:8.
[23]Jenison, *Concerning Gods Certaine Performance*, p. 58.
[24]See the Appendix for a brief sketch of covenant theology's continental beginnings.

interrelationship the dualities, and even antinomies, which followed Puritan stress upon both the evangel and election.[25]

The covenantal story in Puritan thought begins, however, with a failed covenant, the covenant of works. God's initial design for human life promised the granting of reward for human righteousness. But sin destroyed that covenantal relationship—and the covenant of grace, though actually planned in eternity in a covenant of redemption, constituted God's response to the historical event of the fall. It was an act of God's mercy in repair of human misery. When sin entered the world at history's beginning, it did so with such power that only God could redeem and renew. But this indeed God has covenanted to accomplish. Through Christ, God has undertaken to forgive and through the Spirit to refresh, thus dealing with sin to remove both its guilt and its grasp. Here, then, is the covenant of grace, where divine intention of saving mercy is both declared and revealed as bound by a promise. Thomas Shepard elucidated this matter by writing,

> The Covenant is the midst between both God's purposes and performances. . . . For in God's Covenant we see with open face God's secret purposes for times past—God's purpose toward His people being, as it were, nothing else but promises concealed, and God's promises in the Covenant being nothing else but His purposes revealed. As also, in the same Covenant and promises we see performances for the future, as if they were acomplishments at present. Where then is a Christian's comfort but in that Covenant, wherein two eternities (as it were) meet together, and whereby he may see accomplishments (made sure to him) of eternal glory, arising from blessed purposes of eternal grace?[26]

Thomas Goodwin waxed even more ecstatic as he noted particularly the covenant's comprehensiveness, for, he said, it "contains the whole design of God, both of creation, and the instauration of the creature in Christ, and redemption and whatever else."[27]

One important part of this covenant is its mutuality. As covenant it is a compact involving two parties and requires not only divine promising but also human receiving. Peter Bulkeley wrote that it "is not properly a Covenant, where there is not mutuall obligation and binding of the parties one to another by a condition."[28] So God's promises of redemption and renewal are to those who will receive them in faith and respond to them in obedience. The good news is proclaimed, but a requirement is exacted. The declarative and the imperative go together, and exhortation is thus a fully proper part of the covenant's elaboration. "Let us embrace Christ," said

---

[25]See von Rohr, "Covenant and Assurance," pp. 195–203 for a prior discussion, by the author, of this interpretation of covenant in Puritan theology.

[26]Shepard, "To the Reader" in Bulkeley, *Gospel-Covenant*.

[27]T. Goodwin, *Works*, 1:175–76. Quoted in McKee, *Idea of Covenant*, p. 145.

[28]Bulkeley, *Gospel-Covenant*, p. 314.

Thomas Sutton, "that hee may embrace us; let us welcome Christ into our hearts, that hee may welcome us into his Father's kingdome; let us serve him, that hee may preserve us."[29] Here is the covenant of grace in its conditional form, and much was made of it in Puritan covenant theology.

Antinomians among these Puritans objected, holding that under such a conception grace could be rendered uncertain and salvation itself no longer be a free gift. Tobias Crisp criticized the conditional covenant as "but a meer bargain and sale,"[30] and John Saltmarsh alleged that it was in effect simply another form of a covenant of works. "Is this Free-Grace?" he asked—and then exclaimed, "Either place Salvation upon a free bottom, or else you make the New Covenant but an Old Covenant in new terms."[31] But for the covenant theologians this was a new covenant, even as the biblical Gospel proclaimed. This was God's promise of great gifts to the undeserving, benefits never in any way to be earned, and God's covenant commitment to abide by that promise. And if the gifts are to be received in and through faith, still, said Peter Bulkeley, "Faith brings nothing to God of our owne, it offers nothing to stand in exchange for his mercy offered; it receives a gift, but giveth no price."[32] Indeed, explained John Preston, "faith empties a man, it takes a man quite off his owne bottom,"[33] coming to God as an empty hand or an "empty Caske,"[34] seeking to be filled.

Such faith must also be active. The Puritans knew the Epistle of James as well as the letters of Paul and needed no persuasion that "faith without works is dead."[35] So the description of faith could be enlarged by Anthony Burgess to affirm that it "with one hand receiveth all from God, with the other hand sets all graces on work for God."[36] "Wilt thou then," asked Richard Greenham, "have the one part of the covenant, that is, that God should blesse thee in thy seed? Then remember thou also the other part, that thou walk before the Lord and be upright."[37] The covenant does have its conditions, both antecedent and consequent, and thus involves a mutuality of commitment. Peter Bulkeley noted that when God "makes with us a Covenant of Grace and mercy, he doth not then leave us at liberty to live as we list; ... he doth not onely bind himselfe to us, but us to himselfe."[38]

Such ideas spoke satisfyingly to Puritan piety, and preachers used the conditional covenant as an instrument for the proclaiming of the good news,

[29]Sutton, *Lectures on Romans*, p. 72.

[30]Crisp, *Christ Alone Exalted*, p. 34.

[31]Saltmarsh, *Shadows flying away*, p. 135. Quoted in Coolidge, *Pauline Renaissance*, p. 111.

[32]Bulkeley, *Gospel-Covenant*, p. 337.

[33]Preston, *Breast-Plate of Faith and Love*, 1:43.

[34]Preston, *New Covenant*, 2:230.

[35]James 2:17.

[36]Burgess, *True Doctrine of Justification*, 2:261.

[37]Greenham, *Works*, 5:279. Quoted in Møller, "Beginnings of Puritan Covenant Theology," p. 65.

[38]Bulkeley, *Gospel-Covenant*, p. 315.

the calling for faith and obedience, and the providing of assurance to doubting and distressed spirits. The experiences of "wayfaring and warfaring" could readily be caught up in this idiom and the journey of the soul seen in terms of fulfillment of covenant responsibility. Norman Pettit, in dealing with the subject of Puritan thought on "preparation" for conversion, even makes the tentative suggestion that covenant theology may itself have "opened the way for experiential religion." But certainly, he adds, it "provided theological consistency for experiential notions; and in this respect it was an essential ingredient for the emergence of preparation."[39] There was clarity in the covenant's conditions as to the manner in which Christian pilgrims are bound.

Equally the covenant provided an instrument for assurance as it spoke of the binding of God, and the life of piety was also aided by this element of covenant certainty. Thomas Shepard asked, "What is a Christian's comfort, and where doth it chiefly lie, but in this, That the Lord hath made with him an everlasting Covenant, in all things established and sure?"[40] The Christian, in pilgrimage, stands amid many perils, symbolized graphically to Robert Harris by the perils facing Noah of old. When Noah looked outward into the flood he saw "nothing but feare, and death." And when he looked inward "there were no neighbours but Bears and Lyons, and other beasts." But Noah had his Ark, "a pledge of God's care." And so too "stands our case," for "looke wee inward into our selves, there's nothing but guilt, sin, death, rottennesse, corruptions crawling in every roome in the soule; looke we outward … there's nothing before our eyes but confusion and destruction, every place is a sea." But we too have a pledge and, Harris added, "for such as are already enrolled within the covenant … there is not onely a possibility, but a certainty too of their blessedness."[41] God's covenanted promises are truly ground for assurance for the troubled spirit.

Of course the contingent factor is there, the necessity of being in the conditional covenant through the meeting of its conditions, and this led to extended theological analysis and practical advice on the difficult matter of "evidences." But for those who know themselves "already enrolled" there is the immense comfort of the certainty of God's covenanted mercy. Preston marvelled that God "should come to a Compact and agreement with mee, that he should tye himselfe, and bind himselfe to become a debtor to me."[42] But this indeed God had done and in so doing had accepted a bondage beyond compare. Harris told his hearers that they would not want greater binding on the part of their contract partner even if they were dealing with "the veriest sharker, or shifting fellow in a countrey," that great is the

[39]Pettit, *Heart Prepared*, p.11.
[40]Shepard, "To the Reader" in Bulkeley, *Gospel-Covenant*.
[41]Harris, *Way to True Happiness*, 1:23–24.
[42]Preston, *New Covenant*, 2:85.

commitment in covenant which God provides.[43] So here is certainty of divine performance. Preston declared, "If thou art in covenant with God, . . . then thy election is sure; and be sure that God will never alter it, for he is unchangeable."[44] It is not inaccurate to affirm that, in part, the idea of the covenant of grace was employed in Puritan practice to diminish fear of the possible capriciousness of God's action. There is reliability in the covenanting God.

Beyond these psychological benefits there were likewise theological values inherent in the idea of conditional covenant. Puritan divines seeking to be increasingly attentive to the theological implications derived from pulpit proclamation of the evangelical message easily gravitated to the use of the covenant concept, especially since it was also thoroughly biblical in character. In a writing of many decades ago Frank Hugh Foster made the interesting observation that the distinction between the secret and the revealed wills of God was introduced into the Calvinist system in order to save human responsibility.[45] That conclusion might now be shifted to give such privilege to the idea of conditional covenant. Within this structure, with God's offering the gifts of salvation to those who fulfill the covenant conditions, considerable importance is given to the human act. Richard Sibbes declared:

> If you look to God the Father, we are Christ's by donation, if you regard Christ himself, we are his by purchase, . . . if we regard ourselves, we are his by voluntary acceptance of the covenant of grace and by contract passed between him and us.[46]

For Richard Greenham this meant a "willing humbling of ourselves before the face of God,"[47] for "God is not pleased but with voluntary offering."[48] And William Perkins quoted approvingly the voluntarism of Augustine: "He that made thee without thee, doth not regenerate or save thee without thee."[49] There is a deep personalism in the covenant relationship, and God who has drawn near within it lays claim to a personal response. It is in free acceptance that this covenanting God becomes most truly one's own God. Thus faith is seen in personalist terms as a resting upon God or a trusting of God, with increased emphasis placed upon the act of the will, rather than merely the intellect, for self-giving response. And obedience, too, within the covenant takes on a similar character of free and

---

[43]Harris, *New Covenant*, 1:32–33.
[44]Preston, *Life Eternall*, 2:84–85.
[45]Foster, *Genetic History*, p. 319.
[46]Sibbes, "Christian's End," *Works*, 5:308.
[47]Greenham, *Works* (1612), p. 271. Quoted in Pettit, *Heart Prepared*, p. 49.
[48]Ibid., p. 448. Quoted in Pettit, *Heart Prepared*, p. 49.
[49]Perkins, "Gods Free-grace and Mans free-will," *Works*, 1:737.

voluntary action. Peter Bulkeley's description is apt in relating this to God's own rule:

> The Lords government is not a Pharoah-like tyranny . . he rules them by love, as he first wins them by love. He conquers them indeed by a mighty strong hand, but withall he drawes them by the cords of love. . . . Thus when the Lord is in Covenant with a people, they follow him not forcedly, but as farre as they are sanctified by grace, they submit willingly to his regiment.[50]

Further theological implications of the conditional covenant relate to such matters as the significance of God's revealed, as over against secret, will, the broad scope of the atonement accomplished in Christ's death, and the validity of a universal offering of the Gospel promises in the hope of free accepting response. In fact, this pattern of thinking could easily lead in the direction of Arminianism, and Puritan divines were well aware of that threat.

The threat was resisted, however, and the resistance was in the name of the covenant itself. Robert Jenison pointed to two serious absurdities, from the perspective of his inherited Calvinist theology, which were to be found in an understanding of the covenant as merely conditional. The first was that then the benefit persons have by Christ would be as uncertain as that which they once had in Adam and which was "lost when it was left to his owne keeping."[51] Here is a recognition of the fact of human weakness and of one's inability, simply by human will and strength, to turn oneself from sin to faith. In this same regard Thomas Blake noted that if we are in the covenant simply by free will, then Christ "might have been a Saviour, and not one man in the world have been saved."[52]

A second absurdity, said Jenison, would be that the difference "between the Children of God and of this World, as suppose between Peter and Judas, should be wholy made from nature, not from grace."[53] Here is a recognition of the divine sovereignty in election and an affirmation that the chosen are really God's chosen and not simply those who choose themselves. Thomas Sutton affirmed that faith itself is a fruit of election and explained, "Therefore did God chuse us, not because wee were about to beleeve, but that we might beleeve."[54] So the conditional covenant, biblical and beneficial though it may be, was rendered uncertain by the two realities of human weakness and divine sovereignty and needed to be supplemented by another biblical and beneficial affirmation, namely, that God's covenant of grace is also absolute.

[50]Bulkeley, *Gospel-Covenant*, p. 219.
[51]Jenison, *Concerning Gods Certaine Performance*, p. 117.
[52]Blake, *Vindiciae Foederis*, p. 111.
[53]Jenison, *Concerning Gods Certaine Performance*, p. 120.
[54]Sutton, *Lectures on Romans*, p. 60.

Thus time and again there appears in this Puritan covenant theology the emphasis upon God's final, and decisive, efficiency in covenant action. Ezekiel Culverwell noted that the condition of faith to which divine promises of mercy are made was really "an impossible condition to be performed by ourselves," and that therefore it is itself "part of the thing promised," for in the covenant of grace God "freely promised, not onely life, but to give grace to receive this life."[55] Moreover, he added, to think otherwise would really be to take away a chief difference between the covenant of grace and the covenant of works. In various ways this theme of ultimate divine efficiency is then reiterated throughout these Puritan discussions. Robert Bacon held that faith itself, as "infinitely too hard for man," was a branch of the New Covenant, that is, one of its gifts, and thus he could write, "We are not required to bring faith to God, but the Covenant is to give us faith to bring us to God."[56] And many others spoke similarly of God fulfilling the conditions, not only of subsequent sanctification and new life, but also of the prior faith which the conditional covenant requires. Paul Baynes supplied the analogy:

> The same power which raised up Jesus from the dead, is it which bringeth us to beleeve. If one were borne without an hand, none could set a naturall hand on such a body, but the power which createth and maketh a body; so much lesse can any power but the Lords, create this grace in the soule which is as an hand that reacheth into heaven.[57]

Saving grace is thus prevenient, as well as concurring, and the very initiation of the covenant relationship with God is dependent upon it—or, as Preston noted, "till God come and draw a man and change his will the worke is not done."[58]

So the covenant of grace is likewise an absolute covenant, dependent upon the final sovereignty of God's action, and the centrality of that conviction must likewise be recognized in the interpretation of covenant theology. The use of the idea of covenant did not lead Puritan theologians to abandon their Calvinism or to diminish their belief in the reality of God's free election. William Adams Brown once suggested that the covenant concept appealed to federal theologians because it "expresses an obligation voluntarily assumed on either side, and hence not properly to be brought under the sphere of necessity."[59] But whether done "properly" or not, these Puritan theologians did combine their views of the voluntary and their affirmations of the necessary, and the covenant was the connecting bond.

[55]Culverwell, *Treatise of Faith*, pp. 151, 149.
[56]Bacon, *Spirit of Prelacie*, p. 18.
[57]Baynes, *Upon the six Principles*, p. 246.
[58]Preston, *Breast-Plate of Faith and Love*, 1:58.
[59]Brown, "Covenant Theology," *Encyclopedia of Religion and Ethics*, 4:216–24.

Perkins defined the covenant as God's "contract with man, concerning the obtaining of life eternall upon a certen condition" and then portrayed it in his theology as God's outward means for executing the decree of election.[60] William Ames went even farther in his statement on this matter, saying, "in this God onely doth covenant. . . . But if two parties after the manner of a covenant are to be appointed, yet then God only is the party assuming, and constituting, but man is the party assumed."[61]

Indeed, at this point, there was some question as to the adequacy of the covenant terminology, for the implication of the covenant idea could be simply a bilateral *quid pro quo.* When Sibbes once explored this matter, he suggested that the word "testament" might be more adequate for portraying God's actions in Christ, for "a covenant requireth something to be done," whereas "in a testament there is nothing but receiving the legacies given." And yet he could not give up the terminology even at this point, for here is the covenant of grace in its most decisive dimension. It is a "free covenant" which "cometh from God merely of grace" and into which we are brought because "he giveth us hearts to take him for our God."[62]

Puritan covenant theology, therefore, even as the Puritans themselves, lived in "two worlds." These two worlds of the eternal and the historical each laid claim upon the Puritan consciousness, and their separate out-growths in Puritan awareness can be clustered broadly around the poles of predestination and piety. Yet the worlds were also joined, and the covenant of grace, the central form of the covenant conception, served as a compre-hensive connective between the two. But then major questions follow, especially those concerning the theological form taken by the connective as it both reflected and drew together the antinomies emerging from these realms of decree and decision, and these matters we shall need to explore. Involved here also is the issue as to whether ultimately the demand for coherent theological system led to a decisive dominance of either perspec-tive over the other, or whether, on the contrary, there was a living with the paradox. Norman Pettit, seeing the dilemma faced by this covenant theology, reaches the conclusion that "its real significance was its conscious ambiva-lence"[63] in dealing on the one hand with God's omnipotence and on the other hand with human freedom. But underlying these issues is the primary fact that this thinking affirmed two forms of the covenant of grace. A document of the late seventeenth century, reflecting both the Arminian and the Antinomian controversies, commented on the problem caused by the exclusive taking of one side or another on this matter. It said, somewhat plaintively, "Whether the Covenant of Grace be conditional or absolute is

---

[60]Perkins, "Golden Chaine," *Works,* 1:32.
[61]Ames, *Marrow,* p. 102.
[62]Sibbes, "Faithful Covenanter," *Works,* 6:4, 19.
[63]Pettit, *Heart Prepared,* p. 219.

... a very troublesome question. . . . It troubles the Faith of some, the Lives of others, and the Peace of very many."[64] But the Puritans we are examining did not take sides on this issue. They affirmed both sides. The covenant of grace was both conditional and absolute.

INTERPRETATIONS OF COVENANT THEOLOGY

The issue of the roles of divine domination and human participation as interrelated in federal theology has not lain dormant throughout the last century of historians' interest in covenant thought. And one conclusion reiterated in their study has been that of a mitigating influence by the idea of covenant upon Reformed affirmation of the rigors of predestination. This was the claim, in general terms, of J. A. Dorner[65] in 1871, of George P. Fisher[66] in 1896 and of William Adams Brown[67] in 1911. However, the most far-reaching and influential advancing of this thesis came through the work of Perry Miller in the late 1930s and was focused directly on the Puritans themselves.[68] Because of its enormous importance in both scholarly and popular interpretation of Puritan thought over the last five decades, it is useful to explore that view in some detail.

Miller's fundamental thesis is that the covenant concept was developed by Puritan theologians as a "device" for rectifying certain deficiencies in the theological system of John Calvin which they had inherited and for gaining the psychological sense of assurance which these changes could bring. Mainly the deficiencies were in Calvin's views of the nature of God and the grounds for morality. On the one hand, Calvin's God, comprehended as bare sovereignty, was a terror producing reality for the human consciousness. This God was "an unchained force, an incalculable essence," who as far as "personal character" is concerned was an "utter blank to human comprehension," an "inscrutable Divinity." Here was a God to be feared more than loved, a "capricious tyrant" who acts without discernible reason and the possibility of whose favor, therefore, can be a "torturing uncertainty." Then, second, this theological understanding provided no inducement for responsible human behavior, no ground for morality. In Calvin "morality could exist only as a series of divine commands." It was reduced "to an arbitrary fiat," with no inducement "other than the whip and lash of an angry God."

So reads Miller's portrayal of key elements in the theology of John Calvin, to which is then added the clear conclusion that this theology can in

[64]*Covenant of Grace Modestly Asserted*, p. 1.

[65]Dorner, *History of Protestant Theology*, 2:41–42.

[66]Fisher, *History of Christian Doctrine*, p. 348.

[67]Brown, "Covenant Theology," *Encyclopedia of Religion and Ethics*, 4:224.

[68]See "The Marrow of Puritan Divinity" in Miller, *Errand Into the Wilderness*, pp. 1–15. The essay was first published in 1935. See also Miller, *The New England Mind: The Seventeenth Century*, chap. 13. All quotations in the presentation of Miller's views are from these two sources.

no way provide ground for human assurance of salvation. If there is to be that confidence, then "the transcendent God had to be chained, made less inscrutable, less mysterious, less unpredictable." There must be a "caging and confining" of "the inexpressible and unfathomable Being by the laws of ethics." Hence the moral law must likewise be restored to human life in such manner as to enable it to contribute to a sense of salvation's certainty. Its role in the assurance of God's favor must be subject to conditions that are clear and will not be overruled by arbitrariness. Still more, in Miller's view, the task these Puritans faced was to develop such a theology "without losing the sense of the hidden God, without reducing the Divinity to a mechanism, without depriving Him of unpredictability, absolute power, fearfulness, and mystery."

Puritan theologians were, however, equal to this task, and the result was their "covenant of grace." Here Miller chiefly has reference to the conditional covenant, though as a pact which has been brought into being by God's own initiating action. By this instrument, then, these theologians were able to do several necessary things. One was to present a God whose freedom for arbitrary action was limited. By entering into binding covenant commitment to humanity God "has become a chained God—by His own covenant, it is true, but nevertheless a God restricted and circumscribed—a God who can be counted upon, a God who can be lived with." Then further, the covenant is constructed so as to give a prominent place to moral obligation. As covenant it is a contract, thus binding as well upon the human party, and here the basis of moral responsibility is introduced. Works are established as both an indication of faith and an obligation of continuing covenant faithfulness. Morality is therefore mandated as a part of the covenant itself. And still further, since the covenant is essentially a matter of "legal status," a *quid pro quo*, one can "strike a bargain" with God within it and gain assurance of God's favor.

Altogether, then, the covenant was "an extremely strategic device" for stimulating human activity and for providing a sense of security. It was the Puritan "revision of Calvinism" for the obtaining of these ends, in which indeed "a juridical relationship is slyly substituted for the divine decree." And yet all the while there continues in Puritan thought a recognition of the predestining sovereignty of God. It is God, not humanity, by whom the covenant was created; God's "secret counsels" remain; and "the grace which enables us to fulfill the covenant" is itself of God's giving. But "covenant thought kept this divine liberty at several removes, placed it on a theoretical plane, robbed it of much of its terror." Thus, in the last analysis, "the covenant made it possible to argue that while God elects whom He pleases, He is pleased to elect those who catch Him in His plighted word, and that it is up to fallen man to do so." This is Miller's portrayal of Puritan covenant theology.

Assessment of Miller's analysis may be developed in two areas.[69] Initially, there is his portrayal of the thought of Calvin as background for Puritan covenant thinking, and here, it must be said, Miller's account is seriously in error. The teaching of Calvin does not fit into Miller's mold, and Calvin therefore becomes, as David Hall put it, a "stage figure" or "false stereotype" against which Miller "played off the ideas of the New England Puritans, . . . thereby producing a divergence of views."[70] Actually, Calvin's theology was not unmindful of the covenant of grace and made it a prominent, though not central, feature. Calvin never wrote a treatise on the covenant, nor did he devote a separate chapter to it in the *Institutes*, but he read biblical history as the story of God's covenant relationship with a chosen people and then further saw that relationship as one in which there is a mutual binding. God's mercy is a committed mercy and calls for a committed response. All this is disclosed, of course, in the revealed will of God, which for Calvin, as for the later Puritans, was held in close tension with the idea of God's hidden will. Although God has undisclosed secret counsels, there is revelation of the divine nature, intention, and covenantal commitment in Scripture and particularly in Christ. Here are disclosed the mercy and the saving plan of God. Thus it is at least a caricature to speak of Calvin's God as "an unchained force," "an utter blank to human comprehension," "a capricious tyrant."

It is equally fallacious to allege that because of the doctrine of predestination there was no ground for morality in Calvin's theological system. On the contrary, the law in Calvin's understanding is basically "covenant law," that is, law to be used for guidance in moral living by those in covenant relationship. This is the so-called "third use" of the law, the others being law used as an instrument leading to repentance and law as a means of political governance. Actually, Calvin emphasized all three, but particularly is Scriptural law to be understood and followed in relationship to covenant moral responsibility. In the *Institutes* he wrote:

> In all covenants of his mercy the Lord requires of his servants in return uprightness and sanctity of life, lest his goodness be mocked. . . .

[69]Though the scope and brilliance of Miller's portrayal of the Puritan mind make his contributions to be of truly continuing significance in the study of early American intellectual history, several scholars have raised questions over the years concerning the case he pressed for the origin and early use of the covenant idea. See particularly Bogue, *Edwards and the Covenant of Grace*, pp. 4–17; Breward, *Work of William Perkins*, pp. 92–93; Cherry, "Covenant in Jonathan Edwards' Doctrine of Faith," pp. 328–33; Cherry, *Theology of Jonathan Edwards*, pp. 113–16; Emerson, "Calvin and Covenant Theology," pp. 138–42; Hall, "Understanding the Puritans," pp. 37–50; Marsden, "Perry Miller's Rehabilitation of the Puritans," pp. 91–105; McGiffert, "American Puritan Studies," pp. 36–67; Møller, "Beginnings of Puritan Covenant Theology," p. 46; Pettit, *Heart Prepared*, pp. 40, 120, 219–21; Stoever, 'A Faire and Easie Way', pp. 13–14, 192–96; Toon, *God's Statesman*, pp. 170–71.

[70]Hall, "Understanding the Puritans," p. 40, n. 20.

> Consequently, in this way he wills to keep in their duty those admitted
> to fellowship in the covenant.[71]

Calvin cannot be portrayed in Miller's terms, nor can the Puritans be as
radically differentiated from him as Miller proposes.

The further area for assessment is that of Miller's portrayal of Puritan
covenant thought itself. Despite his truly skillful analysis of the Puritan mind
on this matter, certain inadequacies appear here as well. First of all, because
of his desire to portray the covenant as an intellectual "device" deliberately
developed by Puritans to correct Calvinism, Miller largely ignores the
Scriptural sources for the covenant idea. It is highly doubtful that the Puritan
view of the covenant can be properly presented without taking this matter
into substantial account. In the last analysis the Puritans did not create the
covenant idea as an ingenious contrivance for solving a theological problem,
even though they did mold it in the process of use. Rather, they knew it to
be speaking to them out of the biblical story, a part of God's own self-
disclosure, and they believed that the shaping of the covenant conception
must be faithful to this revelation.

In the second place, because of his conviction that Puritanism used the
covenant as a way of reintroducing human action into a system where
presumably persons were immobilized, Miller is led at times to accuse the
Puritans of what might seem to be excessive reliance on moral effort in the
face of their basic understanding of the gift character of salvation. But it is not
their conviction, as Miller alleges, that "they are to be saved for trying." At
most they are to be assured because of their trying, for the role of moral
endeavor was seen as declarative (a fact that Miller does often recognize),
rather than causative, in God's saving plan. Similarly, the call in Puritan
preaching for such effort is hardly a "shamelessly pragmatic injunction"
presumably out of character with faith's central role, for Puritan thought was
never ashamed to urge moral obedience in witness to God's gifts. Thus, even
as Puritanism's emphasis on moral effort was not newly made possible as
consequence of the covenant conception, neither was that effort entreated as
compromising of inherited evangelical way.

Third, related to this emphasis upon human engagement is the undue
stress which Miller places upon the legal character of the covenant and
hence upon its use as a bargaining instrument. The psychology of Puritan
thought and practice is surely complex here and probably contains diverse
elements. But the covenant, as God's self-limitation and entrance into
gracious conditional relations with humanity, is much more in Puritan
feeling than the opportunity for a person "to strike a bargain, to do himself a
good turn, to make a sure profit." The covenant is not simply to be used, but
to be received and appreciated as an act of God's meaningful revelation in

---

[71]Calvin, *Institutes*, 1:808.

history. Norman Pettit has pointed out that acts of "preparation" for conversion, recommended by Puritan divines, are not to be construed, in Miller's manner, as terms of a contract through the fulfillment of which one negotiates with God for salvation.[72] Nor likewise, more generally, can Puritan appropriation of covenant partnership be called, in Miller's words, a "spiritual commercialism." The context for understanding the utilization of covenant conditions must also include other and more comprehensive elements in the Puritan religious consciousness.

Finally, Miller does not recognize the full meaning of continuing divine sovereignty in the covenant. He urges, of course, that though the task of Puritan theologians was to devise an arrangement which would limit divine arbitrariness while encouraging morality and providing security, this was to be done without losing the sense of the hidden God or of God's absolute power. Despite the introduction of predictability, the final mystery must still remain. Yet Miller does not come to grips with the way in which this task was ultimately approached in Puritan covenant thought. His main points are that God's power is preserved because of God's sovereign act of giving the covenant and because its conditions themselves can be met only through the enabling help of God's grace. Both of these indeed are Puritan affirmations, but Puritan struggle with this issue went still one step farther. That was to add the conviction that through God's very action the terms of the covenant are met, for the covenant is both conditional and absolute. Grace is not only enabling, but also efficient, in the fulfillment of the covenant conditions. Miller does recognize that the idea of predestination remains, but this does not lead him to identify the final tension in the Puritan concept of the covenant itself. And this may be because of his distinctive view of the covenant's purpose and origin. For Miller the covenant is mainly the conditional covenant, introduced to limit sovereignty, to encourage morality, and to guarantee security. Such a view must then necessarily place its emphasis upon human responsibility and divine reliability. But for Puritan theology the covenant itself was both conditional and absolute, and covenant understanding thus needed constantly to work with that tension of human freedom and the ultimate sovereignty of God.

Some of these tendencies in Miller's analysis have subsequently been carried to more extreme form in other, less thorough, presentations of Puritan covenant thought. Such popularizations of his views have mainly lifted up the theme of the covenant conditions and the obligation for their fulfillment, painting upon Puritanism an Arminian coloration of the type it so rigorously opposed. For example, Samuel Eliot Morison interpreted it in this manner: "The God of New England ... voluntarily placed himself under a code: the Covenant of Grace. This ... meant that God's redeeming grace was bestowed on any person who sincerely and completely believed in God,

---

[72]Pettit, *Heart Prepared*, pp. 120, 219–21.

and surrendered himself to God. Such a one, no matter how grievously he had sinned, could join the Covenant, and lay hold of Grace."[73] Irvonwy Morgan wrote, "The great merit of the covenant concept for the Godly Preachers was that it simplified the theology of grace and works ... into something practical. ... God made His promise recorded in Scripture and man made his promise of a better life relying on the promises of God. In this way good works and moral effort could be introduced into a theology of grace and faith."[74] Christopher Hill said that "the covenant theology ... was a means of overcoming the absolute decrees, of smuggling 'works' into Calvinism. ... It reestablished moral obligation on a clearer, more rational basis. ... Original sin is all but obliterated by the covenant. ... Conscious effort, conscious morality, conscious struggle to make God's will prevail— such are the lessons of the covenant theology."[75] And Ralph Barton Perry declared, "Through the covenant theology the New England Puritans were possessed of the more congenial creed that God helps those who help themselves."[76] Thus the Miller legacy has in these instances lost all sense of the continuing Calvinism in Puritan covenant thought.

However, in the study of Puritan covenant theology throughout the last three and a half decades certain new approaches and perspectives have also emerged. It is true that the old problem has remained, as interpreters continue to probe the roles of human and divine agency in Puritan covenant understanding. But the context for such probing has, in at least two senses, been altered. First, there has been a more careful searching out of continental antecedents for this covenant thought, with new attention paid particularly to the influence upon it of the early sixteenth century Rhineland reformers. And second, more consideration has been given to the relevant antecedents in England's own Reformation history and to the viewing of later Puritan perspectives, therefore, in the light of earlier English theological developments. Mainly, then, recent research has led to larger engagement with the historical sources of Puritan covenant thought as a means of further clarifying its substance.

A major beginning point for these investigations was Leonard Trinterud's study in 1951 of "the origins of Puritanism," broaching conclusions touching both lines of historical impact.[77] Trinterud affirmed that Puritan covenant ideas originated in what he called the "law-covenant" character of thought in such early sixteenth century Swiss and German Rhineland cities as Zurich, Basel, and Strassburg. Led by Zwingli, Bullinger, Oecolampadius, Bucer, and others, these centers of Reformed Protestantism developed a pattern of theology related to their political

[73]Morison, *Intellectual Life*, p. 160.
[74]I. Morgan, *Godly Preachers*, pp. 120–22.
[75]Hill, *Puritanism and Revolution*, pp. 245–47.
[76]Perry, *Puritanism and Democracy*, p. 96.
[77]Trinterud, "Origins of Puritanism," pp. 37–57.

theory of natural law and social contract, interpreting the divine-human relationship as grounded on divine law and a covenant with God. In such a conception, though grace was affirmed as God's giving, major emphasis came to be placed on human obedience to the law of love for covenant fulfillment. Thus Trinterud could also speak of this covenantal relationship as a "law-contract" structure. Moreover, such Rhineland thinking appeared in contrast to the Genevan outlook as developed shortly thereafter by Calvin where emphasis was primarily upon God's action and the sovereignty of grace. Trinterud put the difference sharply:

> For Calvin, and so in the Geneva Bible, the covenant of God is God's promise to man, which obligates God to fulfill.... In the covenant theory of the Rhineland ... the covenant is a conditional promise on God's part, which has the effect of drawing out of man a responding promise of obedience, thus creating a mutual pact or treaty. The burden of fulfillment rests upon man, for he must first obey in order to bring God's reciprocal obligation into force.[78]

In Trinterud's view, it was this Rhineland conception of the covenant that primarily influenced early English reformers and ultimately Puritan thought. Its initial impact appeared in the writings of William Tyndale, which "show a whole-hearted and systematic adoption of the law-covenant scheme as the basis of his entire religious outlook," for in them "God's promises constitute a covenant, or appointment, by which God promises certain blessings to men on the condition that they keep his laws."[79] From the 1530s on, well down into the next century of English history, this influence continued to be felt, first by such persons as John Frith, John Bale, and John Hooper and then by the Elizabethan Puritans and their seventeenth century successors. Some struggle did occur with the impact of Calvin's theology, but by the mid-seventeenth century the Rhineland view of covenant had triumphed and became the interpretive scheme utilized by the Westminster Assembly of Divines as it drew up its normative and influential Confession.

Although subject to criticism and modification in some of its details, this general interpretation of both the nature and the historical sources of Puritan covenant thought has gathered support from several scholars in the ensuing decades. In 1964 William Clebsch examined the thought of the first group of English Protestant thinkers during the reign of Henry VIII and found a covenant pattern somewhat similar to that which Trinterud had identified. Clebsch did not see as heavy a reliance upon Rhineland influence as did Trinterud, for he pointed also to an ongoing Lollard tradition in England as contributory to these views. But the views themselves were clearly of a

[78]Ibid., p. 45.
[79]Ibid., p. 39.

"law-covenant-contract" character, and their most influential early exponent was William Tyndale. Although initially in his theological work Tyndale was dependent upon Luther and Luther's doctrine of free justification, this outlook changed over the course of the years until ultimately a contractual understanding of salvation emerged in which God, by covenant, was bound to recompense human obedience. Indeed, wrote Clebsch, after 1531 Tyndale was "ever more blatantly interpreting Christianity as a system of rewards and punishments for moral action."[80] In this process, Clebsch maintained, Tyndale, along with others of like mind, ultimately contributed to the founding of English Puritanism, defined as a "theological, religious and moral system" which "regarded scripture as God's law for everyman, binding everyman and God together in a contract that enjoined and re-warded strict morality."[81] So Puritanism is here seen as being more legalistic than evangelical—and Tyndale as a "Proto-Puritan."

In the 1960s Richard Greaves gave further attention to the thesis of Rhineland influence upon Puritan covenant thought and especially to the relation of that influence to the concurrent impact of Calvinist theology upon Puritan ideas.[82] Like Trinterud, Greaves sees the Rhineland covenant conception as contractual in emphasis, with major stress upon the element of conditionality in the divine-human relationship. This he further sees as entering the stream of English thought through the work of Tyndale and his early sixteenth century associates, providing the growing presence of what is termed a "Zwingli-Bullinger-Tyndale tradition" in emerging Puritanism. Calvinism, however, likewise made strong inroads into Puritan thinking, particularly after the publication of the Geneva Bible with Calvin's annotations in 1560, and, without actually denying human responsibility, contributed most fundamentally the idea of covenant as divine promise and eternal gift.

Greaves' thesis, then, is that these two traditions moved side by side through Puritan history and through the development within it of the idea of covenant. The relative influence of each varied, however, in terms of both period and person. As to period, Greaves sees a fusion of the two toward the end of the Elizabethan era, represented in the writings of Fenner, Cartwright, and Perkins. But in the seventeenth century greater divergence occurred. William Ames led the way to a more "distinctively Calvinist" theory of the covenant, whereas John Preston and John Ball moved in the direction of a more pronounced "Zwingli-Tyndale" type of emphasis. Thus the distinction is also among persons within a given period, and Greaves more explicitly classifies a larger number of Puritan theologians of the first

[80]Clebsch, *England's Earliest Protestants*, p. 9.
[81]Ibid., p. 317.
[82]Greaves, "John Bunyan and Covenant Thought," pp. 151–69; and Greaves, "Origins and Early Development," pp. 21–35.

half of the seventeenth century as moderate Calvinists, strict Calvinists, or Antinomians—the latter, of course, being those for whom the Christian life is seen entirely as a gift of grace. On the whole, however, the stricter Calvinism tended to be stronger in the early years of the century, whereas by the third and fourth decades, in Greaves' judgment, the more moderate form incorporating Zwingli-Tyndale emphases began more fully to be accepted. So Greaves seeks by aid of this method of classification to analyze both the nature of Puritan covenant thought and the process of its development.

A still more recent portrayal of Puritan covenant understanding, largely in terms of its Rhineland background, is found in Wayne Baker's 1980 study of Heinrich Bullinger.[83] Central to this discussion is a distinction, made prominent some years earlier by Kenneth Hagen,[84] between testament and covenant. In this usage the term "testament" designates a unilateral gift on God's part, whereas "covenant" refers exclusively to a bilateral divine-human relationship. Thus Calvin's emphasis on divine sovereignty provides a theology of testament, while the Rhineland acceptance of conditionality leads to a theology of covenant. It was this latter outlook, then, that Bullinger proclaimed from his study and pulpit in Zurich. Moreover, a second distinction also becomes important in Baker's discussion, namely, that between single and double predestination. Calvin is seen as a proponent of the latter and Bullinger of the former, and the view is then advanced that whereas single predestination can be held in conjunction with covenant, double predestination necessarily leads to a testament understanding.

With these distinctions in the background, Baker then affirms the impact of Bullinger upon English thought. Initially this influence appeared in Tyndale for whom the conditions of the covenant, namely, faith and piety, were identical to those of Bullinger. But shortly after the time of Tyndale the picture changed, with the influence of the Geneva Bible bringing Calvinism to the fore. This domination by a testament theology then prevailed throughout the Elizabethan period in the thought of such leaders as Fenner, Cartwright, and Perkins, "the crucial doctrine of double predestination ... resulting in the paralysis of the idea of bilateral covenant."[85] But in the seventeenth century the conditional covenant idea was reasserted in the thought of such persons as John Preston and Richard Baxter, despite the continuing Calvinism of others. Moreover, Preston, in Baker's view, was a source for New England covenant thought, and the bilateral covenant conception was thereby spread to the new land as well. So Baker concludes: "The 'new' covenant ideas of the seventeenth century were thus clearly not a further development of Calvinism. Rather, they were part of the other

---

[83]Baker, *Heinrich Bullinger and the Covenant*, pp. 166, 205–10.

[84]Hagen, "From Testament to Covenant," pp. 1–24.

[85]Baker, *Heinrich Bullinger and the Covenant*, p. 200.

Reformed tradition which must be traced back to Zurich, particularly to the thought of Bullinger."[86]

One additional recent study has also explored the "new voluntarism" in Puritan covenant theology, but has approached it in a considerably different manner. This is R. T. Kendall's work on the place of Calvinism in English thought of the first half of the seventeenth century.[87] Perhaps two things come out most strongly in Kendall's treatment of the specific matter here under discussion. First, ignoring the Rhineland sources so strongly emphasized in other approaches, he finds the stimulus to voluntarism in early alterations within Calvinist theology itself. Though Calvin did hold to a doctrine of predestination, he also believed, so Kendall affirms, that Christ in fact died for all persons even though all persons will not ultimately realize the fruits of his atonement. The universality of the atonement, however, does provide a ground for personal assurance when faith simply looks to Christ alone and the magnitude of his saving work. There is no assurance in looking to oneself, but only in looking to Christ's death as pledge, the mirror in which one contemplates one's election. All this began to change, however, through the work of Theodore Beza, Calvin's successor in Geneva, who interpreted the atonement as limited in character, Christ's death being only for the elect, for now assurance must come through personal awareness of the inner presence of that saving faith which is election's sign. And here, says Kendall, is the seed of voluntarism, as the emphasis turns more and more to the obtaining of that faith. Moreover, this voluntarism soon spread to continental covenant theology, since faith was designated a necessary covenant condition—and then through the work of the late sixteenth century Heidelberg theologians it ultimately found its way into English thought.

Second, Kendall explores Puritan covenant theology itself and finds this voluntarism to be so intrusive and predominant a feature that essentially all vestige of Calvinism is lost. This is particularly a consequence of Puritanism's extended use of the "practical syllogism" as a ground for assurance, for now concentration is upon the "reflex act," the application of salvation's promise to oneself by virtue of the internal evidences discerned. It is also a consequence of the doctrine of "temporary faith" which, by admission that one can be deceived by this faith's presumably convincing signs, leads to added effort to attain to a faith that is real. So the Puritanism of both England and New England is read by Kendall as portraying a salvation to be attained (and assured) essentially by human act. Thus for Preston, he says, the covenant of grace has become a covenant of works. For Ames grace is earned by a willingness to consecrate oneself to a godly life. And for Hooker, in New England, God's effectual calling has become meaningless because of the

[86]Ibid., p. 166.
[87]See Kendall, *Calvin and English Calvinism*, especially chaps. 4–5, 7–9, 11.

appeal to the human will. It is true that a doctrine of predestination remains, for these words of Calvinism are not relinquished. But, says Kendall, such predestinarianism is "abstract and formal and bears little connection to the concrete fact that the ground of assurance is godliness, and that that ground being removed removes hope."[88]

Throughout these recent decades, however, there have been other studies more inclined to see a continuation of Calvinism in Puritan covenant thought, and particularly with respect to its doctrine of predestination. In 1963, for example, Jens Møller explored the origins of this theology on the English scene up through the time of Perkins and found Genevan Calvinism to be the major motif.[89] Actually, Møller notes, in addition to the Calvinist strain emphasizing priority of grace in God's covenant dealing there was also the second strain of legal expectation, coming from Zwingli and Bullinger and finding its expression in Tyndale. Like Trinterud before him and Clebsch and others after him, Møller saw an element of the contractual in Tyndale's view of covenant, especially as he developed that more fully in the final years of his life. Although not unmindful of God's promises and grace, Tyndale came more and more to stress "our deeds" as the condition for God's covenant giving. And yet in the ensuing development of English covenant thought this legalism came to have little place. Far more predominant was the view of the sovereignty of God's electing and renewing grace in the divine-human covenant relationship. This, Møller tells us, was in no way to ignore the ethical, for Calvin's covenant conception did not do that, but rather to put the ethical into a different context. So, even immediately following Tyndale, in the theologies of Bale and Bradford, the setting for covenant thinking became the grace of God's free promise. Then soon thereafter, in the thought of the earliest Puritans themselves, such men as Fenner, Cartwright, and Perkins, the theme of covenant was put explicitly under the heading of the execution of God's decree. There was, however, one exception in Møller's judgment. That was the Puritan practice of the vow, in which persons make specific promises in covenanting with God. But, concludes Møller, "on this point only, puritan covenant theology means a deviation from original Calvinism. Calvin's covenant God certainly offered grace and demanded obedience, but he did not recompense obedience by offering grace."[90]

Over the course of recent years Michael McGiffert has also concerned himself in several articles with these issues, finding in the Puritan beginnings of both England and New England a covenant understanding drawing

[88]Ibid., p. 166.
[89]Møller, "Beginnings of Puritan Covenant Theology," pp. 46–67.
[90]Ibid., p. 67.

heavily upon doctrines of divine sovereignty and grace.[91] These tones are present for him as early as Tyndale, and his interpretation here takes exception to those of Trinterud, Clebsch, and Møller. It is true, McGiffert holds, that Tyndale's thought was strongly moralistic, but it was in no way legalistic. Rather, his religious outlook was imbued throughout with a pervasive piety marked by strong evangelical and even experiential emphases, and it is in this light that his practical and moral intensity must be seen. Without question Tyndale had a strong element of conditionality in his covenant understanding, but this did not mean that the covenant was a contractual transaction. The covenant signified a union with God initiated by grace and marked by trust. In this relationship works are expected, though as a sign of fidelity rather than to gain favor. Again, piety rather than legality became their stimulus. They were a part of an already gracious covenant. Underlying this reassessment is also the conviction that covenant as pact and covenant as promise cannot be as easily separated as has been attempted by Trinterud and others sharing his view. Tyndale's covenant includes both.

When McGiffert turns his attention to subsequent English developments he shares Møller's view of the importance of Calvinist ideas for covenant thought within emerging Puritanism itself. This is reflected particularly in his probing of the question of the occasion for the origination of the idea of a covenant of works. Throughout the early decades of the history of covenant thought, both continental and English, only one covenant was understood to exist, the covenant of grace. But by the late sixteenth century this was joined by another, and often chronologically prior, pact of God with humanity, the covenant of works. This covenant was a covenant of law and, whether seen as having its historical introduction in Eden or at Sinai, took the form of a contractual compact. In it the element of conditionality prevailed, and the divine-human relationship was portrayed in terms of a legal *quid pro quo*. So here, in covenant theology, Law and Gospel were now represented by two covenants, those of works and grace. Among the English this concept was first introduced by Dudley Fenner in 1585. McGiffert adduces several reasons for this second covenant's birth, but chief among them is concern to protect from contractualism the covenant of grace. The biblical themes of divine law and its application could not be abandoned, but efforts for their inclusion under the one covenant describing divine-human relations could too easily lead to such infusing of it with conditionality as to degrade the very meaning of grace itself. Thus the covenant is split, contingency is assigned to its legal form, and sovereign

---

[91]McGiffert, "American Puritan Studies," pp. 36–67; McGiffert, "Covenant, Crown, and Commons," pp. 32–52; McGiffert, "Grace and Works," pp. 463–505; McGiffert, "Problem of the Covenant," pp. 107–29; McGiffert, "Tyndale's Conception of Covenant," pp. 67–84.

grace is preserved.[92] As McGiffert reads the beginnings of Puritan thought up through the time of Perkins he sees evidence for this concern to define the saving covenant in terms emphasizing the preeminence of God's gracious giving. These early Puritans remained true to their Calvinist heritage.

McGiffert also looks at a major first generation expression of New England covenant theology, the thought of Peter Bulkeley as set forth in his *Gospel–Covenant* published near the middle of the seventeenth century. Responding in part to Perry Miller's contractualist interpretation, McGiffert not only rejects this characterization, but also affirms Bulkeley's standing in the tradition of "such English legatees of Geneva as William Perkins, William Ames, and Richard Sibbes."[93] The key factor here is again the sovereignty of grace, presented now explicitly in the affirmation that the covenant of grace is absolute. The covenant is also conditional, and one's meeting of the conditions is to be urged, but in the last analysis it is by God's absolute promise that they are to be fulfilled. That which God requires is also God's gift. Within this context, then, McGiffert explores the "problem" of Puritan covenant thought, that is, the tension between the conditional and the absolute. And though Bulkeley managed to maintain the tension, even he reveals hints of the fracturing that was to come when New England Calvinism moved in the eighteenth century in an Arminian direction. McGiffert concludes, "Even while Bulkeley maintains the substance of sound doctrine, the devilish *quid pro quo* teases the margins of his mind . . . in ways that may suggest the ultimately irresistible slippage of Puritanism toward the order of contract."[94]

Perhaps the most comprehensive probing of this tension between the conditional and the absolute in Puritan covenant thought is to be found in a full length study published by William K. B. Stoever in 1978.[95] Although focused primarily on the Massachusetts Antinomian controversy of the late 1630s, this struggle with Anne Hutchinson and John Wheelwright in Boston is placed within the larger context of Puritan theology of both England and New England—and to some extent of even the still broader Reformed tradition itself. And in examining the mainstream of Puritan thinking Stoever is led primarily to the thesis that, in its understanding of the process of salvation, covenant theology held together in close dialectical relationship the roles of human nature and divine grace. This means, of course, that the doctrine of divine sovereignty is not abridged by an admission of human

---

[92]This thesis will be advanced further by McGiffert in a forthcoming essay, "The Making of the Covenant of Works: England, 1585–1610," in a volume to be edited by John Corrigan. The study deals with Dudley Fenner, Josias Nichols, Thomas Cartwright, and William Perkins.

[93]McGiffert, "Problem of the Covenant," p. 124.

[94]Ibid., p. 129.

[95]See Stoever, '*A Faire and Easie Way*', especially chaps. 1, 4, 6, 9.

participation, and Stoever is critical of Miller and others who affirm the necessity of such a conclusion.

The fact is, in his judgment, that the most critical distinction of these Puritan theologians was not one between divine activity and human activity in relation to salvation. Rather, it was a distinction between merit and grace, with the former denied any recognition in the process. But that exclusion is not exactly the same as the exclusion of the participation of human faculties themselves. These are not violated in God's saving act, and the integrity of the human person remains. In the thought of these divines the grace that regenerates is not in conflict with human nature as such, but rather with corrupt human nature. Thus, as the corruption of human nature is corrected by sovereign grace, the human person participates with will and act in conversion and the growth of new life. Faith itself, by which one enters the covenant of grace, is, says Stoever, seen by the Puritans in this light, for though its efficient cause is the Holy Spirit, it is nevertheless also a human act. And as this is then applied to the conditionality of the covenant, it means for these covenant theologians the affirmation of both responsible participation and predestining grace.

It is in general harmony with Stoever's understanding, as well as with those of Møller and McGiffert, that this present study of Puritan covenant theology is presented.[96] The fundamental thesis advanced here is that Puritanism, seeking to be faithful to both the implications of its Gospel piety and the theological requirements of its doctrine of predestination, drew the two themes together within the broad compass of its view of the covenant of grace. Indeed, here were two strains within the biblical presentation itself of the manner of God's covenanting that needed first to be affirmed and then held together in close interrelationship. So the Calvinist heritage of sovereign grace was not compromised through the urging of human participation and agency, nor was that human responsibility rendered insignificant by the proclamation of God's predestining power. Both can be seen as incorporated into the totality of God's gracious covenanting with humanity—so felt these Puritan divines—for that covenant is both conditional and absolute.

From the perspective of this thesis, then, some assessment must likewise be expressed concerning these recent interpretations of Puritanism which tend to de-emphasize its Calvinism. On the one hand, it has been instructive to see the earlier almost totally dominant Calvinist hegemony as a source of Puritan theology corrected by a discovery of the influence of "the other reformation." The Rhineland reformers were indeed known in pre-

[96]Additional instances of emphasis upon a strong continuing Calvinist component in Puritan covenant thought are: Eusden, *Puritans, Lawyers, and Politics*, pp. 28–31; Kevan, *Grace of Law*, p. 40; New, *Anglican and Puritan*, pp. 91–93; Sprunger, *Learned Doctor William Ames*, p. 151; Wallace, *Puritans and Predestination*, p. 197.

Puritan and Puritan England. Ian Breward has even made the claim in recent years that Bullinger's *Decades* were probably read by more English clergy than were Calvin's *Institutes*,[97] a phenomenon undoubtedly due at least in part, however, to Archbishop Whitgift's order that Bullinger be purchased and studied. So the theology of Zurich was known, and although it can hardly be represented as violently in contrast with that of Geneva, a difference of emphasis concerning human participation in the covenant was conveyed. The English were in all likelihood encouraged by this toward what was to become the "pietism" of Puritanism.

But reservations must also be expressed, on the other hand, concerning further aspects of these interpretations. One matter has to do with their tendency to portray Puritan covenant thought in legalistic terms. The covenant is spoken of as contract, and fulfillment of contract obligations is itself seen as obedience to the requirements often pictured as law. Although some of the Rhineland emphasis may have moved in this direction, it is doubtful that such characterization fully fits the subsequent Puritan covenant understanding. Where covenant participation is gift as well as task and religious experience as much as legal duty, a different perspective prevails. So both the predestinarianism and the pietism of Puritan awareness can be seen as refusing a contractual *quid pro quo*.

Yet a further matter is related to this. In these interpretations there is a tendency to ignore the operative element that is of necessity involved in a doctrine of predestination. The Rhineland reformers were predestinarians, and their contribution to Puritan thought thus included a theology of divine as well as human act. Some, such as Bullinger, may have failed to relate this to their own covenant understanding, but to portray the nature of their influence as leading simply to a bilateralism is to reduce predestination for Puritanism itself to mere theory and to ignore the divine agency in the process of salvation which a doctrine of election entails. Such sterilizing of the predestination conviction, however, was hardly a part of either Puritan thought or religious consciousness. Particularly grievous in this misinterpretation is the work of Kendall who dismisses Puritan predestinarianism out of hand as simply an ironic, intellectual remnant in what he portrays as a Calvinist system massively corrupted by a flagrant emphasis on voluntarism. But Greaves and Baker likewise minimize the operative role of predestination within a bilateral view. The fact that predestination is single rather than double does not alter its importance, for single predestination is itself election to salvation involving the necessity and certainty of divine saving act.[98]

---

[97]Breward, *Work of William Perkins*, p. 17.

[98]Wayne Baker feels that, whereas single predestination and bilateral covenant could be jointly affirmed without qualifying the covenant's bilateralism, as was the case for Bullinger, double

And this misunderstanding, then, may be related to one still further aspect of the interpretations under consideration. Central to their portrayal is a distinction made between "covenant" and "testament" suggesting such mutual exclusion of one another that either alone must characterize a pattern of covenant thought. "Covenant" is bilateral and comes from the Rhineland. "Testament" is unilateral and finds its source in Geneva. And the struggle in Puritanism is between the two, for they are incompatible. But the view of Puritan covenant theology being set forth in this study refuses that dichotomy. The genius of the Puritan understanding, so it is here affirmed, lies in its rejection of an "either/or" in favor of a "both/and." Although Puritan covenant theologians indeed came to urge the life of faith and obedience as human responsibility in covenant relationship, they did not thereby abandon their conviction of the ultimacy in this relationship of God's sovereign action. So though it is true that such persons as Preston and Ball, as alleged, looked to human act in their bilateralism, it is also true that they affirmed divine predestination with equal conviction.[99] Thus still further, it is doubt-

---

predestination led to that covenant's "paralysis." He also identifies this latter as "absolute predestination," holding, then, that such a view precluded all possibility of covenant conditionality. See Baker, *Heinrich Bullinger and the Covenant*, pp. 200, 207, 214. But this seems to ignore the fact that single predestination is itself truly predestination, God's determination of some to salvation by divine decree and act. And it also neglects the fact that many Puritan divines were double predestinarians even while affirming a conditional covenant.

[99]Richard Greaves views Preston as one who "leaned toward the Zwingli-Tyndale side" and Ball as even more "representative of a group of men who reassert the fundamental idea of the covenant developed in this Zwingli-Tyndale tradition" (Greaves, "Origins and Early Development," pp. 32–33). These categorizations are in keeping with his division of non-Antinomian Puritans into "moderate Calvinists" and "strict Calvinists," with the former seeing the covenant "more as a pact or a contract" and the latter viewing it "more as a testament or promise" (Greaves, "John Bunyan and Covenant Thought," pp. 152, 158. See also Greaves, *John Bunyan*, p. 98). Yet it must be remembered that, whatever the nature and extent of the "leaning," none of it really threatened the alternative option. In fact, it might be said that for these mainstream Puritans the leaning was simultaneously in both directions. John Ball may be taken as illustration. Although he did emphasize strongly the element of human responsibility in the covenant, he also wrote about the covenant as that in which "God freely promiseth to give what he requireth of his people, and to effect in them what he calleth for at their hands. . . . Righteousnesse and life are promised in the covenant itself" (Ball, *Treatise of Faith*, p. 273). This duality of emphasis can also be seen in Samuel Rutherfurd, another moderate Calvinist in Greaves' classification. Concerning God's saving work Rutherfurd wrote, "He is both without doors knocking and within doors opening, yet he never cometh in, but upon condition we open, which condition is also his own work. He offers Righteousness so the sinner believe, and he works belief that the sinner may have Righteousness" (Rutherfurd, *Survey of Antinomianism*, p. 109. Quoted in *Covenant of Grace Modestly Asserted*, p. 66). And Preston, who "leaned" toward Zwingli-Tyndale, also leaned in the direction of Calvin. He declared, "The Decree of Election . . . is absolute and therefore doth necessarily and infallibly attain its effects . . . God converts the Elect after a manner . . . irresistible" (Preston, *Position of John Preston*, p. 16). So the two themes are put together: "Conversion is irresistible, and yet free" (Ibid., p. 9). And this is also what Perkins, a "strict Calvinist," affirmed.

ful that, as these interpretations from Trinterud onward tend to imply, Zurich bilateralism and Genevan unilateralism were in serious conflict with one another throughout the course of this period of Puritan history, with the former ultimately gaining the upper hand by the mid-seventeenth century. More characteristic would appear to be their dual presence in this Puritan thought. For the mainstream of Puritanism, therefore, it would appear that basically the bilateral and the unilateral were conjoined, human responsibility and divine sovereignty were unitedly maintained, and the covenant of grace was seen as both conditional and absolute.

Chapter 2

THE BEGINNINGS OF THE COVENANT

Puritan theologians frequently made the distinction between a law, a testament, and a covenant as ways of God's working. Often these are combined with one another as, for example, when a covenant is said to lead to the fulfillment of the law or to the receiving of a testament's promise. But they are likewise separable in that each has its distinctive emphasis. A law is a command which depends upon the sovereignty of the law giver and requires subjection whether or not those commanded give their consent. A testament is grounded only on the will of the testator and involves the bequeathing of promised legacies, with no requirement for action on the part of the recipient. A covenant, however, is different from both, for it is a mutual agreement and commitment, in which the consent of each of the participants is essential. This is a central characteristic of covenants between human persons, and when the divine-human covenant is examined, it is found likewise to apply.

GOD'S COVENANTING

The divine-human covenant, said William Strong, "implies two things, something on God's part, which is the promise, and something on man's part, which is the duty, and unto both these consent of parties is required; God's consent unto the promise, and man's consent unto the service."[1] And the mutuality of obligation is so great that the term "contract" may even on occasion be employed, as was done by Perkins, for example, to identify this method of God's working.[2] Yet for all its legality, such a contractual relationhip between God and humanity is not to be conceived simply in terms of the rigidly legal. "Above all other covenants," declared Sibbes, this "contract" is "the sweetest covenant," for the Spirit is likewise at work within it, and "when he saith 'Amen, it shall be so,' then the soul saith, 'Amen, Lord; let it be so.'"[3] This contract of mutual consent and obligation is more than merely contractual and must be seen within the broader frame of the whole Puritan religious consciousness and experience.

There are many reasons proposed in Puritan discussion for God's use of

[1]Strong, *Discourse of Two Covenants*, p. 241.
[2]Perkins, "Golden Chaine," *Works*, 1:32.
[3]Sibbes, "Bride's Longing," *Works*, 6:541.

the covenant manner of working. An overarching conviction concerning this, as God's own purposes are probed, is found in the joyous assertion of Thomas Shepard: "The Lord can never get near enough to His people, and thinks He can never get them near enough to Himself, and therefore unites and binds and fastens them close to Himself and Himself unto them, by the bonds of a Covenant."[4] Still more explicitly the covenant approach was seen in varied ways to involve God's great consideration for human well being. God's use of a covenant, we are told by John Ball, enables the creature to know what to expect from the Creator and what to retribute in return.[5] And because of the reliability of God's action guaranteed by covenant, noted Peter Bulkeley, God uses the covenant "for the stronger consolation of his people."[6] Richard Baxter made the further affirmation that God, by covenanting gifts of goodness and mercy, has made it easier for persons to respond in love.[7]

Above all, however, we hear time and again that God has chosen to work by covenant because to do so is in accord with the rational and voluntary character of the human person. Ball observed that God uses covenants because "such manner of dealing suites best with the nature of the reasonable creature,"[8] a view also expressed by Ames in the *Marrow* when he discussed God's special governance of "intelligent creatures."[9] Sibbes elaborated upon this by pointing out that because God "framed man an understanding creature," he can discern the "better good" of communion and fellowship with God and enter then into covenant relationship.[10] Yet even more, the rational creature is a willing creature, and God's establishing of communion by covenanting is a divine respecting of that central human reality. Sibbes exclaimed, "God honours us by . . . having our consent. Is not this a great honour to us, that he will not perform things without our consent? For indeed he will not accomplish the work of our eternal salvation without it."[11] These actions by consent in covenant are then in fact more valuable by virtue of this free participation. Thomas Blake employed this analogy: "One volunteer that goes out of choice, more honours an expedition, then ten that are prest by power for service."[12] So God acts by covenanting, calling upon the human person to be a freely participating covenant partner. There are thus two consenting participants envisaged in the covenant of grace.

[4]Shepard, "To the Reader," in Bulkeley, *Gospel-Covenant.*
[5]Ball, *Covenant of Grace*, p. 6.
[6]Bulkeley, *Gospel-Covenant*, p. 30.
[7]Baxter, "Christian Directory," *Practical Works*, 5:44.
[8]Ball, *Covenant of Grace*, p. 6.
[9]Ames, *Marrow*, pp. 44–45.
[10]Sibbes, "Faithful Covenanter," *Works*, 6:3.
[11]Sibbes, "Bride's Longing," *Works*, 6:542.
[12]Blake, *Vindiciae Foederis*, p. 6.

The Need for the Covenant

For most Puritan theologians, however, the covenant of grace was not the first covenant in the history of God's relationship with humanity. Rather, as has earlier been suggested, it was given because of the failure of a predecessor, the covenant of works. God originally planned to rely on the perfect obedience of the covenanting partner and had entered into that covenant arrangement with Adam at creation. "Do this and live" was essentially its message, an agreement calling for God's bestowing the rewards of happiness and eternal life in exchange for faithful compliance with the divine command. Here was a thoroughgoing contractual arrangement, a divine-human *quid pro quo*. God would receive obedience, and Adam would receive life. But Adam did not "do" in the manner intended, and the covenant of works was broken.

Actually, some Puritans raised questions about the truly covenantal character of this primordial relationship. Since the biblical text (Genesis 2:16–17) commanding Adam not to eat from the tree of the knowledge of good and evil contained no explicit promise of reward for obedience, but only a threat of punishment for disobedience, some would place it in the category of law rather than covenant. Vavosar Powell preferred to call it a command;[13] Thomas Goodwin saw it as the "Law of Creation;"[14] and Richard Baxter, believing that Adam had also received the promise in a superadded revelation, was willing to say that this "Divine Instrument" was "a Law in one respect, and a Covenant in another."[15] But most of the divines did not scruple so closely on this matter. Anthony Burgess, though granting that the covenant with Adam was "obscurely laid downe" in Scripture, spoke for many when he affirmed that it can nevertheless "be gathered by deduction and consequence." In covenant, Burgess said, God "doth sweeten and mollifie that power of his," which ordinarily is present in the giving of the law, and "ingageth himselfe to reward that obedience, which were otherwise due, though God should never recompense it." This is implied in the Genesis account, so that it can then be affirmed "that God did not onely, as a Law-giver, injoyne obedience unto Adam; but as a loving God, did also enter into covenant with him."[16] Similarly, Adam entered into covenant with God. Mutuality of consent is essential for a covenant to prevail. So, even though this human concurrence likewise is not explicit in the Scriptural statement, William Strong could affirm both knowledge and consent of a far reaching character: "Adam did know the terms of the Covenant by which he

[13]Powell, *Christ and Moses*, p. 2.
[14]T. Goodwin, "Of the Creatures," *Works*, 7:22. Quoted in Kevan, *Grace of Law*, p. 112.
[15]Baxter. *Doctrinal Controversies*, p. 99. Quoted in Kevan, *Grace of Law*, p. 111.
[16]Burgess, *Vindiciae Legis*, p. 119.

stood, and did consent unto them for himself and his posterity."[17] The antecedent to the covenant of grace was the covenant of works.

A further important consideration was the moral content of this covenant, and here two complementary affirmations were insistently made. First, the substance of the covenant of works was to be found in the "natural law" or "moral law" written upon the human heart in the very act of creation itself. Puritan theologians did not hesitate to affirm this universal presence of the divine imprint. Robert Rollock, an early Scottish proponent of the double covenant scheme, maintained that "it could not wel stand with the justice of God to make a covenant with man under the condition of holy and good works, and perfect obedience to his Law, except that he had first created man holy & pure, and ingraven his law in the hart whence those good works should proceed."[18] And John Plaifere said of Adam, "The Law Naturall or Morall, written in the heart of Man, comprehended all Works to be done by him."[19] Scriptural precedent for such conviction was to be found in the first chapter of Paul's Letter to the Romans, where this natural knowledge is accorded to the Gentiles. For these Puritans there was also precedent in Calvin's recognition of a universal "sense of divinity" or "seed of religion."

A problem faced by all those who affirmed natural law, however, was the identification of its precise content. Burgess recognized that "to bound it by the customs of Nations" would leave it most diversified, for "a sin with some was a vertue with others," and to bind it "by reason in every man" could leave its interpretation equally uncertain, for "one mans reason is contrary to anothers."[20] Yet, within the rational nature of all persons there is the underlying sense "whereby things intrinsecally good are commanded, and intrinsecally evil are prohibited."[21] But for clearer and more complete understanding one turns to later revealed legislation, and it can then be said that this natural knowledge is in fact an awareness of what came to be God's written Law, of which the Ten Commandments constitute a basic summary.

So this is the second affirmation. John Lightfoot urged that "Adam heard as much in the garden, as Israel did at Sinai, but onely in fewer words and without thunder."[22] But the thunder was important for fuller hearing, and so Sinai provided the norm. God's law is one law, and humanity from its first moment of obligation has been under its jurisdiction, though this law came in time to be more explicitly stated. Preston said that the covenant "made with Adam" was "expressed by Moses,"[23] and this occurred as he brought about the Law's recording. Such understanding of the content of the

[17]Strong, *Discourse of Two Covenants*, p. 239.
[18]Quoted in E. F., *Marrow*, p. 10.
[19]Plaifere, *Appello Evangelium*, p. 80.
[20]Burgess, *Vindiciae Legis*, p. 62.
[21]Burgess, *True Doctrine of Justification*, 2:387.
[22]Lightfoote, *Miscellanies*, pp. 182–83.
[23]Preston, *New Covenant*, 2:71.

obligations of the covenant of works made it possible for those who found difficulty in giving it the garden's chronological priority at least to assign it a place of logical priority in their theological understanding. This would be true, for example, of Perkins who did not place the covenant of works historically before the fall, but who did put it systematically before the covenant of grace.[24] Ames, on the other hand, though writing in the *Marrow* a systematic statement, located the covenant of works in Paradise and presented an historical progression. This, for the vast majority of divines, became the accepted understanding. Said one, concerning the command-ments, "Though they were not written in Tables of stone until the time of Moses, yet were they writ in the Tables of mans heart in the time of Adam."[25] Another saw a great historical span for the commandments, beginning with the inner promptings in the garden: "The Decalogue is Adams, and Abrahams, and Noahs, and Christs, and the Apostles, as well as of Moses."[26] So natural law and historical law coincide, and their common content comprised the first covenanted human obligation.

The covenant of works was thus also a covenant of nature or a covenant of creation, though here a distinction appears especially between American Puritanism and its English predecessor and counterpart. The term "covenant of nature" was not American in its usage, and John Eusden notes that "the covenant of works as interpreted by American Puritans had little bearing on their interpretation of natural law."[27] Among British writers, however, this identification was more easily made. Robert Rollock and John Cameron were among those in the early seventeenth century who, drawing upon continental sources, introduced the designation "covenant of nature" into the vocabulary of English covenant theology. But on both sides of the Atlantic the Edenic covenant was broadly affirmed, a covenant of works calling for obedience and promising life. And that this was truly a covenant was underscored, as in Ames' explication, by the conviction that even in that primitive beginning God had established "Symboles or Sacraments" to seal the covenant relationship. The tree of life in the garden sealed the reward for obedience, and the tree of the knowledge of good and evil sealed the punishment for disobedience.[28] Yet it was a relationship marked by fragility, for completion required compliance. The law may be written there on the human heart, but Burgess knew that this inward inscription was only for the knowledge of it, and not for the power of it.[29] The first covenanter did not himself generate the power of it, and so the covenant of works was broken.

The fall occurred despite the fact that humanity had been created in the

[24]Perkins, "Golden Chaine," *Works*, 1:32.
[25]E. F., *Marrow*, p. 10.
[26]Burgess, *Vindiciae Legis*, p. 142.
[27]Eusden, "Natural Law," p. 19.
[28]Ames, *Marrow*, p. 48.
[29]Burgess, *Vindiciae Legis*, p. 60.

image of God. There was no defect in creation. The progenitor of the race was "intire and perfect, made after the Image of God in Righteousnesse and true holinesse, furnished not only with a reasonable soule and faculties beseeming, but with divine qualities breathed from the whole Trinity, . . . inabling and fitting him to obey the will of God intirely, willingly, exactly."[30] But though Adam received from God the power to persevere in goodness, he did not receive the grace of perseverence itself.[31] Samuel Rutherfurd commented simply, "Adam was not predestinate to a law glory."[32] So Adam fell in an act of disobedience that Ames saw not only to include pride, ingratitude and unbelief, "but also by violating that most solemne Sacrament, did make show of . . . contempt of the whole covenant."[33] Said another divine, "Adam at that one clap broke all the ten Commandements."[34]

Holding firmly to the belief in God's undiminished sovereignty, even within the covenant relationship, Puritan theology was compelled to deal with the question of responsibility for the fall. This was a troubling issue, and Puritans, like all Calvinists, were charged at times with developing a system in which God was the ultimate sinner. Arminius, who saw Calvin as an infralapsarian and shared with him that interpretation of the relation of God's decrees to the fall, was vigorous in his criticism of the more extreme Calvinist supralapsarians on this matter. Their view, he declared, did indeed make God the author of sin, for the placement of the decree to save before the event of the lapse necessitated the occurrence of the lapse itself.[35] But all Calvinists, whether supralapsarian or infralapsarian, were at times put under this charge, with the fact of predestation seen as necessitating not only the fall, but also the continuation of sin.[36] Puritan response repeated insistently the free factor in the fall. Perkins, a supralapsarian, said that God had decreed and willed the fall, but had not caused it, for the act of divine willing was not a will to effect, but was rather a will not to hinder.[37] He used an analogy: it is "no otherwise, then when a man staying up a staffe on the ground, it standeth upright; but if he never so little withdraw his hand, it falleth of it selfe."[38] Thus he further urged that though the fall was indeed fore-ordained, it was not caused by God, but occurred by "God's operative permission."[39] Ames, emphasizing still further the role of human responsi-

[30]Ball, *Covenant of Grace*, p. 11.

[31]Perkins, "Gods Free-grace and Mans free-will," *Works*, 1:728.

[32]Rutherfurd, *Covenant of Life*, p. 2.

[33]Ames, *Marrow*, p. 49.

[34]E. F., *Marrow*, p. 17.

[35]Bangs, "Arminius and the Reformation," p. 166.

[36]This is an accusation, for example, which Henry Ainsworth attributed to certain Anabaptists. See Ainsworth, *Seasonable Discourse*, p. 28.

[37]Perkins, "Manner of Predestination," *Works*, 2:606, 613.

[38]Perkins, "Golden Chaine," *Works*, 1:18.

[39]Ibid., p. 112.

bility, said, "The principall cause was man himselfe, by the abuse of his free-will," adding, "God therefore was in no wise the cause of his Fall: neither did he lay upon man a necessity of falling."[40] All Puritans accepted the divine permitting, though opinions divided on the decrees. Supralapsarians followed Perkins, but such an infralapsarian as Harris would say that God simply foresaw the fall and did not decree it.[41] At all events, however, even within the most far-reaching conception of the sovereignty of God, the disobedience of the fall was viewed as freely chosen.

The misuse in the garden of divinely endowed qualities had a vastly destructive effect. For Adam and Adam's posterity it brought both guilt and corruption, both liability to eternal punishment and the presence in this life of spiritual death. Puritan theologians, with their bent for the practical, elaborated particularly on the latter aspect of this human predicament. Ames noted that "Originall Sinne ... is the corruption of the whole man," identifying as being affected the understanding, the conscience, the will, the affections of every kind, and the body and all its members,[42] and this litany was repeated by others in a common chorus. When Preston discussed the state of human corruption, he singled out the understanding as especially central, revealing thereby something of his view, shared by many others, of its particular importance in relation to the other faculties. Spiritual death, he said, "is chiefly in the mind and understanding, and not in the will.... Although the will be corrupted, yet whatsoever is in it is carried through the understanding."[43] So this primary faculty has become tainted, even depraved. It has become vain, blind, unteachable, resistant to belief, at enmity with truth. No longer does it understand, or want to understand, the things of God.

Such corruption, however, also pervades the whole person. The will reflects it through pride, inconstancy and outright disobedience. "Our Will," declared Preston, "wil not stoop to God's Will.... We will have plots and projects of our owne." Similarly the conscience is diseased. The conscience should be a "Remembrancer," but "it is a false register," it "sets downe things by halfes," recalling very inadequately our sins. It should be sensitive to the least prick of our failings, but "there is a brawninesse growne over the Conscience." Also "it should stirre us up, and give us no rest," but instead "it lets us fall asleep againe." The disorder spreads additionally to the affections, where "unrighteousnesse and ungodlinesse ... come like a mightie Tempest, like a turbulent wind that carries us away." "Looke to your Delight," he urged, "and see if that be not turned upside down. The Wheele turns quite the contrary way. We delight in things we should not delight in,

[40]Ames, *Marrow*, p. 50.
[41]Harris, *Way to True Happiness*, 1:15.
[42]Ames, *Marrow*, p. 58.
[43]Preston, *Liveless Life*, p. 4,

... in vaine things, in sinfull things, in ... lusts, ... in the falls and sufferings of others."[44] It all adds up to the pervasive corruption that is spiritual death.

Yet there are what Ames called "remainders of God's image." Total depravity, in Calvinist understanding, meant that depravity touched the total range of human faculties, not that the total functioning of any or all of the faculties was depraved. Thus Ames can speak of the continuation of the divine image in both the understanding and the will after the fall. It is in the understanding as a remainder of the natural law within, and from this "there ariseth a certaine force of naturall conscience." It is in the will as "a certaine inclination unto good" by which "at least the shaddowes of vertues are allowed and embraced of all."[45] Preston likewise spoke this language, finding "Truth" still present in the "natural man." It is in the speculative understanding as some knowledge of the nature of the good; it is in the practical understanding as some urging of conscience that the good should be appropriated; and it is in the will and affections as "certaine inclination" toward that good for one's life.[46] Puritan theology did not leave humanity completely bereft—but almost completely, for the remainders are in the last analysis neither large nor of saving power. To Burgess this "relict" of God's image when compared with faith "is but as a glow-worme to the Sun."[47] John Flavel added that whereas "the Light of Reason was at first the bright Lamp or Candle of the Lord," sin has now "melted it down to a Snuff," so that it is no more than "a poor glimmering Light in the best of men" and "almost quite extinguished" in others.[48] Indeed, said Burgess, because depravity is so great the corrupted natural light really becomes "a desperate enemy to the good."[49]

So the human condition in its fallen state really holds out no hope. Perkins wrote, "There is not only an impotency to good, but such a forcible prones & disposition to evill, as that we can do nothing but sinne. . . . And this disposition is not to some few sinnes, but to all sins without exception."[50] It was hardly much consolation for him to say further that "though every sin of itself be mortal, yet all sins are not equally mortal"[51]—an observation utilized in his casuistry. The corruption of original sin, Burgess noted, adheres to us, "cleaving to our Nature, like Ivy to the Tree."[52] The

---

[44]Preston. *Saints Qualification*, pp. 39–63.

[45]Ames, *Marrow*, pp. 62–63.

[46]Preston, *Saints Qualification*, p. 118.

[47]Burgess, *Vindiciae Legis*. p. 68.

[48]Flavel, *Personal Reformation*, p. 3.

[49]Burgess, *Vindiciae Legis*, p. 70.

[50]Perkins, "Gods Free-grace and Mans free-will," *Works*, 1:730.

[51]Quoted in Ian Breward, "William Perkins and the Origins of Puritan Casuistry," *Faith and a Good Conscience*, The Puritan and Reformed Studies Conference (1963), p. 13. See Sprunger, *Learned Doctor William Ames*, p. 164.

[52]Burgess, *True Doctrine of Justification*, 1:23.

understanding is darkened, the will is misdirected, the conscience is clouded, the affections are misapplied. This is the human condition created by the fall.

In a technical sense a certain human freedom remains, that which is essential to human nature as human nature. "Yet," said Ames, that "freedome which pertaines to the perfection of human nature (the ... power to exercise acts spiritually good, and by that meanes acceptable) is not found in this sinful state, unlesse, Remote and Dead."[53] The will at the point of moral exercise is "captive and servile," and from this condition of original sin, then, actual sin itself "flowes ... as an act from a habit."[54] But this bondage is not an exoneration from culpability. The will has such freedom, noted Arthur Dent, that "it sinneth of itselfe," though it is still in "thraldome unto Sinne."[55] So in the grips of spiritual death there is no way for humanity "to patch up a broken covenant"[56] even though pride may dictate that effort. New life can come only through a new covenant, the covenant of grace.

THE ESTABLISHMENT OF THE COVENANT

It is important to note that Puritan understanding of God as a covenanting God was set within an interpretation of the biblical as a record of the historical. Though Puritan theologians contributed their ample share to a using of the Bible for proof text purposes and were at one with Reformed scholasticism in this regard, they also viewed the Bible as the account of God's covenanting labors in the progress of human history. God was at work in the lives of persons and of peoples, and the biblical record recounts that ongoing story. At history's beginning God entered into the first covenant. With its failure God covenanted again, and then the history of Israel and the new Israel became the arena for that second covenant's gradual clarification and application. So this history was a "history of salvation," and the instrument of God's saving action within it was the second covenant, the covenant of grace.

It is interesting, however, that though human history plays so important a role in the outworking of the covenant of grace, the actual origin of the covenant itself was, in this Puritan understanding, not within that historical process. Rather, its beginning was in what might be called "divine history," a kind of meta-history located solely in the life of God. The source of the covenant of grace was a still prior covenant between God and Christ, designated theologically as the covenant of redemption. Thomas F. Torrance has alleged that the use of this concept is a sign of growing abstraction in

[53] Ames, *Marrow*, p. 57.
[54] Ibid., p. 59.
[55] Dent, *Plaine Mans Path-way*, p. 13.
[56] Strong, *Discourse of Two Covenants*, p. 153.

Puritan theology, for in positing something prior to the covenant of grace, that theology made the distinction between God's acts beyond time and God's acts in time.[57] If so, however, it was abstract speculation reaching concrete conclusion, for the ultimate outcome was to draw the Christ of historical revelation more directly into both the substance and the assurance of the covenant of grace. Indeed, Rutherfurd even saw the covenant of redemption as explicitly including temporal, along with eternal, aspects and complicated still more the terminological terrain by subdividing it into a "Covenant of Designation" and a "Covenant of Actual Redemption," the former comprising the covenanted divine plan in pre-history and the latter its historical redemptive enactment.[58] But even apart from that effort at further refinement, the idea of the trans-historical covenant may be seen to have had theological significance for interpreting the historical process, for it explicitly gave a Christological foundation to the covenant of grace, relating it closely to the central Christian conception of Christ's redemptive role in salvation history.

So the covenanting of God and Christ was posited, an agreement "struck Dialogue-wise,"[59] as Thomas Goodwin described it, in which Christ became not only "privy to the Plot" which had existed hidden at "the bottom of Gods Counsel" and in "the depth of all his Secrets,"[60] but also a covenanting participant in its outworking. Though he knew the future cost of the commitment he was undertaking, Christ, in this portrayal, freely covenanted to become the suffering Savior by agreeing to accomplish the redemptive work of the cross. Then, said Goodwin, "as Christ undertook to God, so God undertakes to Christ again, to justifie, adopt and forgive, sanctifie and glorifie those he gives him."[61]

The last part of that statement suggests also another element in this conception, namely, that in the intra-Trinitarian covenanting there was inclusion of those who were to be its ultimate beneficiaries, those who are given to the Son, those who ultimately come to be "in Christ." In fact, some portrayals of this covenant presented it as the covenant of grace itself, since the promises to Christ are likewise to the elect in him.[62] This collapsing of the covenant of grace into the covenant of redemption tended, however, to be more characteristic of the Antinomian wing of Puritanism where there was inclination to see as much as possible in the divine act and to keep the covenant as far away as possible from human contracting. For Puritan theologians as a whole, nevertheless, Christ was known to be the "second

[57]Torrance, *School of Faith*, p. lxxix.

[58]Rutherfurd, *Covenant of Life*, p. 309.

[59]T. Goodwin, "Christ the Mediator," *Works*, 3:138.

[60]Ibid., p. 37.

[61]Ibid., p. 26.

[62]For a contemporary reading of Puritan thought in this manner see Brown, "Covenant Theology," *Encyclopedia of Religion and Ethics*, 4:216–17.

Adam," and one of the significant things about the covenant of redemption is that the promises to Christ include also his posterity. So the beneficial promises are made in the circles of eternity, but are promises touching the life of time. "Here," declared Rutherfurd, "is Covenant-condiscension between JEHOVAH and the Son, of quieting Law, and pitching on a milde Gospel-way."[63] This covenant is not itself the covenant of grace, but it is the source of the covenant of grace. And it provided an additional foundation for comfort. Said William Strong, "It is one of the greatest grounds of faith . . . that Christ is engaged by covenant, unto God, as well as unto us: and therefore he being the Son will be faithful to his Father: And also that God is ingaged unto Christ as well as unto us, and therefore will be faithful to him also, and will not break with the Son."[64] The covenant of redemption undergirds with this strengthened certainty the covenant of grace.

William Perkins defined the new and second covenant with theological formality: "The covenant of Grace," he wrote, "is that whereby God freely promising Christ, and his benefits, exacteth againe of man, that hee would by faith receive Christ, and repent of his sinnes."[65] Less formal and more exuberant language was used by Obadiah Sedgwick:

> There is a gracious Covenant. . . . And when that Covenant is passed twixt God and a person . . . there is a mutuall acceptation . . . as when the woman and man enter into the covenant of marriage. . . . So when the Lord God and a sinner are married to each other, when they are entered into a Covenant, Thou art my God, and none else, my heart is thine, my life shall be thine. . . . The Lord saith unto such a one, And I am thine, and all my mercy is thine, my Christ is thine, my Promise thine: If thou needest any good for soule or body, all good is thine.[66]

The Puritan faithful found much cause for such exuberance in their reflection on this new act of God's covenanting with humanity. Despite the disobedience of the fall, despite the breaking of the first covenant by sin, despite the now corrupted character of the race, God has once again entered

---

[63]Rutherfurd, *Covenant of Life*, p. 296.

[64]Strong, *Discourse of Two Covenants*, p. 130.

[65]Perkins, "Golden Chaine," *Works*, 1:71. Wayne Baker interprets Perkins as holding to a covenant of grace entirely unconditional in character, thus to a testamental view of this covenant. Conditionality, on the other hand, is associated with the covenant of works, which is the agency of law. See Baker, *Heinrich Bullinger and the Covenant*, pp. 205–7. But though Perkins does stress strongly the covenant of grace as God's gift, it is a covenant in which God also "exacteth" from those who are called and to whom the fulfillment is gratuitously given. Perkins is not unaware of the wayfaring and warfaring involved in the soul's struggle in the meeting of covenantal conditions. So in him, as in the others under discussion, the conditional is present along with the absolute, and there is the obligation to respond even as the response itself can be seen as a gift of grace.

[66]O. Sedgwick, *Doubting Beleever*, p. 237.

into the historical scene, not only to renew the broken relationship, but also to establish it in a radically different way. "He hath herein stooped below himselfe," said Bulkeley, "and hath lift us above our selves."[67] Though there is still mutuality of participation in the covenant relationship, it is a mutuality of a different order. Commanding and obeying have been replaced by giving and receiving. Those who once were servants are now adopted daughters and sons. Whereas once all centered on task, now the center is gift. Even in the garden itself God made this change, enrolling into the new relationship those who had so recently fallen—and thus the covenant of grace was entered into human history and into the life of succeeding generations.

Puritan writing often characterized the covenant of grace as a free, sure, and everlasting covenant. An examination of these qualities can reveal in more detail its radical difference from its predecessor, the covenant of works. As free, it is a covenant in which all is of grace. It is not that grace was completely absent from the covenant of works. That covenant was itself understood as created by a gracious act, for even the promise of just reward came from God's goodness. The law might simply have been uncompensated command. Yet in that covenant, said Rutherfurd, the "law is honeyed with love," and "it is mercy that for our penny of obedience, so rich a wadge as communion with God is given."[68] In the second covenant, however, all is of grace. It is not only that God's promises are made out of grace, but more, they are promises of grace. Said Sibbes, "God does not require any answering by our strength, for then he should require light of darkness, life of death."[69] If the covenant of works was a legal covenant, this is now an evangelical covenant in which "the promises that are made, are not made to any worke or vertue in man, but to the worker: not for any merit of his own person or worke, but for the person and merit of Christ."[70]

So in this covenant there is forgiveness of sins: in the covenant of works God condemns sin and condemns the sinner, but in the covenant of grace God condemns sin and spares the sinner.[71] There is also the gift of newness of life which empowers obedience: in the covenant of works it was said, "Do this for life," but in the covenant of grace it is said, "Do this from life," the former injunction delivered to all by God as Creator, the latter by God as Redeemer to those covenanted and renewed "in Christ."[72] This new covenant is what Edward Leigh called "the bundle and body of all the promises."[73] And the overarching promise is in the divine word, "I will be

[67]Bulkeley, *Gospel-Covenant*, p. 46.
[68]Rutherfurd, *Covenant of Life*, p. 35.
[69]Sibbes, "Demand of Good Conscience," *Works*, 7:483.
[70]Perkins, "Reformed Catholike," *Works*, 1:576.
[71]Bulkeley, *Gospel-Covenant*, p. 84.
[72]E. F., *Marrow*, p. 155.
[73]Leigh, *Divine Promises*, title page.

your God." Bulkeley saw here the whole of the Trinity engaged, with the Father's and Son's promises in the covenant of redemption augmented now by those of the Spirit to apply "what the Father hath purposed . . . and the Son hath purchased," by delivering forgiveness and writing the law on the human heart.[74] Sibbes added the further remarkable affirmation that the promises of the covenant extend to one's relation to all creation, so that "there is a covenant betwixt us and the creatures . . . that nothing shall wrong us, but all conduce to our good."[75] Seeing the magnitude of this mercy, it is little wonder that Bulkeley could exclaim, "As the Sun dazles the eye to look upon so glorious a light, so the great things which God hath promised in his covenant, do even dazle the eye of faith."[76] The covenant is of free grace.

The covenant that is free is also sure. It is sure in one sense because it rests not on one's own doing but on the doing of another, that of the Mediator who is Christ, and thus, as the second Adam differs from the first, so this covenant differs from the covenant of works. Rutherfurd wrote, "The first Adam marres all, the second Adam . . . mends all," and then also added, "The first Adam . . . put all things a-reeling. The second Adam received in his arms the whole Creation that was a-falling."[77] It is on this sure foundation of Christ that the second covenant was established. As God-man he was qualified to be Mediator. Said Harris, "He was God for the businesse with God, and man for the businesse with man."[78] Carrying out this "business," then, he provided the redemptive act on which the covenant was based. But the covenant of grace is sure in the added sense that in it are encompassed the committed mercies of God. Puritans often marvelled that God should enter such binding obligation as the covenant entailed, that God should "become a debtor"[79] in relation to humankind. Yet this is what God has undertaken in the covenant relationship, even to the point of swearing an oath, so the Scripture says, to confirm this commitment.[80] So the free mercy of the covenant leads to the self-binding of God and to a covenant that is sure.

Still further the covenant of grace is everlasting and here also differs from the covenant of works. According to an early seventeenth century Puritan document, the covenant of grace is an everlasting covenant which God has "more fixed in his Sonne, than the Sonne and Moone are fixed in the Heavens."[81] Once again the anchorage in Christ is important, now seen as

---

[74]Bulkeley, *Gospel-Covenant*, pp.188–89.

[75]Sibbes, "Privileges of the Faithful," *Works*, 5:262–63.

[76]Bulkeley, *Gospel-Covenant*, p. 52.

[77]Rutherfurd, *Covenant of Life*, p. 225.

[78]Harris, *New Covenant*, 2:157.

[79]Preston, *New Covenant*, 2:85.

[80]G. Downame, *Covenant of Grace*, p. 9.

[81]Quoted in Møller, "Beginnings of Puritan Covenant Theology," p. 62. Møller's listing of the

basis for the covenant's permanence. Whereas the covenant of works was quickly broken in its dependence on finite and weak obedience, the covenant of grace will continue unbroken since upheld by One who is eternally faithful. Because there are two partners to the covenant, this assurance often encountered both theological perplexity and anxious doubt, matters we shall need later to explore. But the underlying certainty was nevertheless strongly affirmed. Bulkeley proclaimed the transition of the soul from the covenant of works to the covenant of grace to mean that "here is a safe harbour. . . . the ship may be tossed, but cannot perish."[82] Sutton shared these sentiments when he exclaimed, "Be glad and rejoyce all . . . unto whom God hath made a covenant and promise. . . . He hath given you the keyes of his Kingdome . . . Though you fall, yet you shall rise againe, therefore you are not to be cast away."[83] For Robert Bolton, the biblical figure of the shepherd tending his flock provided an analogy for this covenant relationship. "The covenant," he said, "is not thus only: as long as you keep within the boundes, and keep within the fould." It is rather that God declares, "This is the Covenant that I will make, . . . if anything bee lost, if a sheepe loose it selfe, . . . I will finde it: If it be driven away by any violence of temptation, I will bring it backe againe. . . . I will heale them, and binde them up."[84] So for persons under the care of the Shepherd the covenant is everlasting and cannot be broken.

There is, however, a still further aspect to this confident affirmation. The covenant of grace embodies divine promises not only to persons, but also to a people, and its everlasting character is likewise a word of assurance to the church. The people are an elect people, for their very existence is a consequence of grace, though in the life of the church itself there may be some who will fall away along with the others who will persevere. Actually, by relating a matter as personal as the gift of grace to the ongoing life of an institution, many of the Puritan divines were led to distinguish between two applications of the covenant of grace. On the one hand, the covenant is applied externally and is available in this sense to all members of the church, to parents and their children, to believers and their seed. Infants of believing parents are sealed in the covenant by baptism and partake of "federal holiness." The church as an institution is thus under God's care. On the other hand, the covenant is also applied within the church savingly or effectually to those who become its full participants. Their identity is often lost in

source as *The Sacred Doctrine of Divinity*, p. 308 is incorrect. It should be Henry Finch, *The Sum of Sacred Divinity*. See McGiffert, "Grace and Works," p. 494, n. 75.

[82]Bulkeley, *Gospel-Covenant*, p. 110.

[83]Sutton, *Lectures on Romans*, p. 403.

[84]R. Bolton, *Comforting Afflicted Consciences*, p. 373.

mystery. Congregational polity sought more industriously to identify them than did presbyterial, but in neither case could the secret counsels of God be fully known. Yet, despite lack of clear identity, the covenant assures the church's continuation. There will always be a "people of God." Because the covenant of grace is everlasting, affirmed Sibbes, the church as the mystical body of Christ will continue. "Always," he said, "God will have some in covenant with him. He will have some to be a God to, when we are gone, so long as the world continueth."[85]

That God's covenant of grace is a covenant not only with persons, but also with a people, is seen in the broad understanding of the covenant's establishment and ongoing history. There are not only Adam and Abraham and Moses, but Adam's posterity, the seed of Abraham, and that entire nation of Moses which laid claim to the name of Israel. There is also the continuation of this people of God in the new Israel centered on Christ. In all instances the criterion for ultimate inclusion is personal saving faith, but the covenant is likewise seen as applicable to the ecclesiastical, if not also political, aspects of ongoing society. The biblical record is the depository of this historical experience, and Puritan theologians analyzed it and portrayed it as the history of the covenant of grace.

William Ames, among others, advanced the major pattern of periodization then generally acknowledged. The covenant was continuous from Genesis through Revelation, though within it are to be found distinct stages of administration. These were identified by Ames as comprising the periods (1) from Adam to Abraham, (2) from Abraham to Moses, (3) from Moses to Christ, and (4) from Christ to the end of the world.[86] The progress of revelation throughout these stages was from cloudiness to light, and the movement in ecclesiastical practice was from primitive to mature. But the progression was in the administration of the one covenant, and thus the whole of the biblical story was stage for this drama of the history of salvation. One major consequence of this outlook was to recognize the continuity in Scripture between the Old and New Testaments. Together they portrayed this history of God's covenant working, and Bulkeley likened them to "the two Cherubims in the temple, which had their faces looking towards the Arke, and were beaten out of one piece of gold," or again to "the two breasts of the Church ... both of them full of sincere milke (as the Apostle calls it ...) fit to nourish the babes of Christ."[87] God's new and everlasting covenant was to be seen as the basis for the continuous history of God's people.

---

[85]Sibbes, "Faithful Covenanter," *Works*, 6:20.
[86]Ames, *Marrow*, pp. 170–80.
[87]Bulkeley, *Gospel-Covenant*, p. 142.

Yet there was one matter which posed considerable difficulty in this Puritan exegesis of the biblical story, the place within it of the Law received and given by Moses at Sinai.[88] The covenant of grace had been initiated, though obscurely, with the race's fallen parents in the garden by what was understood in Genesis 3:15 as the Lord's promise to those parents' posterity for triumph over continuation of the serpent's evil. Then more clearly it was given to Abraham, when in Genesis 17:7 the Lord's word was, "I will fulfill my covenant between myself and you and your descendants after you . . . to be your God." But some four centuries and more later the Law was delivered to Moses in Sinai's thunder, and the question then needed to be pursued as to why God took that action in the course of Israel's history.

Several conclusions were possible, and Puritan theologians differed to some extent on this matter. A few held that the Mosaic covenant was given as a continuation of the covenant of works. Although this view was advanced largely by Antinomians, negative toward all efforts to join law and saving grace, it was also supported by near-Arminian John Goodwin and orthodox divine William Pemble. The mandates of Sinai were a renewal of the covenant law of Eden, now more clearly and explicitly imposed upon the Hebrew people. A second group saw the Mosaic Law as a covenant for Israel subservient to the covenant of grace. Such divines as John Cameron, Samuel Bolton, and Peter Bulkeley wrote in this way. Although under the covenant of grace, declared particularly to Abraham, Israel had fallen on idolatrous ways. God's giving of the Law at Sinai, therefore, was for the curbing of this sin and the restoration of covenant faithfulness. Indeed in this sense it was given also to prepare Israel for the future coming of Christ.

The largest body of Puritan divines, however, viewed the Mosaic Law not as a subservient covenant, but as a genuine part of the covenant of grace itself. John Ball, Anthony Burgess, Thomas Blake, and Samuel Rutherfurd, among others, spoke in this manner, seeing the Law of Sinai as providing the rule of life for those who, already in the covenant, were seeking to walk in the way of the Lord. The Mosaic Law could not be a covenant of works as was the first covenant with Adam, for now it was given to sinners unable to obey out of their own strength, nor was it simply a temporary expedient for Israel's healing. It was, rather, an enlargement of the covenant with Abraham, where the first word was that God will be his God and the God of his descendants, and the second that they shall be obedient as God's people.

[88]For discussion of this issue see Ball, *Covenant of Grace*, pp. 93–118; Blake, *Vindiciae Foederis*, pp. 210–12; S. Bolton, *True Bounds of Christian Freedom*, pp. 127–45; Bulkeley, *Gospel-Covenant*, p. 63; Burgess, *Vindiciae Legis*, pp. 205–6, 220–23; Cameron, *Certain Theses*, pp. 381–84; Pemble, *Vindiciae fidei*, pp. 133–39; Rutherfurd, *Covenant of Life*, pp. 57–81; Kevan, *Grace of Law*, pp. 113–24.

Here now in the Law that way of obedience is more clearly revealed. But even within the Decalogue itself those emphases on grace and law are combined. When the commandments were given, the opening declaration was a reminder of God's graciousness: "I am the Lord your God who brought you out of the land of Egypt, out of the house of bondage." Abraham and Moses belong together. The main body of Puritan divines saw the Law given to Israel as part of the covenant of grace.

Chapter 3
THE NATURE OF THE COVENANT

To speak of the nature of the covenant of grace in Puritan thought is to speak actually of its two natures. Puritan theology was not a rational whole, but was drawn by its own inner impulses into two directions, those generated by the experiential and voluntaristic concerns of Gospel piety and those precipitated by the inherited dogmatic demand for the doctrine of predestination. Evangel and election bequeathed to Puritan theology a double agenda, and the idea of the covenant became, at least in some measure, the point of connection, if not also of reconciliation. So the one covenant has two qualities: it is, on the one hand, the instrument of the mutuality of divine-human commitment and, on the other hand, the instrument of God's sovereign rule in all that pertains to salvation. In the terminology of the Puritans the covenant of grace is both conditional and absolute.

THE COVENANT AS CONDITIONAL

In his portrayal of the covenant of grace Peter Bulkeley emphasized that both commandment and promise are branches of conditional covenant relationship and urged, "The promise is the ground of the duty, and the duty is the way to the promise. . . . Therefore what God hath thus joyned together, let no man put asunder."[1] Certainly there was no desire on the part of Puritan theologians, with the exception of those of Antinomian sympathy, to put asunder these aspects of the covenant, for both the theology of covenant understanding and the psychology of covenant usage pressed for their interconnection. John Ball knew it was as "the thirstie soule" laid hold on "the gratious invitation" and drew near to God in trust for its salvation, that it would be "watered with grace and refreshed with comfort,"[2] a statement containing both theological and psychological implications. The divine mercy of the covenant promise was bestowed on those who fulfilled the prerequisite condition, on those who came by consent into the covenant and were receptive in faith to its gifts. Moreover, to the duty of faith there was added the duty of fidelity. Baxter wrote:

[1]Bulkeley, *Gospel-Covenant*, pp. 157–58.
[2]Ball, *Treatise of Faith*, p. 176.

> The terms or conditions which God requireth of man in his covenant are, consent, and fidelity or performance. . . . He consenteth to be actually our God when we consent to be his people ... but the sincere performance of the duties of the relation which we consent to, are needful afterwards to continue the relation.[3]

The covenant contained and communicated God's promises, but conditionally. In this sense it can certainly be said that the covenant did not so much keep as need keeping. Preston affirmed, "God will be wholly theirs that will be wholly his."[4]

Antinomians warned that this view of covenant could lead to another work-righteousness. To rely on the fulfillment of conditions is to rely on one's own doing, and that is an unstable foundation for covenant security. Even to build on one's faith is to build on both unsatisfactory and improper grounds. Faith itself is subject to hypocrisy, and what is more, as Tobias Crisp urged, justification, the forgiveness of sins, the covenant relationship with God are absolutely given and without condition. "Justification," he said, "is an Act of Christ, it is not an Act of Faith." The act of faith will follow, for by believing on Christ one manifests one's justification. But Christ gives before one believes, and faith itself therefore is only declarative of that giving. Thus Christ, he added, "makes us to be in Covenant, for his own sake, without any condition in the Creature."[5]

The main body of Puritan divines, however, would not permit any such diminution of the role of human decision in the covenant relationship. John Reynolds said that if we do not consent in the covenant, it is "but a Wooing and no Mariage."[6] Thus emphasis persisted for the inclusion of the conditional, a reality which Sibbes enhanced by saying that "we enter into terms of friendship with God in the covenant of grace" and "friends must have the same mind; there must be an answering."[7] Some conditions of the covenant are indeed subsequent or declaratory. But others, it was maintained, are concomitant or even antecedent, though in no case was any condition to be deemed meritorious. An anonymous document dealing with the Arminian issue declared, "The distinction between a Condition, and a meritorious Cause, is no slender and weak Evasion, but a main and fundamental Distinction in this Controversie,"[8] and this was a crucial matter. Puritans, in affirming contingency but in denying meritoriousness, avoided all charges of work-righteousness and yet saved the conditionality of the covenant. It was

---

[3]Baxter, "Christian Directory," *Practical Works*, 5:41.
[4]Preston, *New Covenant*, 1:174.
[5]Crisp, *Christ Alone Exalted*, pp. 84–87.
[6]John Reynolds, *Treatise of the Life of Christ*, p. 465. Quoted in *Covenant of Grace not Absolute*, p. 67.
[7]Sibbes, "Demand of Good Conscience," *Works*, 7:482.
[8]*Covenant of Grace not Absolute*, p. 20.

for them no "weak evasion" to say that God responded to, though did not reward, faith and fidelity.

The conditions of the covenant may not be meritorious, but they are to be taken with utmost seriousness. Richard Baxter, always thorough and precise about these matters, urged that in fact there were certain conditions for the fulfillment of the covenant's conditions, such as, that there be understanding of what is consented to, that it be one's own act, that it be deliberate, seriously done, inclusive of all parts of covenant obligation, performed with the present moment in mind, and done without secret reservation.[9] Baxter's somewhat legal mind thus analyzed soberly the warmth of religious commitment. Not all would be inclined so to dissect passion. But the conditions of covenant were to be taken seriously, and they were also to be seen under the necessity of urgency. Puritan preaching pressed for covenant decision, an evangelicalism that lent itself to stressing the perils in delay. "Take heede of deferring," said Preston, " . . . procrastination in taking the offer of Grace, is the most dangerous thing in the world." He further reminded his hearers that it was also one of the easiest things in the world:

> We thinke to do it in a short time, . . . but it is not so, we are deceived and deluded with it: as Grassehoppers and Butterflies deceive children, when they thinke to lay their hand upon them, they hoppe a little further, and a little further, that in conclusion, they take them not at all; so it is with us, we coozen our selves in that manner, we lose our life, we lose our opportunity to taking grace, because wee thinke it to bee so neere.[10]

Once again difficult theological issues were posed when this sense of urgency was brought into conjunction with the doctrine of God's sovereignty, the tension created by the juxtaposition of piety and predestination. But the tension was possible only because among the convictions of Puritan faith was the belief that the act of faith itself, along with other appropriate human actions, was prerequisite for the covenant relationship. "Every particular soul," Bulkeley affirmed, "must enter into a particular covenant with God."[11] And Ball presented in summary what he understood to be involved in that covenant action: "that we take God to be our God, that is, that we repent of our iniquities, believe the promises of mercy and embrace them with the whole heart, and yeeld love, feare, reverence, worship, and obedience."[12] These were covenant conditions.

To assist and encourage Christian believers in the fulfillment of cove-

---

[9]Baxter, "Christian Directory," *Practical Works*, 5:43.
[10]Preston, *New Covenant*, 2:191–92.
[11]Bulkeley, *Gospel-Covenant*, p. 47.
[12]Ball, *Covenant of Grace*, p. 18.

nant conditions God has established in the church, so it was maintained, both audible and visible means toward grace. There is, of course, the preaching of the Word, as both Law and Gospel. The Reformation tradition had insisted from the outset that faith comes by hearing, and Puritan theology and practice gave strong endorsement to that conviction. Perkins once described the Gospel as "the conduit pipe of the holy Ghost, to fashion and derive faith into the soule."[13] His analogy may not do justice to the personal and subjective element in Christian believing, as indeed it was recognized within this Puritan tradition, but it points clearly to the Puritan sense of the preached word's power. William Twisse once wrote approvingly about "Father Latimer taking notice of some that come to Church to take a nap, yet never the lesse (saith he) let them come, they may be taken napping,"[14] though this was hardly the recommended route to conversion! But when the Word is preached and heard, a means for the encouraging of faith's response is at hand.

Similarly the Word is made visible in the sacraments of the church. Baptism and the Lord's Supper serve as God's instruments for initiating and nurturing the covenant relationship. It is not that grace is tied to the means, nor that the means simply themselves will produce grace. As to the latter, "the means will not do it without the Spirit,"[15] a frequently repeated assertion which keeps the bestowing of grace still in God's hands. As to the former, the Spirit can move freely, and Perkins did not hesitate to voice hope for the salvation of some who lived and died "under popery," for God can utilize extraordinary instruments "when ordinarie meanes of salvation faile."[16] Normally, however, grace comes through the use of the means which God has provided, for this is God's way of loving and providential care. John Rogers wrote:

> God dealeth with us as mothers who nurse their young children; they lap them up warme, and give them both breasts, and so they grow up: so it is between God and us: the Word and Sacraments bee the two breasts of the Church.[17]

It is small wonder, then, that neglect of the means was matter for concern and distress. Walter Marshal complained about the "carnal Gospellers, that being puft up with a Conceit of their feigned Faith, imagine themselves to be in such a state of Perfection, that they are above all Ordinances, except singing Halelujahs."[18] But the more common complaint

[13]Perkins, "Golden Chaine," *Works*, 1:71.
[14]Twisse, *Riches of God's Love*, p. 267.
[15]E. F., *Marrow*, p. 195.
[16]Perkins, "Exposition of the Creed," *Works*, 1:290.
[17]J. Rogers, *Doctrine of Faith*, p. 215.
[18]Marshal, *Gospel Mystery*, p. 274.

was that of Baxter, disturbed over persons in his parish "harping on thi[string," that since one cannot receive grace until God gives it, there is n[need to use the means. Such persons, said Baxter, are "setled in a negle[and contempt of the means of Grace."[19] Even though faith itself, in the la[analysis, is the free gift of God, the means should be used for the obtainin[of it. John Ball provided the analogy:

> Marriage was never held superfluous or unnecessary for the propagatio[
> of mankind, because the reasonable soule is not generated by ou[
> parents, but immediately created and infused by God. That faith is th[
> sole gift of God, wholly infused, not partly acquired by us, should rathe[
> incite, then any way abate our endeavours for attaining it. For faith is n[
> given but in the use of the meanes.[20]

So one needs diligently to attend to the Word and the sacraments—an[then, said Harris, though God "be no way indebted, . . . yet ordinarily he [not wanting to give grace to such a person."[21] Indeed, new life can com[likewise from even more general association with the church, and so h[further counseled:

> Especially apply your selves to the communion of the Saints: A dea[
> coale, put to live coales, will take fire from them, which it would neve[
> do lying in the dead heape: so here . . . sort your selves with such as ar[
> godly, and frequent the ordinances . . . that you may have part in th[
> new covenant.[22]

Thus God provides assistance in evident ways toward one's entrance int[covenant partnership.

In examining the fulfillment of covenant conditions, however, it will b[useful to note a distinction in ways of approach. On the one hand, there is th[question of the "process" by which conversion occurs and the new life [entered and sustained in Christian awareness. This has to do with the natur[of the conditions themselves, the experiences undergone, the feelings o[both anxiety and joy which are known, the traumas and the triumph[involved in becoming a believer and progressing in that state. It has to d[with the stages of the Christian pilgrimage and the nature of the pilgrim's lif[along the way. Here one is concerned with the essence of the covenan[experience. On the other hand, there is the further matter of analyzing an[understanding the nature of the power by which all this is accomplishe[This is the question of "agency" and asks about the extent of the involv[ment of both the Creator and the creature in the process under way. Who [

[19]Baxter, *Saving Faith*, p. 40.
[20]Ball, *Covenant of Grace*, p. 14.
[21]Harris, *New Covenant*, 2:122.
[22]Ibid., p. 23.

at work within it, and by what manner of working? Is the process initiated, sustained and brought to fruition by acts essentially human or divine? What within it is the relationship of the pilgrim's labors and those of God? Here one is concerned with an explanation of the covenant experience. Both issues, those concerning process and those concerning agency, are critical to an understanding of Puritan covenant thought and cannot be completely separated from one another. Yet it may be useful in this chapter, and likewise in the one following, to focus attention as explicitly as possible upon the former rather than the latter, seeking primarily to describe, as both pre-scribed and experienced, the course of the covenanter's journey. A more direct examination of the question of agency will itself be explicitly under-taken at a later point.

PREPARATION THROUGH CONTRITION

The fulfillment of requirements leading to covenant partnership and its continuation is, of course, no simple nor instantaneous act. Despite the immediacy of God's mercy to the believing soul, the process can be long and in the last analysis must be life-long. The renewals of faith and the reiterations of obedience are for the Christian believer never ended. The Christian pilgrimage, in earthly experience, is always in process, for numer-ous obstacles block the way and enactment is continually short of expecta-tion. To move simply from sin to faith is itself a long journey and cannot easily be completed. Sibbes observed that since "there is such a distance between the . . . corruption of man and grace, . . . there must be a great deal of preparation, many degrees to rise by before a man can come to that condition he should be in."[23] Other Puritan divines quite generally agreed. The beginning point and the desired ending point in the pilgrim's progress were a great distance from one another, and the way between was to be traversed only after difficult steps had been taken. The distance was indeed defined by the difference between primary love for self and love for God, the former being overcome and the latter attained only through extended struggle. Thus the movement into covenant partnership and security was no simple nor easy matter. Difficult covenant conditions had to be fulfilled.

First among them—though technically this was more often said to "prepare the way" for the conditions—is heartfelt contrition for one's sins. No person can return to God who is unwilling to turn attention inward and, in self accusation as well as in awareness of divine judgment, enter into the pain of this experience. It is true that, over the course of a Puritan century in both England and America, there were modifications and variations in the extent to which such pain was deemed to be essential.[24] But, throughout, the

---

[23]Sibbes, "Lydia's Conversion," *Works*, 6:522.
[24]See Pettit, *Heart Prepared*, chaps. 3 and 4 for references to this matter in the thought of the

deliberate and disturbing facing of one's sin was a necessary beginning point in the process leading to covenant relationship.

The Reformation tradition had been fully aware of this, with Luther himself having urged that "God kills before making alive." The Puritan theologians saw parallels in everyday aspects of human experience: the surgeon cuts before he cures, the builder digs down before he builds up. So, said Harris, God also "undoes a man before he saves him; marres him before he makes him; and takes him all to pieces, and then ioynes him for ever."[25] Robert Bolton urged that if there is no misery, there is no mercy, and if there is much misery, there is much mercy, adding, however, the further assurance that since mercy is infinite it will ultimately outweigh the finitude of misery.[26] But in the intermediate process misery, once again, is essential. Perkins noted that in the realm of bodily healing "we permit Chirurgians that they should binde us … seare us … lanch and search our members with razours … to cure a bodily disease," and so "will we not give God leave to cure by afflictions the most festred diseases of our sicke soules?"[27] Pain must precede ease. If we take a "physick" for the body, we must also take one for the soul.[28] Indeed, asked Perkins, "How could God wipe away your teares from your eyes in heaven, if on earth you shed them not?" Then he added, "You are as Gods corne, you must therefore goe under the flaile, the fanne, the milstone, and the oven, before you can be Gods bread."[29] Similarly he knew that "there is no greater enemie to faith then pride," and that therefore "he that wil beleeve in Christ must be annihilated, that is, he must be bruised and battered to a flat nothing, in regard of any liking of affection to himself."[30] So terror is a necessary prelude to triumph, though John Rogers also added a further perspective, that "the Lord terrifieth us to make us truely thankefull to him for our deliverance when it comes."[31]

When Puritan theologians related these experiential concerns to the biblical message, they spoke quickly and urgently of the role of the Law in generating such remorse. The Law of God, for all else that it involves, is a mirror to reveal to the sinner his or her sins. Samuel Bolton said that these failings may be seen "in the Glass of the Law." Indeed, he added, it is so fully displayed there that "you can have No Magnifying Glass, to greaten sin above the Greatness of it."[32] And John Bunyan urged, "If thou wouldest …

"English preparationists" and the "American preparationists." The discussion, however, also deals with broader features of the "preparation" process, including the question of "agency."

[25] Harris, *Way to True Happiness*, p. 41.

[26] R. Bolton, *Comforting Afflicted Consciences*, p.350.

[27] Perkins, "Golden Chaine," *Works*, 1:91.

[28] Baynes, *Holy Soliloquies*, p. 14.

[29] Perkins, "Estate of Damnation," *Works*, 1:410.

[30] Ibid., p. 419.

[31] J. Rogers, *Doctrine of Faith*, p. 94.

[32] S. Bolton, *The Sinfulness of Sin*, pp. 27–29. Quoted in Kevan, *Grace of Law*, p. 84.

wash thy face clean, first take a glass and see where it is durty . . . labour first
to see them [i. e., your sins] in the glass of the Law."[33] But the Law is more
than a mirror, for the latter suggests a somewhat quiescent functioning. More
vigorously the Law is a hammer which pounds into awareness and contrition
those who have failed in obedience. The concept of the hammer had both
biblical and Reformation precedents and then was utilized by such a Puritan
theologian as Perkins to urge that this hammering brings (1) knowledge of
the Law, (2) knowledge of sin, (3) compunction of the heart, and (4) holy
desperation of one's own powers.[34] Thomas Goodwin spoke even more
emphatically: "We are fain to make it the greatest of our business to preach
the law, and come with that great hammer to break your bones in pieces first,
that we may then preach the Gospel."[35]

Yet this terrifying could not be accomplished by the Law simply as an
objective and external reality, even though preached and heard. As is the
case with all means of grace, the Spirit must also be present to give the Law
its potency and personal application in sin's revealing and condemnation. So
Preston spoke of the need for experiencing the "spirit of bondage" and said:

> Except the spirit of bondage put an edge upon the Law, put a Sword into
> the hand of the Law, to pricke the heart, to wound the heart, . . . you
> may heare the Law, and the threatenings and curses applyed to you
> tenne thousand times over, and yet no feare bee bred in you, except the
> spirit of bondage joyne with it, that makes it effectuall.[36]

Combined with knowledge of the Law must be an existential recognition of
its relation to one's own personal condition. By this means it then becomes
the way "to enrage and increase sin" in human awareness.[37] Perkins, in
analyzing the processes leading to conversion, identified this as the "beginnings of preparation." These experiences were to open the way, though not
themselves to effect any substantial change in one's ultimate relationship
with God. They were to initiate the process and, as they tamed and subdued
with fears and terrors, they led toward the covenant's initiation.[38] The Law
was terrifying, especially for those outside the covenant, but its terror was a
necessary step in the movement toward salvation.

So here the Law was seen, in Perkins' analogy, as the needle which
makes way for the thread of the Gospel.[39] Or, by employing a different

---

[33]John Bunyan, *The Doctrine of the Law and Grace Unfolded*, p. A5. Quoted in Greaves, *John Bunyan*, p. 111.

[34]Perkins, "Golden Chaine," *Works*, 1:79.

[35]Thomas Goodwin, "Reconciliation of all the People of God," *Works* (1861–65), 5:512. Quoted in Kevan, *Grace of Law*, p. 86.

[36]Preston, *New Covenant*, 1:394.

[37]Kevan, *Grace of Law*, p. 81.

[38]Perkins, "Graine of Musterd-seede," *Works*, 1:628.

[39]Perkins, *Commentarie upon Galatians*, p. 246. Also see J. Rogers, *Doctrine of Faith*, p. 98.

figure, Baynes said that "where the heart is not plowed up and broken," that is, by the Law, "the seed of the Gospel shall never be sowed."[40] Or still again, John Rogers added that "as Elijah was prepared by a whirle-winde and earthquake to heare a still voyce," it is now necessary to be prepared "by the terrible voyce of the Law to heare the sweet voyce of the Gospel."[41] At any rate, whatever the metaphor, the purpose of the proclamation of the Law's requirements was to lead persons in penitence to a receptivity to the Gospel's mercy. Here was "a John the Baptist, to make way for Christ."[42] The Law thus serves an instrumental purpose and opens the way to grace.

One must be careful, however, so these Puritan theologians insisted, lest grace be proclaimed too soon. There is danger in too early a declaration of mercy. Certainly, Blake noted, Gospel cannot be substituted for Law: "evangelical allurements ... can never work on the soul without Law convictions," for "to say the Gospel discovers sin as well as the Law ... is the greatest absurdity."[43] Even more, there is the positive danger of a premature evangelicalism. Robert Bolton despaired over preachers who damaged souls through "stifelling the very first stirring of Legall remorse by healing the wounds of ... conscience with sweet words, before they be searcht and sounded to the bottome."[44] So, argued Burgess, "Take heed, lest thou love the Gospel, because it hath alwayes glad tidings, and thou canst not abide the precepts or threatnings. ... There may be a carnal Gospeller, as well as a Popish Legalist."[45]

In fact, the natural human tendency is one of seeking the good news to the exclusion of the bad, the tendency toward an "easy conscience" which resists facing up thoroughly with the reality, including the multitude, of one's sins. Robert Bolton knew how easy it was to look upon one's sins "as we doe upon the Starres ... [and] see onely the great ones ... here one, and there one."[46] And John Rogers despaired over the many who, even when confronted by the Law, are like the blacksmith's dog "who can lie under the hammers noyse, & the sparkes flying, and yet fast asleepe."[47] The Law must be used diligently to awaken the drowsy and to sharpen the consciences of those inclined to be too easy on themselves. Perkins saw it as the means by which one must search out one's "special and priviest corruptions."[48] Robert Bolton added that the identification of such sins must also be precise and one's confession of them to God specific, for "how is it possible the physitian

[40]Baynes, *Helpe to true Happinesse*, p. 8.

[41]J. Rogers, *Doctrine of Faith*, p. 97.

[42]J. Sedgwick, *Antinomianisme Anatomized*, p. 12.

[43]Blake, *Vindiciae Foederis*, p. 95.

[44]R. Bolton, *Comforting Afflicted Consciences*, p. 324.

[45]Burgess, *True Doctrine of Justification*, 1:279.

[46]R. Bolton, *Comforting Afflicted Consciences*, p. 102.

[47]J. Rogers, *Doctrine of Faith*, p. 99.

[48]Perkins, "Exposition Upon Zephaniah," *Works*, 3:414.

should help him, who only saies, he is not well, but will not tell him where?"[49] So, though the Gospel is the end, the Law must still be the intermediary means, for "those who would come unto Christ . . . must be utterly unbottomed of themselves."[50]

Yet there are degrees of "utterly"—or at least the unbottoming may be said to assume different experiential forms. As a matter of fact, care must be taken lest one so magnify one's sins that they "which are but finite (though many and great)" appear "more and greater then the mercies of God, and the merits of CHRIST, which are infinite." In George Downame's view, for a person "so to be humbled is a fearefull sinne, and perhaps a greater sinne, then any for which he is humbled."[51] But, apart from that extreme, there is the further general recognition, as in Baxter, that "God breaketh not all men's hearts alike."[52] Some require "more hammering" and others less, so that, in John Rogers' perception, "some by one Sermon of the Law . . . are so pulled downe as they cry out they be dammed," while "others be not so much cast downe at three hundred Sermons." But for such a latter person, he added, "if God have a favour" toward him, then "God will lay on more load, terror upon terror, trouble upon trouble, till he have bound him hand and foote and made him tame."[53] Yet not all persons need that terrible troubling. Even Robert Bolton, who was in no way hesitant to recommend a vigorous preaching of the Law, could note, by way of analogy, that two travellers with the same destination might have quite contrasting travel experiences: one may be "tossed with many roaring tempests and raging waves," while "the Other hath a reasonable calme Passage"—and now "they stand both safe upon the shore."[54] So, though "law convictions" are necessary, observed Blake, one cannot make judgments on the ground of their intensity about those so convicted, for "none can judge of the truth of their repentance by the greatness of their trouble."[55]

Thus, all told, the Puritan preacher was advised that he should preach the Law as prelude to the Gospel, but warily. It is not that the latter part of that counsel was always followed. Baxter once claimed that disregard of it was actually the basic cause for the emergence of Antinomianism, which arose, he said, "from our obscure Preaching of Evangelical Grace, and insisting too much on tears and terrors."[56] Likewise one of the major Antinomians, John Saltmarsh, deplored orthodox Puritan preaching, for, in

---

[49]R. Bolton, *Comforting Afflicted Consciences*, p. 210.

[50]Ibid., p. 168.

[51]G. Downame, *Covenant of Grace*, p. 86.

[52]Richard Baxter, *Works*, 1:8. Quoted in Packer, *Redemption and Restoration*, p. 207.

[53]J. Rogers, *Doctrine of Faith*, pp. 92–93.

[54]R. Bolton, *Comforting Afflicted Consciences*, p. 469.

[55]Blake, *Vindiciae Foederis*, pp. 138–39.

[56]Baxter, *An Apology for the Nonconformist Ministry*, p. 226. Quoted in Kevan, *Grace of Law*, p. 11.

his judgment, it contained "usually but a grain or dram of Gospel to a pound of Law."[57] But whether followed or not, the advice to the preacher was to present the Law circumspectly. John Sedgwick said that "the wound should neither be made wider or deeper than the Plaister," adding the observation that in the preaching of the Law "the golden mean is to be observed." "I would not have the Law to be Preached alone by it selfe," he wrote, "without a mixture of some of the Promises of the Gospel. . . . I would have the Law to be Preached, as it was published, for Evangelicall and mercifull intentions. . . . He preacheth the law best who preacheth it with reference to Jesus Christ."[58]

THE CONDITION OF FAITH

More properly, a condition of the covenant is faith, for justification is by faith, as in and through faith one becomes a Christian believer and receives the promises of the Gospel. Contrition, precipitated by the Law, may prepare the way for faith, but it is by faith and faith alone that the gifts of Christ are appropriated and the covenant relationship with God is entered. There can indeed be some question as to precisely where contrition ends and faith begins. Psychological analysis for these Puritans indicated that, as contrition prepared the way, there were generated "hungerings and thirstings of the soule" for Christ and his righteousness as further antecedents to the "closing with Christ" found in the finality of the faith act. Often all such antecedents, including contrition, were viewed as containing the "seed of faith."[59] Yet the distinction remained difficult, and these nascent beginnings were sometimes equally designated as being truly early forms of faith's final ending. In fact, putting the matter in slightly different manner, Nicholas Byfield could write, "It is a truth (though a Paradoxe) that the Desire to believe is Faith."[60] Perkins spoke similarly, though in slightly more cautious manner: "A constant and earnest desire to be reconciled to God, to believe, and to repent, if it be in a touched heart, is in acceptation with God, as reconciliation, Faith, repentance."[61] But apart from the semantics, the process itself was of critical importance. And it ought not to be unduly hastened, despite the sense of urgency, lest it lack the authenticity which comes from a developed awareness of need and a valid hungering and thirsting for fulfillment. Biblical analogies were provided by Timothy Rogers. Faith, he said, should not be "like Jacobs venison, too quicklie found to bee of the right kinde, nor like Jonahs gourd, too suddenlie sprung to

---

[57]Saltmarsh, *Free-Grace*, p. 40.

[58]J. Sedgwick, *Antinomianisme Anatomized*, p. 28.

[59]R. Bolton, *Comforting Afflicted Consciences*, p. 398.

[60]Nicholas Byfield, *Exposition upon Colossians*, 1:4. Quoted in R. Bolton, *Comforting Afflicted Consciences*, p. 376.

[61]Perkins, "Graine of Musterd-seede," *Works*, 1:638.

continue long, but like the water of Bethlehem, much longed for & hardly obtained."[62]

Antinomians protested. Faith, they said, was not a condition of the covenant, for the covenant as God's gift had no prerequisite conditions. "Faith is not given before the Covenant," wrote Vavasor Powell, "but in, with and through the Covenant." Christ must first be present within the soul to enable the act of faith, so that "then its Christ in us, that brings us to Christ out of us."[63] Faith, as a manifestation of what has already transpired, has rather the function of assuring those in covenant of their covenant standing and of the fact that the covenant blessings are theirs. Saltmarsh said, "Christ is ours without faith, . . . but we cannot here know him to be ours but by believing,"[64] and thus he defined faith as "being perswaded more or lesse of Christ's love."[65] For the main body of covenant theologians, however, the covenant was conditional, and its primary condition was faith. John Rogers rejoiced that "God hath highly honored" faith, noting that "he made it the onely instrument of our salvation, there being no other condition of the Covenant of Grace, but believing."[66] The *sola fide* of Luther's early Protestantism was not ignored in this latter day manifestation.

With faith occupying so central a place in the covenant, much Puritan writing dealt with several issues involved in understanding its fundamental nature. A general definition was offered by John Rogers:

> Faith . . . is the mightie worke of the holy Ghost, whereby a sinner humbled by the Law, and quite driven out of himselfe, by or upon the gracious and sweet voyce of the Gospell, and the free and unpartiall offer of mercy from God in Christ, comes in time to cast himselfe upon Christ, and to trust him as the All-sufficient and onely meanes of his salvation, and withall is willing to be subject to him all his dayes.[67]

Rogers' definition began with an affirmation of faith's origin as a "mightie worke of the holy Ghost." Since this relates to the issue of "agency," rather than that of "process," consideration of its implications will be deferred. But the remainder of the definition describes the character of saving faith and can serve as background for our discussion.

The subject of this faith is first identified as "a sinner humbled by the Law, and quite driven out of himselfe." Thus, as has earlier been noted, saving faith, in Puritan understanding, must be preceded by that "unbottoming" of the self which comes through an earnest confrontation with one's

---

[62]T. Rogers, *Righteous Mans Evidences*, pp. 22–23.
[63]Powell, *Christ and Moses*, p. 61.
[64]Saltmarsh, *Free-Grace*, pp. 188–89.
[65]Ibid., p. 93.
[66]J. Rogers, *Doctrine of Faith*, p. 255.
[67]Ibid., "Epistle to the Reader."

sins. But then after self-reliance has been destroyed, said Rogers, the person of faith "comes in time to cast himselfe upon Christ, and to trust him as the All-sufficient and onely meanes of his salvation." This is the central element in faith's act. However, many issues, even controversies, were involved in the Puritan understanding of it.

The first set of issues focused on the differentiation of faith as trust from other forms that faith may assume. Justifying faith, for instance, is not simply the faith of intellectual assent. To define it in this way would make it too wide, for "even the devils believe." So it is not the "common faith" or "historical faith" possessed by many, conceivably including elect and reprobate alike, in which the identifying feature is knowledge of God's Word and assent to its truthfulness. This intellectual affirmation is important and is a prerequisite for the full faith that justifies, but alone it has no saving power. It is not enough even to believe that Christ is the Redeemer, for he becomes so for oneself only as he is trusted as one's own. *Assensus* falls short of *fiducia*. Ames said that the object of faith is Christ and "not the truth of some sentence."[68]

Nor is justifying faith to be identified with the "temporary faith" which sometimes approximates it. Perkins saw this faith as going beyond intellectual faith in that by it one not only affirms the Word, but "rejoyceth inwardly in it . . . and bringeth forth some kind of fruit." Yet because "it is grounded on temporary causes," such as desire for praise or for profit, it will ultimately pass away.[69] John Rogers compared this temporary faith to one's coming to a merchant's cellar to buy wine, but though one tastes and approves, one still goes away without making a purchase, for the cost is deemed too high. Such a person, Rogers said, as he applied his analogy to faith, "will not pay the Lords price."[70]

Nor, still further, is justifying faith to be identified with the faith of assurance. The latter was given a role of large importance in both Puritan theory and practice, and much thought and effort were expended toward "making one's calling and election sure." But this confidence of being actually and certainly within the covenant was not itself even a part of the faith that saves. "Justifying faith," said Robert Bolton, "is not . . . to be assured of pardon; but to trust wholly upon the mercy of God for pardon."[71] If the identifying of justifying faith with "historical faith" makes its scope too wide, the inclusion within it of a "faith of assurance" would render that scope too narrow. John Rogers saw two acts of faith: the first was "an accepting of Christ, a leaning upon him, and a laying hold of him offered by God," and the second comes when one is "perswaded that he is one of those

---

[68]Ames, *Marrow*, p. 117.
[69]Perkins, "Exposition of the Creed," *Works*, 1:125.
[70]J. Rogers, *Doctrine of Faith*, p. 14.
[71]R. Bolton, *Comfortable Walking with God*, p. 320.

that Christ dyed for." The first is saving faith, and the second is assuring faith. But, added Rogers, "There be [those] that doe truely beleeve in Christ, and that to salvation, . . . that yet are not come to be perswaded that Christ is theirs."[72] William Ames, whose affirmation of the richness of faith's experience led him to stress strongly the certainty of God's grace which it could provide, also was aware that that particular assurance "is wanting in some, for a time, who notwithstanding have true Faith lying hid in their hearts."[73]

So the condition of the covenant is faith as confidence in God, not faith as confidence in one's own salvation. It is the "faith of adherence," not the "faith of assurance." For Baxter this assurance could come only through a certainty of one's faith of adherence, that is, only if I am able "to believe that I do believe." But, he observed, for this to be salvation's requirement could end up in an absurdity: "If I am bound to believe that I do believe, then also I must be bound to believe, that I believe, that I do believe, and so on." Faith cannot be "its owne specifying Object."[74] Indeed, declared John Downe, the object of faith must be "the person of the Mediator" and not "present grace and future glory."[75]

Thus saving faith, as Rogers put it in his definition, is the act in which one comes "to cast himselfe upon Christ, and to trust him." It is not simply assent, for even more it is reliance. Francis Taylor took note of the fact that the Latin word for faith, *fides*, "comes not from *Credo* to beleeve, but from *Fido* to trust."[76] Though faith may include belief, it is finally an act of "affiance" in which relationship to God is not simply through the mind, but through the whole person. This is a "resting upon God," and John Downe affirmed, "Faith is such a Rest, and such a Rest Faith."[77] Though there were some exceptions, particularly where the tendency was to lift up somewhat more prominently faith's intellectual aspects, Puritan theologians on the whole emphasized strongly this fiduciary element. It is not that affiance develops as a consequence of faith; rather, faith includes and even reaches its completion in the act of trust. The promises of God find their ultimate acceptance in the yielding of the heart. So trust is the crown of faith and is necessary for salvation. Ames could write: "To believe in God is . . . to cleave to God, to leane on God, to rest on God. . . . Faith is the first act of life, whereby we live to God." Moreover, it is "an act of the whole man" in which one "must needs cast himself upon God in Christ as a sufficient and faithfull Savior."[78]

[72]J. Rogers, *Doctrine of Faith*, "Epistle to the Reader."

[73]Ames, *Marrow*, p. 8. See also p. 117.

[74]Baxter, *Saving Faith*, p. 67.

[75]Downe, *Definition of Justifying Faith*, p. A2.

[76]F. Taylor, *Justification Cleared*, p. 268.

[77]Downe, *Definition of Justifying Faith*, p. 164.

[78]Ames, *Marrow*, pp. 5–7.

The Westminster Confession expressed this general view by declaring that faith is an "accepting, receiving, and resting upon Christ alone."[79] The term "receiving," however, points to one further feature in the Puritan understanding of affiance: such trust is in no way an active righteousness; rather it is a passive emptiness before God, open to be filled. Faith is an empty hand to receive the other graces which God bestows. Francis Taylor could even say, "God chose faith to apply Christ to us, because it is the emptiest of all ... graces."[80] Thus the covenant is entered by this trusting faith which rests, relies, and receives. Though justifying faith ultimately becomes obediential, it justifies not by such obedience, but by its passive receiving from God.[81]

A second set of issues has to do with the ground on which such faith rests, and the distinction between the faith of adherence and the faith of assurance contributes to Puritan discussion of this matter. The faith of assurance may find its ground in subjective experience, but the only adequate ground for the faith of adherence, said the Puritan divines, is the objective reality of God's promise in God's Word. Without exception they claimed and proclaimed the conviction that saving faith cannot have as unstable a foundation as one's own senses or awareness. Sense is fragile and can be deceiving, and though it is the necessary avenue for the gaining of such evidences as may provide assurance for the soul concerning its status with God, it cannot be the ground on which that status itself is established. The faith that justifies, the faith that adheres to God in trust, the faith that is entrance into the covenant, must rest on a firmer foundation, the covenant promises themselves. Culverwell declared that for believers "the onely firme ground of this saving Faith, is Gods truth, revealed in his Word, ... this generall pardon proclaimed in the Gospell to poore sinners." Others build "on the outward change of their life, which often is found deceitfull."[82] And Obadiah Sedgwick noted succinctly, "We have more reason to suspect our own testimony, then to distrust God's invitation and promise."[83]

Moreover, there may be times when sense is not only deceiving, but is discouraging, offering no awareness of God's presence or grace. But then, again, there is ground for faith in the objective reality of God's Word. Arthur Dent provided the analogy of a man being tied high on a steeple, fearing when he looked down, but being reassured when he saw his supports on looking up. So, said Dent, "When we looke downeward to our selves, wee have doubts and feares: but when wee looke upward to Christ and the truth of his promises, wee feele our selves cocke-sure, and cease to doubt any

[79]"Westminster Confession of Faith," XIV, 2. Schaff, *Creeds of Christendom*, 3:630.

[80]F. Taylor, *Justification Cleared*, p. 268.

[81]Burgess, *True Doctrine of Justification*, 2:244.

[82]Culverwell, *Treatise of Faith*, pp. 21, 26–27.

[83]O. Sedgwick, *Doubting Beleever*, p. 127.

more."[84] Baynes observed that the important matter "is not the manner of apprehending, but the thing apprehended." Thus, he said, "A trembling palsie hand may take the thing which a more steddie one doth take, . . . so a heart of faith which yet shaketh and doubteth through much unbeleefe, may take Christ, as well as a heart doth which is more fully perswaded."[85] And this is especially the time, when a feeling of God's love is absent, that faith is an heroic act. Timothy Rogers observed that "it is nothing for a child being dandled in the lap, to think his father loves him; but when his father frownes and lowres upon him, then to be perswaded of his love is something indeed."[86] But, once more, the ground for that persuasion is in God's promises. Robert Bolton counselled, "Bee it so then, that thy Faith hath lost its hold-fast, that for the present thou findest no feeling . . . cast thy selfe upon the sure Word of that mighty God, who hath established all the ends of the earth."[87] The foundation for saving faith within the covenant is not sense or feeling, but "the truth and tenderheartedness of Christ, in the promises which can never faile."[88]

A third set of issues in Puritan probing of faith's character has to do with the way in which this trust may be psychologically understood. In Rogers' definition faith is a response to "the gracious and sweet voyce of the Gospell and the free and impartiall offer of mercy from God in Christ." But seen in terms of the operation of the human faculties, what is the nature of that response? In such saving faith what are the roles and the inter-relationships of the intellect and the will? Though this was not a priority matter for Puritan preaching, it was a matter of concern for Puritan reflection, and not a little effort was applied to its exploration.

In general three major positions can be identified. The first stressed the role of the intellect, making the mind the locus of faith, a view largely characteristic of Reformed scholasticism. For Beza, Zanchius, Piscator, Maccovius, Gomarus and others, faith was essentially the mind's exercise of its God-given ability to know the truth of the divine Word. Justifying faith was a conviction of the truth about God, including the truth about "the free and impartiall offer of mercy from God in Christ" to which Rogers referred. Faith was *assensus*, and *fiducia* came only later as a consequence of this intellectual assent. This interpretation of the nature of faith seems, however, to have had few full-fledged followers among Puritan theologians. One was George Downame. The faith that justifies, he affirmed, is the belief "that Christ is the Saviour of all that believe in him," and this he called a "lively assent to the promise of the Gospel." So faith, he wrote, "is a perswasion of the mind," whereas affiance, which then later follows from it, "is an affection

[84]Dent, *Plaine Mans Path-way*, p. 243.
[85]Baynes, *Helpe to true Happinesse*, p. 194.
[86]T. Rogers, *Righteous Mans Evidences*, p. 204.
[87]R. Bolton, *Comforting Afflicted Consciences*, p. 364.
[88]R. Bolton, *Comfortable Walking with God*, p. 320.

of the heart."[89] Affiance, for Downame, was important, as were other consequences of faith, such as hope, zeal, peace, joy, thankfulness, obedience, patience, and love. But justification is by assent to the truth of the Gospel.

The major Puritan figure who moved in this direction, however, was William Perkins. Though Perkins often showed more concern than did the continental scholastics for the place of the will and the role of trust in the divine-human relationship, he still shared their basic definition of faith. He wrote, "The place and seat of faith . . . is the minde of man, not the will: for it stands in a kinde of particular knowledge or perswasion, and there is no perswasion but in the minde," and then further affirmed faith to be that act in which "we give assent or credence to Gods word."[90] Central to faith is "to know the points of religion, . . . the summe of the Gospell, especially the promise." But this faith "must not be idle in the braine," and so it then works "to apply the promise and withall the thing promised, which is Christ, unto our selves."[91] All told, this is faith mainly as an intellectual act. Perkins' honoring of the understanding as the principal faculty of the soul, "serving to rule and order the whole man," can be seen in his viewing of it as placed there by God "to be the waggoner in the waggon."[92]

A second and quite different view of the locus of faith was that of William Ames who saw it as an act of the will. Ames was a voluntarist in his understanding of human nature and is separate in this regard from the mainstream of Reformed theologians. For Ames "the prime and proper subject of Divinity is the Will," since "this life is a spiritual act of the whole man, whereby he is carried on to enjoy God, and to doe according to his will,"[93] and this perspective immediately has implications for the nature of faith. In faith one finds an act of embracing the good, not simply of affirming the true, and will therefore takes precedence over intellect. Faith always presupposes a knowledge of God and of the Gospel, but these truths are not themselves the object of faith. God is the object of faith, and even more it is God "not as he is considered in himselfe, but as we by him doe live well." So Ames developed explicitly the conviction that since faith "is the first act of life, whereby we live to God," and indeed "in Christ . . . must needs consist in union with God," it is something "which an assent given to the truth concerning God can in no wise doe." Further, since this involves casting oneself "upon God in Christ as a sufficient and faithful Saviour," it is something that cannot "in any measure" be done by "an assent of the understanding," but rather requires "a consent of the will."[94] Ames went

[89]G. Downame, *Covenant of Grace*, pp. 77, 94, 78.
[90]Perkins, "Exposition of the Creed," *Works*, 1:125–26.
[91]Perkins, "Treatise of Cases of Conscience," *Works*, 2:15.
[92]Perkins, "Discourse of Conscience," *Works*, 1:517.
[93]Ames, *Marrow*, pp. 2–3.
[94]Ibid., pp. 5–7.

farther than any other major Puritan figure in subordinating the intellect and in attributing to the will a central role and responsibility in the act of saving faith.

The majority of Puritan divines, however, held to a third and intermediate view, affirming a significant place for both intellect and will in faith's act. When Culverwell defined justifying faith as "a beliefe of the Gospell, whereby I receive Christ offered unto me in the same," he knew it to include both an "assent of the minde and judgement to the truth of the Gospel," and "a consent with our heart, and will, . . . whereby indeed he is become ours, and wee his."[95] Such a view of the two loci of faith in mind and will was then expressed over and over again. John Rogers made the duality fully explicit by saying that we should understand "the seat of true faith, to bee the whole soule of man, not the head onely, or the heart onely," for such faith "is begun in the head, but not perfected till it come in the heart."[96]

A major spokesman for this view was John Preston who claimed that first the mind believes the promises and then the will embraces them. He found an analogy for this justifying faith in the entering into marriage. There must first be an act of the mind to believe that there will be a marriage partner, and then there must be the will to embrace that partner in the marriage relationship.[97] Preston did not diminish the role of belief in faith, and even at one point defined the covenant faith of Abraham as believing that "a Messiah shall be sent," enlarging further upon this by saying that "the condition that makes every man a partaker of the Covenant of grace" is the belief not only that God was so committed, but "that he hath exhibited, and sent him since."[98] But saving faith also involves trust, for unless Christ "be taken by us, he doth us no good, he is not made ours."[99] Indeed, Preston likewise made a great deal of this role of the will in faith. We must not "trust in Christ by halves,"[100] he said, but rather, the will's acceptance of Christ must be (1) "compleat," excluding "all wishers and woulders," (2) "deliberate," excluding all those that will "take CHRIST in a good moode, on some sudden flash," and (3) "free," excluding those who take Christ "meerely for servile feare, at time of death, in the day of sicknesse and trouble."[101] Such trust Preston then illustrated with an episode from ancient history:

> There was an action that Alexander the Great did . . . When hee was
> sicke, there comes a friend that was alwaies close with him, that was a

---

[95]Culverwell, *Treatise of Faith*, pp. 14–17.

[96]J. Rogers, *Doctrine of Faith*, p. 23.

[97]Preston, *Breast-Plate of Faith and Love*, 1:17, 52.

[98]Preston, *New Covenant*, 2:113.

[99]Preston, *Breast-Plate of Faith and Love*, 1:51.

[100]Ibid., 2:151.

[101]Ibid., 1:22.

Physician, and he prepared him a Potion; but before the same came to him, there was a Letter delivered to him, that that very Potion was poyson: when his friend came with his Potion in his hand, he takes the Letter that was sent to give him notice of the Treason, and drinkes off the Cup with one hand, and reaches the Letter with the other, so he dranke off the Cup before he shewed the Letter. Here Alexander trusted him, if he had failed him, he had lost his life; but hee shewed that he trusted him. In such a case, if thou be able to trust GOD, if thou canst put thy selfe upon him, if he faile thee, thou art undone, in such a case; this is to trust in GOD.[102]

Here both will and intellect are involved in the believer's act of faith. Baxter provided an overall descriptive term by calling it "a believing fiducial consent."[103]

One further related consideration is important. Despite the duality of emphasis, there was often a tendency to give the intellect a position higher than the will. In general it may be said that these Puritan theologians saw the will as following the commendations of the intellect, choosing what the mind has decreed to be good. Ball could say, "What the minde judgeth best the will followeth best." He even affirmed that "the only cause why men are not willing to submit unto Christ, is because they are not thoroughly . . . inlightened in their minde," adding that "the first sinne of our first parents was an errour."[104] So there is still an intellectualist bent in this mainstream Puritan thought despite its inclusive emphasis upon mind and will. Preston wrote, "The Lord ruleth nowhere as a King, but where hee rules first as a Prophet, that is, except he first perswade the heart by an inward enlightening, that it is best for the heart to be subject, the will and affection will never yield."[105]

Thus Puritan divines, as they dealt with these various issues, interpreted faith to be an act ultimately of affiance, in and by which the believer, through both intellect and will, places trust in God and relies on God for the grace which in mercy will be given. Sibbes developed a portrayal in which, with a slightly different phrasing, he enunciated these major ideas. Faith, he said, accomplishes four things. First, it empties the soul of all reliance on its own strength, for "in the new covenant, since Adam's fall, all our strength is in the 'second Adam,' our Head." Second, it moves out to fasten upon that new source of strength, for it "is a uniting grace as well as an emptying grace." Third, it draws from that source the strength that it needs. It is "like a root;

[102]Ibid., 2:169.
[103]Richard Baxter, *Catholick Theologie*. Quoted in Packer, *Redemption and Restoration*, p. 292.
[104]Ball, *Covenant of Grace*, pp. 333–35.
[105]Preston, *Golden scepter*, 2:13.

when it knits to Christ, it . . . draws virtue from him." Finally, it has the power "to make things present," that is, to bring into present experience the sense of the love of God and the renewal of life which God gives.[106]

The latter is particularly important, for the Puritan consciousness was oriented to a redemption in the midst of this life as well as to a redemption for the life that is to come. Faith and hope were to be distinguished, for though faith is the basis for a hope that looks to the future, it is also the path to a proleptic realization of that which hope foresees. The Puritan may have lived in two worlds and understood himself to be a "stranger and pilgrim" in one, but there was nevertheless a continuity between the two and both were under the merciful governance of God. So faith could make divine things present, even in the midst of the pilgrimage, and grace this life with a foretaste of that which is to come. John Bunyan knew faith to be "the onely instrument through the Spirit, that doth deep the soul in a comfortable frame, both to do and to suffer for Christ" as the soul then also engages "in its progress heaven-wards."[107]

A final element in John Rogers' definition of faith applies directly to the present actions of this life and says that in casting oneself upon Christ in trust, one "withall is willing to be subject to him all his dayes." The faith that is passive in receiving must also be active in doing. Samuel Bolton wrote that "the law sends us to the Gospel, that we may be justified, and the Gospel sends us to the law againe to enquire what is our dutie being justified."[108] For these Puritans there was no faith without its being active in works. If faith is the means of entering the covenant, it is also charged with the responsibility for keeping the covenant through the faithfulness which it can supply. Bulkeley declared that in no way does faith prescribe to God, but answers God and applies itself to God's offer, taking the conditions which God sets forth, that is, it accepts mercy and submits to God's rule.[109] And God's rule calls for the active exercise of the new quality of life given. John Rogers saw here a genuine distinction between a pseudo and an authentic faith. The former, which is but a formal profession of religion without true godliness, is a "raggamuffanly Faith that hath a sorry ragged reformation, and some shewes of some vertues, but none sound and substantiall." By contrast, "True Faith is a Lady or Queen, attended by a great traine of many excellent vertues: shew me thy Faith by thy workes, shew a great Lady by her traine; even this great Lady Faith by that great traine of graces."[110]

[106]Sibbes, "Commentary on Corinthians," *Works*, 3:518–19.
[107]Bunyan, *Law and Grace*, pp. 117–18.
[108]S. Bolton, *True Bounds of Christian Freedom*, p. 98.
[109]Bulkeley, *Gospel-Covenant*, pp. 335–36.
[110]J. Rogers, *Doctrine of Faith*, pp. 381–82.

THE CONDITION OF OBEDIENCE

We are now in the position to identify a final condition of the covenant of grace—the condition of repentance or obedience. In the Reformed theological tradition the term "repentance" was used in a twofold manner. First, it referred to contrition under the Law, the preparation for conversion. This was "legal repentance," the plowing up of the heart for the sowing of the seed of the Gospel. Properly speaking, it was not a covenant condition, but a pre-condition, preparing the way for the covenant condition of faith. In a second sense, however, repentance was a condition of the covenant, that is, as "evangelical repentance" flowing from faith and involving a conscious correction of life. Legal repentance was characterized by a "worldly sorrow," a horror of conscience in awareness of wrath. Evangelical repentance reflected a "godly sorrow" which, though indeed occasioned by one's sins, sprang from awareness in faith of God's grace and goodness. And this also included the committed effort to forsake sin and to live a life faithful to God.

The word "repentance," in its New Testament usage, meant literally a turning around and going in the opposite direction. These Puritan readers of the New Testament knew, therefore, that more than fear was necessary for the repentant life. That life must also have the positive characteristic of seeking fuller obedience to God's way. Ames wrote, "Although this repentance doth alwayes bring griefe with it for sins past and present, yet it doth not so properly or essentially consist in griefe, as in turning from, and hatred of sin, and in a firme purpose to follow after the good."[111] In evangelical repentance there is to be more reformation than remorse. The Christian's life can in no way be casual in its moral responsibility nor relapse into carelessness because it is comforted by God's freely given forgiveness. Justification must lead to renewed concern for purification. Said William Woodward, "The garments of Christ's righteousness must not be made a cloak for sin."[112] So the Christian must struggle to bring forth the fruits of a new life. For Perkins this "turning unto God" had two parts, first, "a purpose and resolution of heart never to sinne any more," and second, "an holy labour in mans life and conversation to purifie and clense himselfe from sinne."[113]

Both Puritan theory and experience knew this purification to be no easy accomplishment. The conquering of sin must be complete, its eradication entire. So Dent could note that such repentance cannot be simply the "cursory saying of a few praiers a little before death." "It is," he added, "no ordinary three houres matter."[114] Repentance requires a major assault on the

---

[111]Ames, *Marrow*, p. 114.

[112]William Woodworth, *Lord our Righteousness*, p. 76. Quoted in Kevan, *Grace of Law*, p. 208.

[113]Perkins, "Estate of Damnation," *Works*, 1:372.

[114]Dent, *Plaine Mans Path-way*, pp. 276–77.

sin in one's life. "We must yield him universal obedience in all things," urged Bulkeley, for Christ "cometh to lay waste the whole kingdome of sinne, all must be downe, not a stone left on that Babel."[115] Turning the figure in the opposite direction, Nathanael Cole declared that "as a City besieged, if but one gate stand open, the enemy will enter in, as if the whole wall were downe; so if we leave any one sinne not repented of, it is a sufficient gap to let in the divell with all his troupe."[116] Strategically one can well begin by attacking one's "master-sinne," for "if the roote be plucked up, soone will the branch wither."[117] But the reformation must also be searching and comprehensive, leading explicitly to the seeking out and destruction of those "neere and deere" sins which are so hard to set aside. Bulkeley put it directly: "Canst thou part with thy Absalom, thy beloved lust, and be content that God should set up his kingdome in thy whole soule? Then God is over thee, and thou in covenant with him."[118]

So evangelical repentance, as remorse and reformation, is a condition of the covenant. It is a condition in a way different, however, from that attributed to faith. The latter is a condition for entrance into the covenant. As such it is antecedent to, or at least concomitant with, the granting of grace. Faith is the casting of oneself in trust upon Christ which receives, as an open hand, the restored relationship. But repentance then must follow as a condition of the covenant's continuation, a living out of this relationship in faithfulness. It is a consequent condition and in a certain sense a declaratory condition. Those who through faith are entered into covenant with God are called upon to keep that covenant through fidelity. The covenant relationship involved not only *credenda*, things to be believed, but also *agenda*, things to be done. Greenham declared that "where we looke for the like mercie, we must performe like dutie."[119] And Preston warned, "Think not that thou canst take Christ divided, that thou canst take him half, and leave the other part, that thou canst take him as a Saviour, and not take him as a Prophet, and a King."[120] In the last analysis, being in covenant meant being under God's sovereign rule. When God "invites us to come and enter into Covenant with him, he doth not offer himselfe to be a God to us to blesse us, without being a God over us, to order and govern us."[121] Baxter saw the "sum of the covenant" in the words of God to Abraham, "I will be thy God, and thou shalt be my people." But for God to be our God meant, among other

---

[115]Bulkeley, *Gospel-Covenant*, p. 220.
[116]Cole, *Godly Mans Assurance*, p. 147.
[117]Ibid., pp. 146–48.
[118]Bulkeley, *Gospel-Covenant*, p. 220.
[119]Richard Greenham, "Exposition of the XVI Psalme," *Works*, 5:326. Quoted in Møller, "Beginnings of Puritan Covenant Theology," p. 65.
[120]Preston, *Saints Qualification*, pp. 319–20.
[121]Bulkeley, *Gospel-Covenant*, p. 346.

things, that God is to be to us an "absolute Owner."[122] "When God became a Saviour," wrote Blake, "he did not cease to be a Sovereign."[123]

These views are in accord with those of Calvin himself and constitute a major emphasis in his shaping of the Reformed tradition. As noted earlier, Calvin was no stranger to these covenant ideas. Although he did not make the covenant theme a central organizational theme in his theology, he readily appropriated the biblical portrayal of God's working as covenant action. And in that covenant there were both mercy and mandate. In commenting on Genesis 17:2 Calvin wrote, "The covenant of God with Abram had two parts. The first was a declaration of gratuitous love. . . . But the other was an exhortation to the sincere endeavour to cultivate righteousness."[124] As also noted earlier, the repository of that exhortation was the divine Law. The Law could lead to legal repentance and be a preparation for faith, and it could become a political means for the restraint of sin. But in its "third use" it was to be a guide for the Christian's conduct, a rule for evangelical repentance, a directory pointing the path to the believer's righteousness. In this, as well, Calvin prepared the way for his Puritan successors, though in their hands the Law became an even more precise instrument for such purpose. Luther, too, had spoken about the third use of the Law, but for him, it has been observed, this was more "like a compass, indicating the general direction of the journey, not like a map prescribing certain roads."[125] The Puritan divines, certainly more than both Luther and Calvin, saw in it a detailed directive.

Constituting that directive were the mandates of the Old Testament and New Testament alike, with the ancient Law seen as adopted and renewed by Christ. Though Christ is Savior, he also lays claim for obedience upon those whom he saves. Thomas Manton wrote that "as Christ came to raise the comfort of the creature to the highest, so also the duty of the creature to the highest."[126] Actually, in the view of Burgess, Christ gave no new laws, but interpreted and clarified the old, as a painter who works over an old painting to restore to freshness its former glory.[127] This means, then, that the law of Christ is at one with the ancient Law of the covenant of works, "which matter is scattered through the whole Bible, and summed up in the Decalogue . . . so that evangelical grace directs a man to no other obedience than that whereof the law of the Ten Commandments is to be the rule."[128] In

[122]Baxter, "Christian Directory," *Practical Works*, 2:200.

[123]Blake, *Vindiciae Foederis*, p. 47.

[124]Calvin, *Commentary on Genesis* (Genesis 17:2). Quoted in New, *Anglican and Puritan*, p. 92.

[125]H. H. Kramm, *Theology of Martin Luther* (London: J. Clarke, 1947), p. 61.

[126]Thomas Manton, "Sermon on Ephesians 2:10," *Works*, 2:400. Quoted in Kevan, *Grace of Law*, p. 176.

[127]Burgess, *Vindiciae Legis*, p. 117.

[128]E. F., *Marrow*, p. 144.

its formal definition on this matter the Westminster Confession said, "The moral law doth for ever bind all. . . . Neither doth Christ in the gospel any dissolve, but much strengthen this obligation."[129]

So the Christian believer was both free from the Law and under the Law. There was freedom from it in the sense that no longer was fulfillment of the Law a requirement for justification nor the Law itself an instrument of threat of punishment. Freedom from the covenant of works meant freedom in this sense from the Law. But the Christian was under the Law as a participant in the covenant of grace, where its obligation for fidelity in covenant keeping prevailed. Burgess declared, "We hold the Law as a rule still to walk by, though not a Covenant of works to be justified by."[130] And Samuel Bolton affirmed, "The Law is void for the damnatory, not its directionary power, we are not under the curse, but yet the commands."[131]

Once again Antinomians protested, insisting that Christian believers are not under the Law at all and that the liberty of grace and the commandment of the Law cannot exist together. If the commandments are put to the believer, contended John Eaton, "Wee confound the Old Testament with the New: we bring back the full grown heir to Schoole again to be whipped of his Schoolmaster."[132] These laws were simply for the time of childhood, so Antinomians claimed, and not for that of maturity in Christian experience. They have now been abolished in favor of the greater inner spiritual power which God's grace provides. Said Walter Cradock, "The Lord Jesus hath broken and dissolved those little childish lawes, . . . those A.B.C. lawes."[133] Robert Towne added that "the nature of the Spirit is freely to conform the heart and life to the outward rule of the law . . . without the help of the law."[134]

In response, however, the divines insisted that the "law within" was not enough. "Antinomians," said Rutherfurd, "make all duties a matter of courtesie."[135] There must be something more binding, more firm, and this is "Law-obligation." It is true that the Christian now has the Law "written upon the heart," placed there more effectively than was the natural law in creation. But the heart can be deceitful, and the internal Law must therefore be tested by the outer written Word. Moreover, "the disposition of the heart unto good, by means of the Law written there, may be quickened and put forwards by the voice of the Law from without."[136] The Law, as Calvin himself had said, is a spur to action, a goad needed even by the Christian

---

[129]"Westminster Confession of Faith," XIX, 5. Schaff, *Creeds of Christendom*, 3:641.
[130]Burgess, *Vindiciae Legis*, p. 206.
[131]S. Bolton, *True Bounds of Christian Freedome*, p. 76.
[132]Eaton, *Honey-Combe of Free Justification*, p. 114.
[133]Walter Cradock, *Gospel-Libertie*, p. 18. Quoted in Greaves, *John Bunyan*, p. 116.
[134]Robert Towne, *The Assertion of Grace*, p. 138. Quoted in Kevan, *Grace of Law*, p. 168.
[135]Rutherfurd, *Spirituall Antichrist*, 2:29.
[136]Bulkeley, *Gospel-Covenant*, pp. 128–29.

believer in the midst of lassitude and sloth. It was thus in accord with common opinion when John Sedgwick deplored the "Law-destroying and Dutie-casting-down course" of the Antinomians.[137]

Hence persons in covenant with God are to be confronted with obligation and encouraged in duty. Harris said that for the Christian who claims "I goe two or three mile to heare a Sermon," the further question remains, "Will you goe as farre to doe a Sermon?"[138] Good works in obedience to the Law are essential. They are a mark of faithfulness and an important part of the Chrisian's pilgrimage to salvation. Ball affirmed that "obedience to all Gods Commandements is covenanted, not as the cause of life, but as the way to life. Faith ... is obedientiall.... It is altogether bootlesse, for men to thinke of entring into Covenant with God, if they be not resolved to obey in all things."[139] Thus there is a combination of Gospel and Law in this conditional covenant, the one leading to faith and the other to obedience, both of which are covenant conditions. Both conditions are to be supplied by the Christian in fullness. Though he knew it to be "wittily spoken," Samuel Bolton was attracted to and found "some truth" in the exhortation:

> Live as though there were no Gospel; die as though there were no Law; passe the time of this life in the wildernesse of the world under the conduct of Moses; but let none but Joshua bring thee over to Canaan, the promised Land.[140]

MOTIVATION FOR COVENANT ACTION

One further matter must be examined in this exploration of the Puritan use of the conditional covenant, namely, the nature of the motivations which might underlie human covenant action. As the Christian believer pursues the pilgrimage of a covenanted life, how can the goals and purposes which give it impetus best be understood? What indeed should those goals and purposes be from the standpoint of a Christian apprehending of God and God's way? If one is called upon to respond to God's Word in faith and obedience, what reasons might justify and motivate that response? Several themes emerge in Puritan discussion of this issue, though there is also a main direction in which much of Puritan thinking on motivation seems to move.

Some among the divines spoke, at least in part, the language of an Augustinian Neo-Platonism. "Man was made for happinesse," wrote Harris, "neither can his heart ever bee at rest till it hath pitcht upon something which ... can make him happy.... A false god makes but a false hap-

---

[137]J. Sedgwick, *Antinomianisme Anatomized*, "To the Reader."
[138]Harris, *New Covenant*, 2:147.
[139]Ball, *Covenant of Grace*, pp. 19–21.
[140]S. Bolton, *True Bounds of Christian Freedome*, p. 106.

pinesse." However, those in covenant with God "have laid hold of true happinesse in him."[141] Preston too developed this theme, emphasizing particularly in his sermons published under the title, *The New Covenant*, that God's "all-sufficiency" permits one's heart to be satisfied with God alone, for here the highest good can be provided. One may search for satisfaction in many other ways, "but the creature is finite, and therefore is not able to fill the soule." This can be done only by God who is infinite, and the reason "why he is onely able to doe it," said Preston in a tellingly Augustinian phrase, "is because the soule is made for him." With such an appraisal of human longing and fulfillment, it was an easy step to exhortation: "then let your hearts be satisfied with him alone, let them be filled with him, let them be so bottomed upon him . . . that you neede not goe out from him to fetch any comfort from any creature whatsoever."[142] One motivation, therefore, was psychologically comprehended, and, at least in some Puritan thought, a goal for seeking and maintaining the covenant was the fulfillment of spiritual longing.

More common, however, was the language of "reward," drawn particularly from the biblical message. Calvin had found there that God will reward the service which we render, though such reward is due to God's goodness and not to human merit. So, he said, God makes promises to recompense us "to stir us up to take courage better to serve him, seeing that our labors are not lost before him."[143] This reward of which Scripture speaks was then, the Puritans affirmed, "not . . . as if it were the wages of a servant, but as it is the inheritance of sons."[144] It was not improper, therefore, in the eyes of many, to focus on the approbation which God has promised to those who maintain the covenant relationship in faithfulness. If the Law is still applicable to the believer in "its Minatory part" as a goad for one who "needs the whip," said John Sedgwick, it is also applicable "in its Promissory part," so that the godly may "have an eye to the recompense or reward, though not . . . in a way of merit."[145] Undoubtedly Baxter went farther in this direction than did any others, for his distinctive view of justification, which envisaged it as perfected by the good works of the believer, lent itself to the interpretation that God rewards the merit of the faithful. But even Ames, for whom the idea of merit was anathema and who maintained that "the chiefe end is Gods glory," could see acceptability for one's being "secondarily stirred up to doe his duty, by looking on the reward," for "this is not strange from the Sonnes of God, neither doth it in any part weaken their solid obedience."[146]

Yet, in the last analysis, all seeking for personal self-fulfillment must be

[141]Harris, *New Covenant*, 2:184–86, 190.
[142]Preston, *New Covenant*, 1:9, 45, 61.
[143]Calvin, *Opera*, 26:481. Quoted in Hoekema, "Covenant of Grace," p. 161.
[144]E. F., *Marrow*, p. 181.
[145]J. Sedgwick, *Antinomianisme Anatomized*, p. 11.
[146]Ames, *Marrow*, p. 195.

subordinated to that chief end of which Ames spoke. Perhaps the two can be reconciled, so some felt. George Downame argued that since our justification is an element in God's Kingdom of Grace and our sanctification is an objective of God's will, our desire for this salvation is itself a desire that God be glorified. And Peter Bulkeley felt that "a man in Covenant with God may do many things for himselfe, ayming at the furtherance of his own good, both spirituall and temporall," which then are "not in opposition, but in subordination to God and his glory." But the latter part is crucial, and Bulkeley added, "That last and main end must sway all other ends."[147] Thus despite expressions implying anthropocentric motivation in some of the Puritan writings, with their commendation of such goals as happiness and reward, the controlling emphasis in this theology was theocentric, setting ultimately the glory of God as prime consideration.

Here again the essential Calvinism of the Puritan outlook prevailed. Christian thought must not be based on the welfare of the human creature, though that welfare according to the Scriptures is of great importance in God's sight, but rather it must be grounded on the glory of the divine Creator, whose will rules over all. *Soli deo gloria* was a byword for all seventeenth century Calvinism, and Puritanism remained fully under its sway. When Ames discussed the goal for the Christian's life, he wrote that it was more excellent to live well than to live happily, adding the further comment that "that which ought chiefly and finally to be respected is not blessednesse, which respects our profit, but goodnesse, which is referred to Gods glory."[148] Even those who had commended the motive of search for spiritual happiness came to subordinate this to, or at least to coordinate this with, a theocentric view. Harris said that if it comes to a matter of competition between one's self and God, then one should let everything go, even "life and all, rather than God, and his glory."[149] And Preston knew that in the final sense the desire "proper to the saints" is the desire to be made a new Creature not only "out of the beauty and taste of it," but also "out of a desire to please God and glorifie him."[150]

So God is to be honored and served and loved for God's sake, rather than one's own, that is, because God is God. Genuine grief over sin is not worldly sorrow out of anxiety about personal punishment or pain, but distress over the displeasing of the holy God. Rutherfurd saw this as acting out of "the aw of heaven" which then "hath a stronger impression then the terrour and aw of hell."[151] Obedience to the Law should rest on the fact that it is God's Law, even as such obedience is also an expression of thankfulness for God's gifts of mercy. On the whole, then, the commitments of the covenanted Christian

---

[147]Bulkeley, *Gospel-Covenant*, p. 222.

[148]Ames, *Marrow*, p. 2.

[149]Harris, *New Covenant*, 1:68.

[150]Preston, *Saints Qualification*, p. 306.

[151]Rutherfurd, *Covenant of Life*, p. 217.

are to be for the doing of whatever is God's will. The proper question to be asked of oneself by a Christian believer is not, "What will God give to me?"—but rather, "What shall I give to God?"[152] Said Perkins, "I will imploy my soule which he hath redeemed with all the powers and faculties thereof, as weapons of righteousness for the advancement of his glory."[153]

THE COVENANT AS ABSOLUTE

To see all of these conditional, and indeed human, factors in the covenant relationship is, however, to see only one side of this reality. Here the stress has been on human responsibility in the meeting of covenant requirements in order that God's conditional promises may be fulfilled, a view of the covenant of grace most congenial to the evangelical impulses of Puritan piety. But intersecting this view of the covenant was that fed by the impulses, not so much from devotion as from doctrine. The doctrinal heritage of the Puritans gave high priority to the central Calvinist affirmations of deep-rooted human depravity and unconditioned divine sovereignty. Thus, as the implications of these theological convictions were applied to the covenant understanding, the contingency of conditionality was overlaid by the assurance that by God's irresistible power the covenant goals would be realized. Predestination joined piety in shaping the covenant conception, and to accommodate its requirements the covenant was deemed to be absolute.

For Puritan theology this assurance was as rooted in the biblical message as was the evangelical proclamation of the conditional promise. The biblical Gospel presented the promises of forgiveness and new life offered to the repentant sinner who would receive them in faith, but that divine Word also told of promises to which no condition was attached. John Ball noted that "the Covenant in Scripture doth sometimes signifie an absolute Promise of God, without any stipulation at all" and cited as example God's covenant commitment to Noah after the flood, "promising freely, that he would never destroy man and beasts with a universall deluge of water any more." But then Ball also added, "Of this kind is the Covenant wherein God promiseth that he will give his elect faith and perseverance, to which promise no condition can be conceived in mind, which is not comprehended in the Promise it selfe. Heb. 8.10."[154]

The Hebrews text to which Ball referred is a quotation from Jeremiah 31 which served in Puritan understanding as a central instance of God's free and absolute covenant commitment: "The time is coming, says the Lord, when I will make a new covenant with Israel and Judah. . . . I will set my law

[152]E. F., *Marrow*, p. 182.
[153]Perkins, "Mans Imaginations," *Works*, 2:478.
[154]Ball, *Covenant of Grace*, p. 3. See also Cameron, *Certain Theses*, 1st thesis.

within them and write it on their hearts; I will become their God and they shall become my people."[155] Here is the divine promise of a new being, without requirement attached. It is simply by God's intention and by God's action that this shall come to pass. There is promised, without any prerequisite or qualification, a new spiritual and moral existence despite all previous and present sin. A similar expression, equally drawn upon in this Puritan usage, was found in the "words of the Lord" of Ezekiel 36: "I will give you a new heart and put a new spirit within you; I will take the heart of stone from your body and give you a heart of flesh. I will put my spirit in you and make you conform to my statutes, keep my law and live by them."[156]

Such passages grounded the Puritan conviction that God's sovereign mercy will refresh and renew, and that in the last analysis this covenanting action was fully in God's hands. William Prynne commented on a similar biblical promise in Jeremiah 32, which affirms, "I will give them one heart and one way of life . . . for their own good and the good of their children. . . . I will enter into an eternal covenant with them, to follow them unfailingly with my bounty."[157] His observation was that this "is not a mutuall and reciprocall covenant, wherein God covenants for himselfe to us, and wee covenant againe for our selves to him. . . . But it is an intire covenant, made by God himselfe, to us, and to himselfe: this covenant therefore being only the covenant of God."[158] Jenison noted that "in regard of the word and worke of the ministery," thus in the evangelical proclamation of the Gospel, "things may goe with Iffs and Ands," with the result that "the conditions in regard of man (whose actions . . . are voluntary) may, or may not be done or performed." Yet, he added, "as they are Gods workes . . . and effects of his Election," God "speaks of them without Iffs, and promiseth them absolutely, yea and accordingly worketh and effecteth them himselfe."[159] The covenant of grace, therefore, can be viewed from two directions. From one perspective the covenant is conditional, but from another it is absolute.

It is not, however, as though it were either conditional or absolute. Puritan theology rejected at this point the "either/or" and affirmed a "both/and," with the connecting link found in the fulfillment of the conditions themselves. The distinctive feature of the covenant as absolute is that it becomes God's means of bringing to completion the covenant as conditional. For God's chosen there is the divinely covenanted commitment that the conditions will be fulfilled by God's own doing, and this commitment is without conditions. Indeed, said Sibbes, this is the most significant reason for the covenant being called a "covenant of grace." It is not simply because the things promised conditionally, such as forgiveness and new life, are

[155]Jeremiah 31:31–34.
[156]Ezekiel 36:26–27.
[157]Jeremiah 32:38–40.
[158]Prynne, *Regenerate Mans Estate*, p. 37.
[159]Jenison, *Concerning Gods Certaine Performance*, p. 57.

promised as gifts of grace to the receptive believer, but even more because one's very receiving is made possible by God's further giving. "All," he said, "is of grace in the new covenant, merely of grace. God requires not any answering by our strength. . . . It is ourselves that answer, but not from ourselves, but from grace."[160] Or again he noted, "The covenant of grace is so called, because God is so gracious as to enable us to perform our own part."[161] Hence in the covenant, wrote Prynne, "God himselfe hath absolutely undertaken to doe all that for us which he requireth and expecteth from us."[162] And this is great consolation, for it gives surety to the fulfillment of the conditional covenant itself. "Conditional promising," said Baynes, "doth not hurt the certainty, but when the condition is doubtful; now the condition is out of all doubt, for God hath absolutely promised to work it in us; Hee is the author and finisher of Faith, hee will confirm us, he will perfect his good work."[163]

This need for God's absolute help in the fulfilling of covenant conditions is due to the impotence for good which characterizes humanity's fallen state. Clearly there is no innate capacity to be obedient to God's Law of active righteousness, but equally there is inability to manifest before God the trust and receptivity which constitutes faith. Asked Burgess, "Doth not the Gospel, when it bids a man beleeve, speak as impossible a thing to a man's power?[164] Jenison knew the conditions of the covenant of grace to be "no lesse hard" than those of its predecessor and of such nature that they could not be performed aright "by our owne strength."[165] Bacon added that "if God should stay to make good the Covenant till we bring faith to the Covenant, the Covenant would be of none effect."[166] Thus the doctrine of depravity made impact here upon Puritan covenant understanding. To affirm unaided capacity for faith and repentance would be horrendous heresy, the theological folly variously designated Pelagian, Papist, or Arminian.

This reading must also be given to even such a biblical text as the invitation of James 4:8, "Draw nigh to God, and he will draw nigh to you." Joseph Caryl commented, "This and the like Scriptures shew us our dutie not our abilitie. . . . And though we are invited to come to God, yet till God comes to us, we cannot come to him. We are spoken to, under the tenour, and in the language of the Covenant of grace, which giveth the strength for every dutie it calls us to."[167] As the human condition renders impossible, therefore, the purely human fulfillment of the covenant conditions, God gives in the

[160]Sibbes, "Demand of Good Conscience," *Works*, 7:483.

[161]Sibbes, "Bowels Opened," *Works*, 2:183.

[162]Prynne, *Regenerate Mans Estate*, p. 54.

[163]Baynes, *Commentary Upon Ephesians*, p. 447.

[164]Burgess, *Vindiciae Legis*, p. 14.

[165]Jenison, *Concerning Gods Certaine Performance*, p. 61.

[166]Bacon, *Spirit of Prelacie*, p. 18.

[167]Caryl, *Heaven and Earth Embracing*, p. 23.

covenant those absolute promises which are without condition and become ground for the covenant's ultimate completion. In an anonymous document of the late seventeeth century one divine wrote, "I cannot imagine how any condition can be attached to those Promises: *I will write my Laws in their hearts . . . and I will take the stony heart out of their bodies,* unless free will be granted."[168] But free will, with implied ability to move oneself from sin to faith, was in no way to be granted, and the absolute promises were offered without condition, the further and ultimate gift in the covenant of grace.

So whatever may be God's requirements as covenant conditions, their fulfillment is now promised. If the condition is faith, then that will be provided, for, asked Jenison, "is not faith one those lawes, which God hath promised to put into our hearts? . . . Yea, Hee worketh it both for habit and for act."[169] Richard Resbury observed that God would not only give "life upon beleeving," but also enable one "to believe unto life."[170] Again, if the condition is repentance, that too will be provided, for, said Jenison, "God doth promise it. . . . Yea he also works it. . . . So that he both appointed it, to be preached, and works it by preaching."[171] Indeed grace must precede true repentance. Godly sorrow cannot emerge out of a graceless heart, nor can a holy resolution of amendment of life be in an unholy person. This too is one of the "lawes" written on the heart. Bacon believed that this repentance was called godly sorrow "because it is the work of God in us."[172] A biblical illustration of such sorrow was found in the repentance of "the good Thiefe on the Cross," of whom it was affirmed that he "was not illuminated because he did confesse Christ, but hee did confesse Christ because he was illuminated."[173] Still again, if the condition is perseverance in obedience, that "Constancy without which no Crown," this likewise will be provided, for in the last analysis, said Jenison, "God will neither turne from us, nor suffer us to turne from him, though others fall away."[174] Prynne objected to those who alleged that there is no "certainty in our perseverance," for "we are fickle and unconstant," by affirming that constancy itself is part of the absolute and unconditional promises of God.[175]

The fulfillment of the conditions of the conditional covenant, therefore, is guaranteed by the promises of the covenant as absolute. Bacon affirmed that the covenant of grace "commands no more than it gives,"[176] and thus one can have confidence in the adequacy of the gift. Ball spoke of this

---

[168]*Covenant of Grace not Absolute*, p. 24.

[169]Jenison, *Concerning Gods Certaine Performance*, p. 66.

[170]Resbury, *Gangrene of Arminianism*, pp. 9–10.

[171]Jenison, *Concerning Gods Certaine Performance*, pp. 69–70.

[172]Bacon, *Spirit of Prelacie*, p. 19.

[173]E. F., *Marrow*, p. 188.

[174]Jenison, *Concerning Gods Certaine Performance*, p. 75.

[175]Prynne, *Regenerate Mans Estate*, p. 48.

[176]Bacon, *Spirit of Prelacie*, p. 18.

covenant characteristic by saying simply, "God giveth what he requireth: Mans duty is his free gift of grace."[177] Hence, urged Sibbes, "if God will be our God, there will be grace given to take him for our God."[178] This means that "He chooseth us, and then we choose him. He knoweth us, and therefore we come to know him. He loveth us first, and then we love him. He singleth us out to be a peculiar people, and we single out him above all things to be our portion."[179] This is the covenant of grace as absolute.

One particular form taken by this emphasis upon God's sovereignty in saving covenant action is found in the Christological center of much Puritan thought. The covenant of grace, Harris affirmed, is a covenant made with Christ and then, in Christ, with "all Christian men and women" who are to be its participants. It is first with Christ as the head of the Church in which "God gives unto his Sonne . . . a people from all eternity, that he should redeem them," and then it is "with us" as God "fits us in Christ for himselfe and brings us home to himselfe."[180] This takes us back to the intra-Trinitarian covenant of redemption as source for the covenant of grace. Nevertheless the two are not coalesced. While emphasizing the mutuality of promises contained in the covenant between God and Christ, the main body of Puritan divines continued strongly to affirm the mutuality of promises between God and the covenanting believer. Antinomian diminution of the latter was emphatically denied. Yet the connecting link between the two sets of promises remained very much evident: covenanting believers are "in Christ" and have been from all eternity. Thus the eternal covenant with Christ is also an eternal covenant with those who have been elected to receive his redemption. Ultimately the application of this redemption will be through the means which God has chosen to employ, that is, through the conditions of the covenant of grace. But the election of those so to be favored has been determined before all ages in God's covenant with Christ. Preston pointed out that there were two Adams, that God had made covenant with both, and that in each there were others involved. All had fallen, of course, in the first Adam. "But," he said, "there is a second Adam, and all that are saved, are members of him . . . he kept the covenant, and therefore if he stand, they shall stand also."[181]

A sense of organic connectedness between Christ and the believer was part of this perception, even as the biblical portrayal suggested. Rutherfurd developed it, for example, in this comprehensive observation:

> God choosed the noble royall Family, Christ the Head, and all the
> Branches in Him. . . . We were in Christ as the tree is in the seed, as all

[177]Ball, *Treatise of Faith*, p. 239.
[178]Sibbes, "Faithful Covenanter," *Works*, 6:9.
[179]Ibid., 6:19.
[180]Harris, *New Covenant*, 2:160.
[181]Preston, *Life Eternall*, 2:87.

Rose trees and the Vine trees are in the first Rose tree and the first Vine tree, created of God, virtually. For because God choosed us, therefore shall we be in Christ by faith: yea and he choosed us and ordained us to be in Christ by faith, when He gave us to the Son to be keeped by him.[182]

William Strong added, "The promises are primarily made to Christ, and are his inheritance, and secondarily ours, only by vertue of our Union with him."[183] As Christ incorporated all future believers into himself in the counsels of eternity, this determined the covenant actions yet to occur in the passage of time. God's covenant with Abraham, for example, was prepared in this divine pre-history. Perkins, whom Richard Muller has recently interpreted as maintaining a "soteriological Christocentricity,"[184] said that "the promises made to Abraham, are first made to Christ, and then in Christ to all that beleeve in him, be they Jewes, or Gentiles."[185] And Edmund Calamy wrote even more explicitly:

As one King makes a league or covenant with another by an Embassadour, so Abraham represented Christ, for the promise of eternal life . . . made before the world began. . . . Therefore before Abraham had his being [he] received the sign or token of this covenant . . . whereas the covenant itself was made with Christ from all eternity, and those elect . . . in every age . . . hath been in Christ.[186]

The historical, therefore, is incorporated into the counsels and decrees of the eternal, and the participants in the covenant of grace are those who in Christ have been elected for this favor. Predestination lies behind covenant composition, and in this way as well the covenant of grace is absolute.

[182]Rutherfurd, *Covenant of Life*, pp. 305–6.
[183]Strong, *Discourse of Two Covenants*, p. 249.
[184]Muller, "Perkins' *A Golden Chaine*," p. 77.
[185]Perkins, *Commentarie upon Galatians*, p. 184.
[186]Calamy, *Two solemne Covenants*, p. 7.

Chapter 4
COVENANT AND THE *ORDO SALUTIS*

Even as a person's natural life progresses from infancy to adulthood, so the spiritual life of the Christian believer encompasses a wide span of development. Initiation, progress, fulfillment—these are as much a part of the individual's growth in the life of the spirit as they are landmarks of maturing in the life of the flesh. As natural life is itself "in progress," so the life which transcends the purely natural also must move from stage to stage. There is, therefore, an "order of salvation," a development in the life of the spirit, and each of its stages, biblically designated, must be seen—so Puritan divines maintained—as incorporated within the covenant of grace. God's gracious covenantal acts, bringing spiritual life to birth, nurturing it in the years of struggle, and then leading it to final fulfillment are a powerful part of this progress, even as are the covenanted responses of believers as they share in the responsibilities for this pilgrimage.

Hence the covenant, seen as an instrument of salvation, relates in all stages to the *ordo salutis*. Here is the beginning with its "calling," the actions of God that initiate the Christian's life. Here are the gifts of "justification" and "adoption" which, when properly received, provide new relationship with God. Here are the further developments of "sanctification" and "glorification" in which the Christian's life is brought, through divine-human cooperation, both to expression and to completion. These encompass the alpha through omega of Christian spiritual existence, and all parts thereof must be comprehended within the framework of the covenant of grace.

COVENANT AND THE NEW BEING

George Downame once wrote, "To do that good which he would not, or not to do the evil which he would, are signes of a Carnall man, whose will is not regenerate, and contrariwise, not to do the good which he would, or to do the evil which he would not, are signes (though sins) of a faithful man whose will is regenerate."[1] This statement identifies a significant Puritan priority. "Being" is more critical to the character of the Christian person than is "act." In normal expectations act will be in accord with being, but the vagaries and varieties of human behavior do not necessarily keep it so. Those

---

[1] G. Downame, *Certainty of Perseverance*, pp. 286–87.

of carnal being may occasionally surprise and those of regenerated being may even more frequently disappoint, but the underlying intention outweighs the deed. In this sense the heart is more central for identification of a person's true nature than is the hand, though heart and hand would most often coincide.

In the life of every person, then, there has been, or yet is, the need for a new heart, a "heart of flesh" with the "stony heart" removed, a heart with the Law written upon it, a heart that is renewed, restored, recreated by God. But such restoration can come to pass. If in fallen humanity the heart has turned away, now in God's covenanted restoration it can be brought back to its proper love and true destiny. Harris spoke of God as not only the "heart maker," but also the "heart mender" through whom the new heart can come to be. This, again, is central. Harris was concerned about persons who would "have their faces faire, their skin smooth" but would be inattentive to the heart. Yet since the heart "is the source and spring of all our actions," that must be cleansed first. "To what purpose," he asked, "is it to wash the bucket, so long as the spring is foule?" But heart-cleansing, heart-mending, heart-recreating are the commitment of God. "In his covenant," said Harris, "he undertakes it."[2] So the giving of the "new being" is God's first act in that process of salvation carried out through the covenant of grace.

In their standard theological terminology Puritan divines customarily saw this initial stage in the *ordo salutis* as that of "calling" or "vocation," the first summoning of persons into the new life of God—though also, as in Ames' *Marrow*,[3] this first step was discussed under the categories of "conversion" and "regeneration." It is significant, from the standpoint of our analysis of the nature of Puritan covenant understanding, that Ames likewise combined here the themes of the conditional and the absolute. "Calling," he said, involves initially the offer of Christ. This is the proclamation of the Gospel in which the promises "are propounded to all without difference, together with a command to believe them." Then the receiving of the promises is by an act of faith in which one "doth now wholly leane upon Christ as his Saviour, and by Christ upon God." But the receiving also has its "passive" aspects "whereby a spirituall principle of grace is begotten in the will of man," an act emanating from God's predestining sovereignty. So calling itself "doth not in any sort depend upon the dignity, honesty, industry, or any indeavour of the called, but upon the election and predestination of God only." At this point especially do the terms "conversion" and "regeneration" apply, for in Ames' understanding it was by God's sovereign act that the will was so altered, the heart so regenerated, as to bring about the "conversion of the whole man." All this constitutes the beginning of the Christian pilgrimage in "calling."

[2]Harris, *New Covenant*, 1:18, 26.
[3]Ames, *Marrow*, pp. 110–13.

Here is the initial fulfillment of God's promise to provide a new heart. In this regeneration there is the generation of a new being. Though evidences may sometimes fail fully to discriminate, the change is truly there. John Forbes used the delightful analogy of the scents of an "Apothecaris shop." The unregenerated individual, he said, may draw these to him as he passes by, though he carry none of its "odoriferous things" on his person. But the regenerate purchaser is different, for the work of God on the elect is the "imparting of the things witnessed to the soule, and making it reallie to possess it."[4] So life at its center is transformed. It takes on a new quality, a new character, a new being. Preston said that God implants in the human person a new instinct which can be satisfied only by embracing Christ. It is "as the Iron cannot rest till it come to the Loadstone, and as the stone cannot rest till it come to the center."[5] This new instinct then becomes a new direction, "for to be a New Creature is nothing else, but to be turned up-side downe, when a man changeth his course, . . . when he sayles to a quite contrary point of the Compasse, when the Rudder of his life is turned."[6]

This analogy also had further implications. The change which God gives to the ship of one's life is not that of a new vessel or even of new sailing conditions, but rather simply a new course as provided by a rudder turned a new way. With regard to one's natural dispositions, "only the oldnesse is to be taken away, but the nature it selfe is to continue." These dispositions are "like the wind to drive the Ship," which must be utilized under any course upon which the vessel is set. The crucial matter is the control of the rudder, and there "only godlinesse must sit at the Sterne."[7] The new heart sets life upon a new course, a direction designated by God. Changing the analogy, Preston likewise noted that the meaning of being a new creature "is not that the substance of a man is changed, but the order and frame of his soule is altered. There are the same strings, as it were, but there is a new tune."[8]

Such fundamental alteration can occur because the new being is really the consequence of a union of Christ and the believer. When Ames discussed the subjective aspect of "calling," he saw it as that part of salvation's beginning in which "Christ is joyned to man and man to Christ."[9] Perkins likewise listed this union as a special work of grace even prior, "in order of nature," to conversion.[10] Puritan theology was not always consistent on some of the details connected with this matter, and Perkins particularly seemed to have thought of conversion in a more comprehensive way. In "A Reformed Catholike," for example, he developed the idea of a twofold

[4]Forbes, *A Letter for resolving*, p. 28.
[5]Preston, *Breast-Plate of Faith and Love*, 1:103.
[6]Preston, *Saints Qualification*, p. 323.
[7]Ibid., p. 391.
[8]Ibid., p. 324.
[9]Ames, *Marrow*, p. 112.
[10]Perkins, "Graine of Musterd-seede," *Works*, 1:627.

conversion, the first being an act of God in regeneration and the second an act in which one "turnes himself" in repentance.[11] And when he discussed conversion in "A Graine of Musterd-seede," he spoke of it as occurring gradually by stages or degrees, to be likened to the dawning of the day.[12] But beneath all such conceptions of the turning of direction in human life was the fundamental affirmation, resting on biblical declaration, of the union of Christ and the believer. John Cotton, for whom this was particularly important, defined "our effectual calling" as being "the Spirit of God taking possession in our hearts and working this Faith in us . . . that maketh us one with Christ."[13]

The beginning of the Christian's new being must also be seen under one further perspective. Within the practices of the church the historical rite of introduction into new life has been the sacrament of baptism, and this likewise played its role in Puritan thought. In Puritan understanding, it is true, the sacramental tended to be subordinated to the evangelical, for Puritan divines were concerned over the personal more than over the institutional, and the formalities of ecclesiastical heritage were thus generally interpreted in their relationship to personal faith. Still the sacramental had strong significance, biblically grounded and traditionally conveyed. Ames could speak of baptism as the "Sacrament of Initiation or Regeneration" which, as it "doth seale the whole covenant of grace," also in a personal way "doth represent and confirme our very ingrafting into Christ."[14] This is not to be interpreted in the classical sense of a regeneration produced by the baptismal act. The Reformed theological tradition had long rejected that. But it is to be seen as sacred solemnization of God's covenant with those incorporated thereby into the visible Christian family, a sealing of both God's promises to them and their believing response. With particular reference to the conditional aspect of the covenant of grace, Baxter looked upon baptism as being to its parties in mutual commitment the same as "what solemnization of marriage is to them that do before consent."[15] And Perkins explicitly declared, "in this washing of Baptisme, there is propounded and sealed a marveilous solemne covenant and contract: first, of God with the baptized . . . secondly, of the baptized with God."[16]

It is not that baptism was necessary for salvation. "God hath appointed the sacraments to be seals for us, not for himself," wrote Sibbes. "He himself keepeth his covenant whether we have the seal or no."[17] But receiving the seal conveys powerful confirmation of God's covenanted goodness and

[11]Perkins, "Reformed Catholike," Works, 1:614.
[12]Perkins, "Graine of Musterd-seede," Works, 1:627.
[13]Cotton, Covenant of Grace, p. 19.
[14]Ames, Marrow, p. 181.
[15]Baxter, "Christian Directory," Practical Works, 5:44.
[16]Perkins, "Golden Chaine," Works, 1:74.
[17]Sibbes, "Faithful Covenanter," Works, 6:22.

becomes significant representation of the gift of new being with which the process of growth in Christian life begins. For persons of maturity this sacramental solemnization of entrance into covenant means that the sealing is of the believer's faith as well as of God's faithfulness. But the sacrament is also for the children of believers who by their parents' faith are brought through baptism into the visible church and signified therein as sharing in covenant with God. That covenant, so the biblical message affirmed, was for believers and their seed, and thus the seal of the covenant must extend to the latter as well. In the earlier times of Israel that seal was circumcision. Now it is baptism, under the prescriptions of the New Covenant. "Whence," wrote Sibbes, "we see a ground of baptizing infants, because they are in the covenant. To whom the covenant belongs; the seal of it belongs." God is "the God of our children from . . . conception and birth."[18]

Certain problems were posed here for Puritan thinking by allegiance to the doctrine of predestination, particularly the question of the relation of a broadly administered baptismal seal to the selective grace of an absolute covenant. Therefore much effort was given, especially by New England divines, to sorting out that issue.[19] Yet despite the difficulties, not only was the significance of baptism affirmed as an identifying sign, but also its helpfulness was attested for accomplishing salvation's goal.[20] The Cambridge Platform of 1648 confidently claimed that the children of believers baptized in their infancy

> have many priviledges which others . . . have not: they are in covenant with God; have the seale thereof upon them, viz. Baptisme; & so if not regenerated, yet are in a more hopefull way of attayning regenerating grace, & all the spirituall blessings both of the covenant & seal; they are also under Church-watch, & consequently subject, to the reprehensions, admonitions, & censures therof, for their healing and amendment, as need shall require.[21]

Here the sacramental is joined with the evangelical, and the emergence of the new being is likewise seen as aided and abetted by this rite of the church. God, who deals in personal immediacy with the soul, also works mediately through the means divinely established.

Thus in the many ways of the mysterious workings of God there is "effectual calling," the giving of the new heart, the regeneration of the soul, the initiation of what for the Christian believer is to be a new life. Ball provided for it a definition lifting up also the experiential aspect: "Effectuall

---

[18]Ibid.

[19]For a discussion of this matter see Holifield, *Covenant Sealed*, pp. 143–59.

[20]See Pettit, *Heart Prepared*, chap. 4. His interpretation of Hooker, Shepard, and Bulkeley is questioned, however, by Holifield.

[21]"Cambridge Platform," XII, 7. Walker, *Creeds and Platforms*, p. 224.

Vocation on Gods part is the powerfull invitation and assured drawing of the weary and thirsty soule unto Christ, that in him it might finde refreshing and comfort."[22]

COVENANT AND RELATIONSHIP TO GOD

If the *ordo salutis* begins in "calling," it moves on immediately to "justification" and "adoption," the formal, theological way of saying that sins are now forgiven and a new status for the individual is established in God's sight. Probably no aspect of Christian doctrine was more strongly empha-sized in the time of Protestantism's sixteenth century beginnings than was the idea of justification. For Luther it was the heart of the Gospel, the key to biblical understanding of the divine-human relationship, the centerpiece of theology, and in its Protestant interpretation a major point of difference with the doctrine of the Roman Catholic Church. Little wonder, then, that Puritan theologians would attach similar central significance to this matter of the faith. Burgess wrote that justification is "the very Marrow of Doctrinal and Practical Divinity. . . . Its the Centre wherein all theological truths do meet. Its the Ocean that by its several streams watereth and refresheth the Paradise, the Church of God. Its the Ark of Faith, all Religion is kept pure, while this is kept pure."[23]

There was the problem, of course, that it had not always been kept pure, and Burgess therefore noted that since the death of Luther "there presently rose up many, perverted in minde, and set upon it, as those thieves upon the man going to Jericho, leaving it wounded and half dead."[24] Certainly a part of the theologian's task in the seventeenth century was to attempt to restore this doctrine to better health. But the task was to be undertaken not without difficulty and opposition. On either side of mainstream Puritan thought were to be the critical and contending views of the Arminians and the Antinom-ians. Likewise from within the very heart of orthodoxy itself such a Puritan stalwart as Richard Baxter was to add considerable dispute to the discussion, as to lesser extent did others inside the fold. Yet the doctrine was central, and in the theological effort to clarify and preserve it much agreement emerged.

The first thing to note is that justification was kept clearly separated from sanctification in major Puritan thought, an important theological matter. In experience they may be concurrent, but in theological understanding they represent two different, though complementary, aspects of the way in which life under God can be portrayed. If the former is a relational matter, the latter deals more concretely with essential change in one's life, for in justification one is freed from guilt, whereas in sanctification one is freed from corruption.

[22]Ball, *Covenant of Grace*, p. 347.
[23]Burgess, *True Doctrine of Justification*, 2:114.
[24]Ibid., 1:4.

The one is based on an act of God from "without us," while the other is based on an act of God "within us." In the former one benefits from imputed righteousness, in the latter from a gift of inherent righteousness. In justification one is accepted by God and given title to God's Kingdom, whereas in sanctification one is morally renewed by God and fitted for God's Kingdom. Moreover, in terms of the fulfillment of covenant conditions, justification is by faith alone, while in sanctification the person of faith is likewise called upon for obedience.

In sum, justification and sanctification are closely connected and yet different. Burgess pointed out, in his criticism of Roman views on this matter, that renovation must be joined with justification, but one is not justified by having a new nature given. His analogy said: "The water hath both moistnesse and coldnesse in it, yet it doth not wash away spots as it is cold, but as it is moist."[25] The principal benefit of justification, however, is that it does wash away the spots, that is, through the goodness of God's viewing it makes a sinful and unacceptable person acceptable in God's sight. By virtue of the merits of Christ's satisfaction this has become the miracle of saving grace. He was the "Samson strong enough to bear the weight" of human sin in God's sight.[26] So now, said Sutton, "we dare to stand before God" since Christ stands "betweene us and our sinnes" and "is our buckler wherewith we are protected from judgement, . . . emboldened to goe and appeare at the Tribunall of God, and are there pronounced just."[27] Christ's atonement leads to justifying grace—the Puritans, like Luther, saw this to be the center of the Christian proclamation.

When Puritan divines parsed this out more completely, however, they were led to a double emphasis in their understanding of justification. Both are included in the comprehensive definition provided by Cole: "Justification . . . is the absolving of a sinner, beleeving in Christ, from sin, and the guilt thereof, and the imputation of the righteousness of Christ unto him: and the acceptation to life eternall, freely, for the merits of Christ."[28] On the one hand, there is the "absolving . . . from sin and the guilt thereof." Christian thought has developed variant views about the ground and manner of divine remission, but consistently, in its historical expressions, it has stressed the significance of such forgiveness in one's relationship with God. Sin leads to separation and to judgment. Forgiveness means restoration and peace. The biblical message itself proclaims a forgiving mercy. So one major element in Puritanism's understanding of the Christian believer's restored relationship is God's removal of this barrier to friendship. "Justification" is a legal term and implies the passing of a sentence. The sentence upon the sinner is

[25]Ibid., p. 16.
[26]Ibid., p. 17.
[27]Sutton, *Lectures on Romans*, p. 131.
[28]Cole, *Godly Mans Assurance*, p. 26.

therefore one of acquittal. It expresses the words often spoken by Christ himself: "Your sins are forgiven you." Here is the fulfillment of a chief promise of the covenant of grace.

On the other hand, justification was likewise viewed as including what Cole designated "the imputation of the righteousness of Christ . . . the acceptation to life eternall," again a conviction coming out of the biblical heritage. Theologically analyzed, this "clothing" of the sinner as righteous in God's sight was the positive counterpart of the removal of guilt by forgiveness. George Downame saw its necessity in terms of the consequences for eternal salvation: "If justification be nothing else but bare remission of sinne, then is there . . . no acceptation as righteous: a freedome from hell, but no title to heaven."[29] In the sentence which God passes in justification, wrote Ames, "he doth absolve the sinner from sin and death, and accounts him righteous unto life."[30] Imputation was one of the promises of the covenant of grace, and Christ's faithful obedience was understood to be accepted by God as one's own. Downame found a biblical analogy in Rebecca's act of clothing Jacob in the raiment of Esau, commenting, "So the Lord justifieth us by putting upon us our eldest brothers righteousness."[31]

Criticism of this doctrine of imputation soon appeared, however, from outside the Puritan fold. Socinians objected on the ground that if Christ's righteousness were to be imputed to the sinner, there would be neither need for one's own personal righteousness nor in fact anything for God to forgive![32] William Penn, the Quaker, shared these views and added that "Justification by an Imputative Righteousness" is "meerly an imagination, not a reality."[33] Some Puritan responses proposed that only the passive righteousness of Christ, that is, his suffering and death, was imputed, whereas his active righteousness, that is, his lifelong obedience, was not. Thus imputation could not be considered as obviating the need for both forgiveness and personal obedience. However, the major body of divines continued to affirm the twofold imputation. Perkins had indeed brought the two ideas together in his earlier discussion of the matter, saying that "Christ in suffering obeied, and obeying suffered."[34]

A more serious confrontation on this matter developed in connection with the growth of Arminian influence upon Puritanism's theological left wing. Here one finds John Goodwin as the most distinguished and published representative, though he refused to be identified in the full sense as

[29]G. Downame, *Treatise of Justification*, p. 33.

[30]Ames, *Marrow*, p. 115.

[31]G. Downame, *Treatise of Justification*, p. 16.

[32]Even within Puritan orthodoxy there was lack of clarity as to how the two parts of justification, forgiveness and imputation, were related to one another. See Burgess, *True Doctrine of Justification*, 1:17.

[33]William Penn, *Sandy Foundations*, pp. 32–33. Quoted in Greaves, *John Bunyan*, p. 82.

[34]Perkins, "Reformed Catholike," *Works*, 1:567.

an Arminian.[35] The basic thrust of the Arminian movement was to reduce the potential exclusiveness which orthodoxy posited in God's decrees and correspondingly to give to the human person a freer and stronger voice in the determination of salvation. Goodwin shared fully in these goals and from his London pulpit throughout the mid-seventeenth century persistently provoked his more orthodox brethren into controversy on these issues.

Part of the discussion centered on the doctrine of justification and, within it, the question of imputation. Goodwin did not reject out of hand the idea of imputation, but rather sought to reinterpret it in line with more liberal views. For one thing, the concept of Christ's righteousness being imputed was quite unacceptable. Like all liberal critics he felt this left no place for remission: "It evacuates that high and soveraigne power of God . . . whereby he forgives sins."[36] In addition, in his judgment, it destroyed the need for repentance and took away the necessity for Christ's death, since the transfer of his active righteousness would have been sufficient to redeem one's status in God's sight. In fact, so he charged, this kind of imputation even reduces the covenant of grace once again to a covenant of works, and one might as well say that "there was no second Adam, really differing from the first, as no second Covenant differing really from the first, and that mount Sina in Arabia, is the same mountaine with Sion in Judea, and that the Spirit of bondage is the same as the Spirit of Adoption, and Isaak and Ishmael were but the same Child."[37] This is heavy indictment, especially of a concept ardently maintained by Antinomians, among others, for whom nothing was more anathema than any form of work righteousness! But then that was not out of keeping with the theological cannonading of the times. John Goodwin's own view of imputation, with its Arminian components, was accused equally in counter-charge as leading back to a covenant of works.

His positive portrayal of justification restricted it to forgiveness, "an acquitting . . . and setting a man free from the guilt and penalties due to such things as were laid to his charge."[38] Yet, though imputation of Christ's righteousness was rejected as a second part of justification, imputation itself had a place. But it was imputation differently interpreted, being the imputation of the believer's faith as righteousness in the sight of God. This is again a biblical concept, resting especially on Paul's statements about the faith of Abraham in Romans 4, and John Goodwin, along with others of Arminian sympathy, saw it as the connecting link between divine mercy and human responsibility.

The essential nature of imputation, as developed here, rested heavily upon its "as if" aspect. Wrote Goodwin, "A thing may be said to be imputed

[35]John Goodwin, "Letter of October 15, 1651 to Richard Resbury." Quoted in Jackson, *Life of John Goodwin*, p. 274.

[36]J. Goodwin, *Imputatio Fidei*, 1:151.

[37]Ibid., p. 157.

[38]Ibid., p. 77.

to a man when he is looked upon or dealt with, as if he had some true worth or qualification in him." In this way God can impute righteousness to a person, looking upon that individual "with the same grace and favor, wherewith he would looke upon him if he were properly and legally righteous indeed."[39] The human condition for this imputation is faith. Though God required perfect obedience under the first covenant, in the covenant of grace the condition of justification is faith in Christ, a simple relying upon him. It is then through this act that, by imputation, the believer can become fully acceptable in God's sight. This brings the person of faith into that desirable pristine state which would have been accorded to one who had complied with all the original commandments of God for righteous works. Since faith is the condition of the covenant of grace, Goodwin affirmed that "God lookes upon a man who truly beleeveth, with as much grace and favor, and intends to doe as graciously and bountifully by him, as if he were a man of perfect righteousness,"[40] that is, "as a perfect righteousness should have ben under the first Covenant."[41]

This imputation of faith for righteousness is not intended to provide a meritorious ground for justification. In Goodwin's view this would be a serious misrepresentation, for "He that is justified by Faith, is not justified by the inherent dignity, or merit of that which justifyeth him, but by the free and gracious acceptation of it by God."[42] In fact at this point Goodwin turned back again to the basic foundation of all justification, Christ's own sacrificial and saving work. The possibility of justification by faith, with its imputation of that faith as righteousness, exists only because of God's prior acceptance of Christ's suffering righteousness for human redemption. Here, incidentally, Goodwin took sides for "the infinite valour of Christs passives," as against "an imaginarie exaltation of his actives," when he discussed Christ's work, but the "righteousness" of this work is not to be imputed. So Goodwin could conclude, with a certain dialectical flair, "A believer may be said to be cloathed with the righteousness of Christ, and yet the righteousnesse of Christ it selfe not be his cloathing, but only that which procured this cloathing unto him," which meant to him that "God cloaths no man with the letter of it, but every man that believes with the Spirit of it," for it "is that for which righteousness is imputeth for every man that believeth."[43]

Here was a formidable confrontation with mainstream Puritan thought, and in defending the idea of the imputation of Christ's righteousness Burgess wrote candidly of its rejection by Arminian protesters, "This is a Camel ... that they cannot swallow."[44] Theological understanding of

[39]Ibid., 2:55.
[40]Ibid., p. 176.
[41]Ibid., 1:14–15.
[42]Ibid.. p. 148.
[43]Ibid., p. 17.
[44]Burgess, *True Doctrine of Justification*, 2:293.

justification, so affirmed John Goodwin and his associates, must be adjusted to accommodate the belief that salvation is truly in human, as well as divine, hands. The doctrine of imputation was one battleground on which that struggle took place.

At the other end of the Puritan theological spectrum was the Antinomian movement, and from these quarters as well emerged views of justification troubling to the main body of divines. Major disagreement was due to the Antinomian insistence that justification was not an act occurring in human historical experience, but rather an event located in the eternal counsels of God. By viewing the covenant as absolute, without contingent historical conditions, and by correspondingly collapsing the covenant of grace into the pre-historical covenant of redemption, Antinomians saw the divine promise of justification fulfilled before all time in God's covenanting with Christ. Those whom God has chosen in eternal election are "in Christ" and are recipients of the promise, but the covenant is of Christ's doing. "What ever promise there is which hath any condition in it," wrote Saltmarsh, "it is ours in him, that is in Christ, who was the onely conditional and qualified person for all the promises."[45]

So justification was viewed in Antinomian thought as an immanent, rather than a transient, act of God, that is, confined in its nature to God's inner and eternal life and not a part of God's external acts in time. As such, therefore, it rested in no way upon the believer's faith. Justification occurring in eternity antedates faith as a temporal act. Indeed, one is not justified by faith, but by Christ, and faith then becomes declarative of what has already been given. "Faith," said Powell, "is not given before the Covenant, but in, with and through the Covenant."[46] And Crisp related it to justification by noting, "We do not believe that we may be justified, but we do believe, and truly believe when we are, and because we are justified."[47] Faith, therefore, was essentially a "faith of assurance," and the struggle for faith was a search for confidence rather than for conversion.

Much in this view of the nature of justification was obviously unacceptable to major Puritan divines and was strongly protested, particularly on the grounds of the historical character of Christian experience and of God's saving deeds within it. Burgess saw in Antinomian "eternal justification" a confusion of the "decree and purpose to justifie" with the justifying act itself, but only the former is to be found in the counsels of eternity.[48] Blake urged that such a view "overthrows the redemption wrought by Christ," for then he "did not purchase, . . . but only published," and under those circumstances "was a messenger from God . . . but no Saviour."[49] And if faith is simply

[45]Saltmarsh, *Free-Grace*, p. 105.

[46]Powell, *Christ and Moses*, p. 60.

[47]Crisp, *Christ Alone Exalted*, p. 86.

[48]Burgess, *True Doctrine of Justification*, 1:188.

[49]Blake, *Vindiciae Foederis*, pp. 131–32.

declarative, then the whole historical experience again has no serious significance and, as Burgess expressed it, "our Justification by faith, shall be but a copy fetcht out of the Court-roll, where the sentence of Justification was passed already."[50] One disgruntled divine, anti-Roman as well as anti-Antinomian in his convictions, ventured the judgment that Antinomianism "hath found a shorter cut to heaven than the Catholicke Church ever heard of."[51] Leo Solt, in comparing mainstream Puritan theologians with the Antinomians, observed that the former "believed that salvation was possible," whereas the latter "believed that it had already come."[52]

If Arminianism and Antinomianism posed problems on the theological extremes, further dispute concerning justification was also added by the much respected Richard Baxter from within the citadel of orthodoxy itself. Baxter's deep anxiety was over the threat of Antinomianism. As a military chaplain in the 1640s he had seen its spread and experienced its excesses, and this had significant impact on his theological development. Haller writes,

> [He] found too many men in the army so overpersuaded that they had Christ within that they had but to reach forth their hands and retake paradise, or whatever else they might erroneously conceive to be rightfully theirs, at once, just as they had taken Bristol or Basing or Worcester, ... an error from which he was to spend years trying to rescue them, on the crucial point of justification.[53]

Baxter's theological response was not only to reject the extremes of Antinomianism, but also to lean sufficiently in the direction of Arminianism to be accused of simply basing the act of justification on the fulfillment of the "new law." His fundamental deviation from orthodoxy was thus seen as "Neonomian."

There is unquestionably some truth to this allegation, but Baxter's total view was by no means a simple legalism. Rather, he worked out in considerable complexity the relations of faith and works, mercy and merit, Christ and commitment in salvation's process, seeking throughout to accord an important place to human responsibility while likewise maintaining the pre-eminence of divine grace. His distinctive conjoining of the divine and the human can be seen especially in two aspects of his doctrine of justification, in both of which he was criticized by his orthodox colleagues for stressing too strongly the human part.

First, there was the development of the new covenant itself and the

[50]Burgess, *True Doctrine of Justification*, 1:198.
[51]Francis Wortley, *Characters and Elegies*, p. 14. Quoted in Solt, *Saints in Arms*, p. 41.
[52]Solt, *Saints in Arms*, p. 37.
[53]Haller, "New Model Army," p. 20.

believer's entrance into it. Differing from others in his view of God's governance, he saw God's law as flexible and subject to change by God's act as new circumstances might require. This indeed has happened as the result of the fall and Christ's subsequent redeeming acts. Where orthodoxy taught that Christ satisfied the eternal law in the sinner's place, making possible the imputation of his righteousness, Baxter affirmed that Christ satisfied the Lawgiver and so procured a change in the law. This new law is the law of the new covenant, which requires faith and brings justification to those who exercise it. So two kinds of righteousness are necessary for entrance into the new covenant: the righteousness of Christ which has brought the new law and the faith of the believer which is then imputed to him for righteousness, a view similar to John Goodwin's. The former he considered "legal" righteousness and the latter "evangelical," and they must remain together. Baxter combined them when he wrote, "Christ's Righteousness is reputed the meritorious Cause. . . . And our Faith is reputed the Condition . . . all that is required in us to our Justification." But he also added the crucial comment, "Are we in any way Justified by our own performed Righteousness? Answer: yes."[54] Or again he wrote, "To affirm that our Evangelical or New Covenant Righteousness is in Christ, and not in ourselves, or performed by Christ, and not by ourselves, is . . . a monstrous piece of Antinomian doctrine."[55]

Second, Baxter developed a view of justification as a continuous process which likewise drew criticism for its involvement of human effort. If one decisive moment in justification was its time of beginning in faith, "constitutive justification" in his terminology, an equally decisive moment will come at the culmination of life's journey in the "declarative justification" of the last day when final judgment takes place. And throughout the journey there is "executive justification," the bestowal of promised benefits and rewards along the way. However, in this lifelong process under the care of God's covenant there must be faithful covenant-keeping in order to reach the promised goal. A dead faith, Baxter knew, does not justify; it must live through its works. So he could write: "Our first faith is our Contract with Christ. . . . [But] all Contracts of such nature, do impose a necessity of performing what we consent to and promise, in order to [receive] the benefits. . . . Covenant-making may admit you, but its the Covenant-keeping that must continue you in your priviledges."[56] Thus, he added, "Faith, Repentance, Love, Thankfulness, sincere Obedience, together with finall Perseverance, do make up the Condition of our final Absolution in Judge-

---

[54]Baxter, *Justifying Righteousness*, p. 88.

[55]Baxter, *Aphorismes of Justification*, p. 111.

[56]Richard Baxter, *Of Justification*, pp. 123–24. Quoted in Packer, *Redemption and Restoration*, p. 297.

ment, and our eternal Glorification."[57] When confronted by criticism over this alleged "Romanizing" of the theology of salvation, he candidly said, "If this be Justification by Works, I am for it."[58]

So Baxter moved into this "Neonomianism" as he countered the less disciplined enthusiasms of Antinomianism. Leo Solt offers this contrast between Baxter and the Antinomian Saltmarsh:

> Baxter liked to compare the covenant between man and God with the marriage contract between husband and wife . . . [where] although mere consent is the only condition of first possession, yet the faithful performance of marriage duties . . . is necessary to continue the marriage. The counterpart to Baxter's analogy in Saltmarsh's theology would be the case of the abducted maiden. The maiden's fear would have been converted by her abductor's love to faith, and her startled incredulity at her own abduction would have changed to an assuring belief that it really had happened and was not just a wishful dream. The Baxter analogy was essentially legalistic; with Saltmarsh it was outside the pale of the law.[59]

Perhaps other Puritans, one might add, would have opted for some "abduction" within marriage itself, where love's spontaneity transcends the obligatory and brings further freedom and joy. In any case, orthodox Puritan divines sought to provide theological correctives. The doctrine of justification needed to be protected against excessive reliance on legal constraint, as well as against excessive abandon to unstructured grace.

Thus, on the one hand, Burgess could write, "Take heed of confounding faith with obedience. . . . our justification consists in our receiving from God, not giving to him."[60] Justification is by faith and not by works. Baxter was repudiated on that score by his orthodox colleagues as, with more animus, were John Goodwin, all Arminians, Socinians, and representatives of the Roman way. Whether the alleged ground for justification be evangelical works, faith imputed for righteousness, infused grace, or out and out merit, the overwhelming response was the same: justification is not based on any human condition of worthiness. To those holding any such notion the bitter comment directed at the bishops of the Council of Trent would no doubt have been held to apply: "Because they did not follow the Starre of the Scripture [that is, in their decree on justification], they came not to the lodging where Christ was."[61] In justification Christ was where the grace of God was, and grace is never earned.

On the other hand, George Downame could write, "Although the Robe

[57]Richard Baxter, *Confession*, p. 56. Quoted in Packer, *Redemption and Restoration*, p. 298.
[58]Baxter, *Justifying Righteousness*, p. 163.
[59]Solt, *Saints in Arms*, p. 34.
[60]Burgess, *True Doctrine of Justification*, 2:244.
[61]Ibid., 1:6.

the Christian as no "idle condition," but as a "busy trade."[81] And Preston's confidence in justifying faith's productive power led to the affirmation that "he that beleeves in the greatest degree the promises of pardon and remission, I dare boldly say, he hath the holiest heart, and the holiest life."[82] Here is no timid "back door" concession. Works of moral worth are a valued and necessary part of total Christian responsiveness. Like Calvin the Puritans maintained that though one is not justified by good works, neither is one justified without them.

Justification and sanctification, therefore, go together. The new relationship to God in faith and the living out of its obligations in faithfulness are each a part of the one total Christian experience provided in the covenant of grace. And the latter part, like the former, is dependent on God's giving. Here, as well, is the fulfillment of covenanted promises and a change in human existence brought about by divine power. The more concrete elaboration of this idea took several forms, even as had its expression in the Scripture itself. From one perspective this is union with Christ, as Paul had affirmed in that "mysticism" which constituted part of his Christian experience and its explication. "We must have Christ as it were borne in us, 'formed in us,'" Sibbes wrote. "Certainly the same Spirit that sanctified Christ doth sanctify every member of Christ; and Christ is in some sort begotten, and conceived, and 'manifested' in every one that is a Christian."[83] Or again, writing in terms specifically related to central covenant conviction, he said, "Whosoever God is a God to, there will be a transforming unto God, a transforming unto Christ, in whom God is our God ... for we are predestinated to be like God incarnate."[84]

Likewise sanctification was understood as the inner working of the Spirit, "a secret and yet sacred blast of the Spirit of God breaking in"[85] and leading to purification and moral endeavor. Cotton affirmed that "the Spirit sanctifying draweth us into an holy confederacy to serve God in Family, Church, and Commonwealth."[86] Still further, the gift of sanctification was interpreted, in much used biblical terminology, as the presence of the Law within, that is, the divine Law now written upon the human heart. To grant this was God's basic covenant promise, and one form of its fulfillment is in the sanctified life. Of the Law Samuel Bolton wrote, "while it is a rule without us: it cannot make us holy, it must be a rule within us." But this has occurred by God's working. So "the law is a principle within us first, and then a patterne without us: we are not made holy by imitation, but by

[81]Sibbes, "Art of Contentment," *Works*, 5:185.
[82]Preston, *New Covenant*, 2:103.
[83]Sibbes, "Fountain Opened," *Works*, 5:486.
[84]Sibbes, "Faithful Covenanter," *Works*, 6:15.
[85]Strong, *Discourse of Two Covenants*, p. 102.
[86]Cotton, *Covenant of Grace*, p. 23.

of Christ's righteousness be that wedding garment which covereth our nakedness, and maketh us accepted before God; yet it will not cover us unlesse we put it on; and it is put on by faith."[62] So Antinomianism was equally repudiated, and the collective Puritan voice reaffirmed not only Luther's *sola*, but also his *fide*, when he laid down the central Protestant affirmation that justification is by faith alone. The gifts of forgiveness and imputation may be generously given, but they are not one's own until they are personally received, even though by a beggar's, rather than a laborer's, hands.[63] No doubt with Antinomian claims in mind, Bulkeley noted that "though God purposed to justifie us before the world was" and though prior to our believing there occurred "the attonement and obedience which Christ hath performed for us," faith is nevertheless an essential condition "antecedent to our actuall justification."[64] It is in one's personal historical experience and through one's personal trustful receiving that this gift of the covenant of grace can become truly one's own.

For one to receive this gift in faith is to be entered both completely and continuously into God's favor. Justification is a relationship, a condition of being under God's forgiveness, acceptable in God's sight. Condemnation has given way to acquittal, guilt to imputed righteouness, and one's "possession" is God's mercy. But this, said Puritan divines, is wrought *simul et semel*, "at once" and "but once," and thus there is both a completeness and a continuity to be found in the justified state.[65] Justification is complete in the sense that, given "at once" and not in stages, it admits of no degrees. It cannot be divided or be partial. Burgess wrote, "It is impossible that sin should be forgiven divisibly, and by parts: so a man should be at the same time under the favour of God and under his hatred."[66] Sanctification, growth in moral life, can be by degrees, but not justification as a relationship. Preston compared it with marriage and said simply, "Either you are married, or not."[67]

Justification is also continuous in that, given "but once," it remains as the Christian's relationship to God despite all the falterings and failings of one's ongoing life. The Arminians spoke of a mutable justification, holding that if faith is lost then justification is lost, with restoration contingent upon the renewal of belief. Puritan theology rejected this, for the covenant is not only conditional, but also absolute. One's personal assurance of justification may fluctuate, influenced by the changing moods of confidence and doubt, but for God's elect justification itself remains secure. Burgess' analogy affirmed that "the Sunne may be in an eclipse, but not removed from its

[62]G. Downame, *Certainty of Perseverance*, P. 270.
[63]Burgess, *True Doctrine of Justification*, 2:244.
[64]Bulkeley, *Gospel-Covenant*, p. 358.
[65]G. Downame, *Treatise of Justification*, p. 7.
[66]Burgess, *True Doctrine of Justification*, 1:152.
[67]Preston, *Saints Qualification*, p. 431.

orb."[68] So recurrence of sin does not destroy this fundamental relationship, though one must regularly continue to seek fresh forgiveness, since "there is no pardon of any new sin, without a new act of faith and repentance."[69] Even the loss of faith itself, in the inner struggles to which no person is fully immune, cannot cancel the condition of divine favor, for "justification is an act of God . . . and dependeth upon his eternall counsel. . . . To imagine that our justification is interrupted so oft as the act of faith is interrupted is a dreame."[70]

In the classic *ordo salutis* "justification" is followed by "adoption," again a state of relationship. Ames defined it as "the gracious sentence of God whereby he accepts the faithful for Christ's sake, unto the dignity of Sons." This did not loom large in Puritan theological discussion and was understood essentially as a further enhancement of the relationship established in justification. Ames noted that the faithful have the "title of redemption" by justification and the "title of Son-ship" by adoption. Redemption is the foundation, but adoption, he wrote, "doth ad a certaine manner of excellency and dignity."[71] Both reflect the condition of being in God's favor, the fulfillment of a major promise within the covenant of grace.

COVENANT AND THE MORAL LIFE

The promises of the covenant of grace carry the believer along still farther, however, on the pathway of Christian experience in the journey toward salvation. Next in the *ordo salutis* is "sanctification," and this, like justification, is committed in covenant by God. "Among the greater and more principall promises," wrote Ball, are those "which God hath made concerning our Sanctification . . . that he will enable them that believe, to bring forth fruits of amendment, and perfect the good works done in them day to day. This is the covenant which God hath made with his people."[72] If justification represents a relational change, sanctification represents a real change in the believer. Here sin is not pardoned, but purged. To sanctify is to make holy, to endow with a new character and quality of existence, and particularly so to purify as to bring into and sustain in being a new order of moral life. Ames used for it the term "new Divine creature" because, he said, it is "a new principle of life, communicated by God unto us" and "resembles that highest perfection which is found in God."[73]

In the theological disputes of the sixteenth and seventeenth centuries the charge was sometimes levelled against the more orthodox theologians of

[68]Burgess, *True Doctrine of Justification*, 2:147.
[69]Perkins, "Manner of Predestination," *Works*, 2:634.
[70]G. Downame, *Certainty of Perseverance*, p. 292.
[71]Ames, *Marrow*, pp. 120–21.
[72]Ball, *Treatise of Faith*, p. 62.
[73]Ames, *Marrow*, p. 127.

being unconcerned about the Christian's inner moral condition, nothing of outward moral behavior. And in instances of particular scholasticism this seems in certain measure to have been true. The was defined as intellectual assent, and a purely forensic doctrine of cation so emphasized the believer's presence before God clothed garment of Christ's righteousness as to leave little interest in the de ment of the believer's own. But the piety of Puritanism could not live that view of the Christian Gospel. The "wayfaring and warfaring" directed above all at the attainment of godliness of life. And this, like th of pardon, was to be realized through the covenant of grace. The cove said Bulkeley, is not only a consolation, but also "a foundation to godlinesse and holy walking before God."[74]

Thus Puritan theology was concerned with good works—and genuinely and consistently so. It is an utter misrepresentation of b Puritan thought and motives to allege, as one critic has done, that "thou the Puritan with great scorn and fanfare cast good works out the front do and haughtily refused them any part in the accomplishment of justificatio he nevertheless quietly and meekly welcomed their return by the back doc to dispel his doubts and to quiet his scruples and to confirm his justifica tion."[75] It is true that good works were in no way contributory to justification, and it is true also that good works were looked upon as one of the many available evidences of one's justification, but there was nothing quiet nor meek nor covert about the Puritan endorsement of them for the Christian's life. Christian experience is simply truncated, even inauthentic, without a vigorous and dedicated moral expression. Though moral works are not "the way" to salvation, they are the manner of the believer's "walking in the way."[76] "We are not saved by good Works," wrote Marshal, "yet we are saved to good Works as fruits and effects of Saving grace."[77] Faith without works is dead, and justifying faith must be a living faith. Where faith is genuine it leads to no quiet withdrawal from the moral scene. "Faith and holiness," said Bulkeley, "can no more be separated, then light can be separated from the Sunne."[78] Daniel Dyke made the observation that "though Faith be alone in justification, yet not in the justified. . . . Faith is a fruitfull Mother of many daughters, and Love is the first borne."[79] So faith must be "incarnated into works, and become flesh as it were,"[80] looking to its model in Christ. With faith thus active and energetic, Sibbes saw the life of

[74]Bulkeley, *Gospel-Covenant*, p. A2.
[75]Reilly, *Elizabethan Puritan's Conception*, p. 29.
[76]E. F., *Marrow*, p. 168.
[77]Marshal, *Gospel Mystery*, p. 148.
[78]Bulkeley, *Gospel-Covenant*, p. 332.
[79]Dyke, *Commentary on Philemon*, p. 103.
[80]Burgess, *Vindiciae Legis*, p. 43.

implantation."[87] Here is again the inner path to outward works. "When the law is written on the heart," said Robert Traill, "it is copied out in life."[88]

Puritanism may have had its share, and at times more than its proper share, of moralism and even legal repressiveness. Certainly, at least, it emphasized the importance of disciplined demeanor and conduct under careful self-control. It had its "guides to godliness" and its recommended rules and moral mandates. Its divines knew well how to instruct their parishoners in the details of "walking in the way of the Lord." But the other side of the Puritan coin was its enthusiasm for experience and its sense of the divine redeeming and ennobling power at work in the life of the believer. Preston's ecstacy is expressive of this mood and its theology:

> Christ leads them into his Sellar, as it were, and makes a mans heart glad with Flagons of wine, that is, with the consolations of the Spirit; I say, it quickens him, and makes him zealous, and ready to every good worke, when he hath once tasted of this Wine, his case is like Elihues, he cannot hold it in, but hee must breake forth into good workes, into holinesse of life.[89]

So in sanctification there is at work a divine power, pregnant and productive. When truly experienced, it becomes the motivating and generating ground for the Chistian's behavior. That power, which is God's love, works its wonders within the soul and leads to the soul's own working of wonders in the world. Sibbes wrote, "We have his love first shed abroad in our hearts, inflaming the affections, . . . and then we send back a reflex of love to him. Love is bountiful. All obedience comes from love."[90] Thus experience of God's love leads to new commitment and conduct. Sibbes again put it confidently: "the sense of the love of Christ in pardoning sins will constrain one to a holy violence in the performing of all duties."[91]

Yet such sanctification is also portrayed with a real measure of restraint. Though the change to holiness is genuine in the Christian pilgrim's life, it is by no means complete. The "entire sanctification" which John Wesley was later to affirm as possible for the Christian believer is not anticipated in this Puritan thought. Ames asserted that the perfection of sanctification was not to be found in this life "unlesse in the dreames of some fantastick persons,"[92] an early reference to the type of thinking that led to more full-blown mid-seventeenth century Antinomianism. It is rather that sanctification is a process, and God makes one holy by degrees.

[87]S. Bolton, *True Bounds of Christian Freedom*, p. 126.

[88]Robert Traill, "A Vindication of the Protestant Doctrine Concerning Justification," *Works*, 1:278. Quoted in Kevan, *Grace of Law*, p. 208.

[89]Preston, *New Covenant*, 2:177.

[90]Sibbes, "Life of Faith," *Works*, 5:368.

[91]Sibbes, "Salvation Applied," *Works*, 5:399.

[92]Ames, *Marrow*, p. 128.

There is no *simul et semel* for sanctification as is the case for God's works in justification. The gift of new life does not occur all at once, nor is there a once-and-for-all quality attached to it. "The Lord is slow in his works, but sure," explained Harris, "sure but slow." So he counselled his hearers, "That grace which at first was but a sparke ... becomes afterwards a great flame, a shining lamp.... God will doe it, but you must give him time."[93] It is true that the Christian believer is called a "new creature," yet "not because he is perfectly new, but that is the end he lookes to."[94] For this gradual growth in sanctification the analogy of restoration of health was employed: "Sinne is a sicknesse, and God is the Phisitian; a wound and God is the Chirurgian.... He cures our sicknesse and sores perfectly: but not suddainely.... He forgives all our iniquity and that is done entirely ... but this is by degrees."[95] Yet though it is slow, it occurs. Said Cotton, "There is growth in grace; this sanctification is not bed-rid."[96] So God "dispelleth the darknesse of sinne and ... doth more and more perfect the light begun, till it come to glorie."[97] For that point of final perfection, however, thought Ames, the language itself might be changed: "In this life we are more properly said to have sanctification then holinesse, and the life to come: holinesse only, and not sanctification."[98]

A major reason for Puritan insistence upon the gradual and growth character of sanctification was its realistic recognition of the continuance of sin in earthly experience. Despite all the divine overpowering of sin in redemption, regeneration, and renewal, there are still the "stubs and reliques" of original corruption that make defective even the deeds of the godly.[99] Greenham was convinced that "wicked motions and affections shall never be out of us as long as we live, for they are almost continually boyling and walloping in us,"[100] and Baynes was aware that such sin "doth fight against the worke of grace, more than water fighteth with the heat of fire."[101] Thus the Christian's life is one of perpetual struggle. The sanctified may well be renewed and "tend unto perfection," but still they must engage in a "spirituall war" and likewise continue to seek "a dayly renewing of repentance."[102] Indeed, the condition of struggle is aggravated by the very fact of renewal, for regeneration brings greater spiritual sensitivity to bear on one's self understanding, and thus "a regenerate man is ... guilty of more known

[93]Harris, *New Covenant*, 1:45.
[94]Preston, *Saints Qualification*, p. 378.
[95]Pemble, *Vindiciae fidei*, p. 74.
[96]Cotton, *Covenant of Grace*, p. 106.
[97]Baynes, *Lords Prayer*, p. 58.
[98]Ames, *Marrow*, p. 127.
[99]Anthony Burgess, *Spiritual Refining*, 1:639. Quoted in Kevan, *Grace of Law*, p. 213.
[100]Richard Greenham, *Works*, p. 307. Quoted in Kevan, *Grace of Law*, p. 93.
[101]Baynes, *Help to true Happinesse*, p. 92.
[102]Ames, *Marrow*, pp. 128–29.

sins than an unregenerate."[103] So though the redeemed life is under grace, it is still in a contrary grasp. Luther's *simul iustus et peccator* was very much reaffirmed in this Puritan thought. In describing the condition of one who has received the "new birth," Dent could say, "The new worke and the old, flesh and spirit, grace and corruption, are so intermingledly joined together in all the faculties of the soule and body, as that the one doth ever fight against the other."[104]

In this fight grace gains a certain upper hand. "In the very first instant of the conversion of a sinner," wrote Perkins, "sinne receiveth his deadly wound in the root, never afterward to be recovered."[105] Sin no longer reigns in the faithful as it does in those untouched by grace. "Sin is pulled downe from his Regency," said Preston, "it may assault thee as a Rebel, but it comes nò more as a Lord, as a King."[106] This is what sanctification is all about: through it sin is "broken, subdued, and mortified" and the image of God is so restored in one that "there ariseth a strong tye . . . to be addicted wholly to God and to Christ."[107] But this again is conquest only in the midst of continued struggle. Even the faith of the believer, so crucial for the renewed life, can wax and wane. Dyke noted that it can become "lazie," and "then it is Holy-day and Vacation-time with her till she can recover her selfe again."[108] Sin persists throughout the pilgrimage. Thomas Gouge believed that it "hath so lamed and crippled us, that we shall never perfectly recover our legs while we live; but shall go lame to our graves."[109]

This emphasis upon the continuance of sin in the midst of grace was ground for further theological conflict with Antinomianism. The spiritualizing tendency of the latter, with its claim for the utter domination by Christ over the life of the Christian, lent itself easily to a minimization of sin's presence and power. Major Antinomian expression here had to do with the comprehensiveness of the obliteration of sin through Christ's sacrifice and the imputation of his righteousness. "Now, beloved," affirmed Crisp, "our Scape-Goat hath carried our sins into a land of forgetfulness."[110] By the transfer of the burden to Christ and by the transfer of his righteousness to the saints, the sins of the latter are wiped out completely from God's view. Eaton held that God "made the just a sinner, that he might make sinners just, that is perfectly righteous in the sight of God freely."[111] Or again he urged that

---

[103]Thomas Goodwin, *Works*, 4:169. Quoted in Kevan, *Grace of Law*, p. 102.

[104]Dent, *Plaine Mans Path-way*, p. 15.

[105]Perkins, "Reformed Catholike," *Works*, 1:562.

[106]Preston, *Saints Qualification*, p. 359.

[107]Ames, *Marrow*, p. 128.

[108]Dyke, *Commentary on Philemon*, p. 134.

[109]Thomas Gouge, *Principles of Christian Religion*, p. 228. Quoted in Kevan, *Grace of Law*, p. 213.

[110]Crisp, *Christ Alone Exalted*, p. 512.

[111]Eaton, *Honey-Combe of Free Justification*, p. 303.

Christ has so prevailed over sin that he has "extinguished" it as is extinguished "a sparke of fire cast into the wide Sea." Thus "God doth cast all the sins of the faithfull, into the bottome of the Sea, ... that from thenceforth they may never appear before God any more."[112] Then came the further implication, that believers themselves need not be troubled by their shortcomings nor grieve over them in repentance, for they truly have no existence in the awareness of God. It would be a denial of the power of God to be contrite in this manner—and even the petition for forgiveness in the Lord's Prayer is to be seen not as acknowledgement of sinfulness, but as simply the seeking for strengthening of personal assurance of God's ever present favor.[113]

The orthodox objected that God still sees sins in believers. God may not condemn the persons of the faithful, for they have been accepted in covenant, but even in the faithful there is continuing sin needing repentance, and this is subject to the condemnation of God. Eaton, however, had his reply:

> But how comes God to see them in us, after hee hath covered them out of his own sight? These Objectors answer, By looking under the covering. But I would gladly know of them, wherefore did God cover them out of his sight, if hee peepe under the covering to see them againe? Or, I would know of them, whether God so cover our sinnes out of his owne sight, as men cover things with a net, that lie as naked to view as they did before they were covered?[114]

But Burgess had his own response to such argument: "The sinnes of godly men cease not to be sins, though they are justified. We may not say, that in Cain killing of another is murder, but in David it is not."[115]

Such dispute was also aggravated by the tendency in Antinomianism to merge the categories of justification and sanctification, attributing to the latter some of the characteristics of the former. As Ernest Kevan writes,

> The Antinomian authors ... allowed themselves to be swept away into enthusiastic ... deductions. From the forensic language of justification, they made inferences about the spiritual condition of those who are justified; from the premise of the believer's perfect standing, they drew the conclusion of the believer's perfect state.[116]

It is not difficult to see this occurring in such an affirmation, for example, as that of Eaton when he declared, "There is no spot left, there remains nothing

---

[112]Ibid., p. 30.

[113]See Stoever, 'A Faire and Easie Way', p. 140.

[114]Eaton, Honey-Combe of Free Justification, p. 57.

[115]Burgess, True Doctrine of Justification, 1:78.

[116]Kevan, Grace of Law, p. 97.

to be purged in Purgatory."[117] Incidentally, Baxter, whose antagonism to Antinomian perfectionism led him to denounce it as "unsavory stuff," seems to have balanced things in the opposite direction. Kevan observes, "Baxter . . . uses the language of sanctification to expound the doctrine of justification, and, as a result, takes away from justification that perfection which truly belongs to it."[118] But major Puritan divines sought to keep a clear distinction between the two and, once again, were able to affirm, along with God's pardoning and perfecting power, the continuance of sin.

If this led to conflict with Antinomianism, so did the Puritan call for contravening sin with obedience to the Law in the development of the godly life. Antinomians were charged with fixing "their discourses upon the promisory part of the Scriptures, not at the same time attending to the preceptive part."[119] They were "Promise-Preachers, and not duty-Preachers; grace-Preachers, and not repentance-Preachers."[120] Such allegations were valid, for the Antinomian was indeed "against *nomos*," critical of legal prescriptions for obedience, in movement toward manifestation of Christian righteousness. The way to moral life is through the power of the Spirit, inwardly possessed. There must be freedom from constraint, for the Christian life is a life of liberty. Crisp felt that "to be called a Libertine, is the gloriousest Title under Heaven," for a Libertine is "one that is truly free by Christ."[121] As to the Law, this to Saltmarsh was but an "empty, weak means of prevailing against sin, like the mighty sails of a ship, without either winde or tyde. . . . it is Christ crucified, which is the power of all, and in all."[122] But such critique was anathema in major Puritan understanding. James Durham deplored those preachers who "disdain and account it below them to stay a while and talk with Moses at the foot of Mount Sinai, as if they could . . . by one Falcon-flight come at the top of Mount Sion, and there converse with and make use of Jesus Christ."[123]

The Puritan divines did not disdain staying a while to converse with Moses. Without denying the power of the Gospel and its divine promises of grace, these preachers found continuing place for the Law in the proclamation of their message. The Law was not cancelled by the fall and the establishment of the covenant of grace. It can still be preached to Christian believers, both as continuing call to repentance, for sin remains, and as instruction in the ways of covenant obedience. Even Cotton, whose tenden-

[117]Eaton, *Honey-Combe of Free Justification*, p. 32.

[118]Kevan, *Grace of Law*, p. 95.

[119]Burgess, *True Doctrine of Justification*, 1:A3.

[120]Blake, *Vindiciae Foederis*, p. 189.

[121]Tobias Crisp, *Works*, 1:114. Quoted in Kevan, *Grace of Law*, p. 244.

[122]Saltmarsh, *Free-Grace*, p. 68.

[123]Durham, *Exposition of the Ten Commandments*, "To the Christian Reader."

cies were more toward the Antinomian view than were those of any other major New England preacher, could write:

> If any therefore shall accuse the Doctrine of the Covenant of free Grace of Antinomianism, and say, it teacheth men freedome from the Law of Moses; . . . we see how false such an aspersion would be; . . . the children of the Covenant of grace will only tell you, that they are free from the Covenant of the Law but not from the Commandment of it.[124]

Ernest Kevan has proposed this relationship: "The Antinomians held that the Law was abrogated, the Baxterians, that the Law was modified, and the [other] Puritans, that the Law was established."[125] This meant that even in the process of sanctification itself there was abundant place envisaged for Law, duty, and obedience. The Law is a "rule of Sanctification."[126] There is the "necessity of duety, towards God, our Neighbour, Our Selves."[127] And as to obedience, this is obligation both in and out of season: "We must sometimes doe duties out of obedience, although we want both a heart to it, and a heart in it."[128] Indeed, constrained obedience may assist in inflaming the heart, at least so felt Obadiah Sedgwick:

> The ingenuous Scholar will write one line more, and the desirous Archer will make one shot more: So the sincere heart, hee will assay yet more in duty, perhaps frequency in duty (saith he) may breed fervency in duty.[129]

Yet the process of sanctification did not really require that. There was fervency fully furnished by God through the gift and the power of the Spirit. And there was spontaneity. "Good duties," said Sibbes, "come from unsound Christians as fire out of flint; but they flow from the child of God as water out of a spring."[130] So the Puritan understanding of the way of sanctification emphasized both liberty and duty, both spontaneity and obligation. It may be asked finally, then, how these were joined together. One thing to note is that they certainly were not deemed to be contradictory. "The obliging rule, and government of the Law," wrote Rutherfurd, is by no means "contrary to the sweet cords of Gospel-love, by which the Spirit kindly draweth, and gently leadeth the Saints in the way of Sanctification."[131] But the more positive response has to do with the nature of

---

[124]Cotton, *Covenant of Grace*, p. 87.

[125]Kevan, *Grace of Law*, p. 137.

[126]S. Bolton, *True Bounds of Christian Freedom*, p. 98.

[127]G. Downame, *Treatise of Justification*, p. 436.

[128]S. Bolton, *True Bounds of Christian Freedom*, p. 202.

[129]O. Sedgwick, *Doubting Beleever*, p. 166.

[130]Sibbes, "Divine Meditations," *Works*, 7:190.

[131]Rutherfurd, *Spirituall Antichrist*, 2:68.

obedience itself. Some obedience can be that of mere submission, a compliance with law because it is law. It is not that this is to be entirely eschewed, for there may be times when such "legal obedience" is the only possible way. Then, however, God's Law is a "heavy yoake" to be borne. But the obedience of the Christian in the life of grace is more properly an "evangelical obedience," out of such new inward principle as transforms submission into delight. And then "it is naturall to obey," for "we do not obey meerly because it is commanded . . . but out of principles which God hath implanted in us sutable to the commands. . . . The command is the rule . . . but grace is the principle within; the heart and command answer one another."[132]

Rutherfurd felt that "in this new obedience, the spirit so oyleth the wheeles of free will" that obeying "is as free, con-naturall, delightfull, being sweetened with the love of God, as if there were not an awing Law." Then "the beleever obeyes with an Angell-like obedience" as "the Spirit . . . supplyes the Lawes imperious power with the strength and power of love."[133] In the language of the Westminster Confession this was "yielding obedience . . . not out of slavish fear, but a child-like love, and willing mind."[134] Thus the Puritan theologians sought to enunciate a way in which spontaneity and obligation could be conjoined in the manifestation of sanctification in the Christian's life. Their task was to avoid legalism on the one hand and libertinism on the other. What this effort required was an affirmation of responsibility for Christian duty which acknowledged the impulses of Christian liberty. And these emphases they drew and maintained together with remarkable consistency. Samuel Crooke's phrasing comprehended it well:

> From the Commandement, as a rule of life, we are not freed, but contrariwise [we are] enclined and disposed, by [God's] free spirit, to the willing obedience thereof. Thus to the regenerate the Law becommeth as it were Gospell; even a law of liberty.[135]

The final stage in the *ordo salutis* is that of "glorification," the ultimate realization of the destiny toward which the whole process of salvation has been moving. Ames said that it is also called "beatification, blessing, life eternall, glory, the kingdom of our Lord and Savior Jesus Christ, and an immortall inheritance." Actually, when Ames discussed this in the *Marrow* he did not focus primarily on eternity, but viewed it in terms of its anticipations in this life, treating preeminently the question of the believer's personal assurance of the blessings to come. But the state itself is that of life

---

[132]S. Bolton, *True Bounds of Christian Freedom*, pp. 219–20.
[133]Rutherfurd, *Spirituall Antichrist*, 1:318.
[134]"Westminster Confession of Faith," XX,1. Schaff, *Creeds of Christendom*, 3:643.
[135]Crooke, *True Blessednesse*, p. 85.

in eternity, when "Perfect Glorification is the taking away all imperfection from soule and body, and communication of all perfection."[136] As thus portrayed, glorification is a completion of sanctification, the culmination of the progress in holiness. Burgess saw it as a state in which justification itself, with its imputation, would then cease, "for having perfect righteousness inherent in ourselves, we shall need no covering."[137] Drawing upon an idea from Augustine, Perkins spoke also about the immutability of this perfection, saying that "In this estate the liberty of wil is a certain freedome, only to will that which is good, and pleasing to God. . . . perfect liberty . . . cannot will that which is evill."[138] Here, in Puritan faith, is the culmination of the whole process of human renewal under God's covenanting care, the final fulfillment of the promises of the covenant of grace.

[136]Ames, *Marrow*, pp. 129–33.
[137]Burgess, *True Doctrine of Justification*, 1:284.
[138]Perkins, "Gods Free-grace and Mans free-will," *Works*, 1:739.

of Christ's righteousness be that wedding garment which covereth our nakedness, and maketh us accepted before God; yet it will not cover us unlesse we put it on; and it is put on by faith."[62] So Antinomianism was equally repudiated, and the collective Puritan voice reaffirmed not only Luther's *sola*, but also his *fide*, when he laid down the central Protestant affirmation that justification is by faith alone. The gifts of forgiveness and imputation may be generously given, but they are not one's own until they are personally received, even though by a beggar's, rather than a laborer's, hands.[63] No doubt with Antinomian claims in mind, Bulkeley noted that "though God purposed to justifie us before the world was" and though prior to our believing there occurred "the attonement and obedience which Christ hath performed for us," faith is nevertheless an essential condition "antecedent to our actuall justification."[64] It is in one's personal historical experience and through one's personal trustful receiving that this gift of the covenant of grace can become truly one's own.

For one to receive this gift in faith is to be entered both completely and continuously into God's favor. Justification is a relationship, a condition of being under God's forgiveness, acceptable in God's sight. Condemnation has given way to acquittal, guilt to imputed righteouness, and one's "possession" is God's mercy. But this, said Puritan divines, is wrought *simul et semel*, "at once" and "but once," and thus there is both a completeness and a continuity to be found in the justified state.[65] Justification is complete in the sense that, given "at once" and not in stages, it admits of no degrees. It cannot be divided or be partial. Burgess wrote, "It is impossible that sin should be forgiven divisibly, and by parts: so a man should be at the same time under the favour of God and under his hatred."[66] Sanctification, growth in moral life, can be by degrees, but not justification as a relationship. Preston compared it with marriage and said simply, "Either you are married, or not."[67]

Justification is also continuous in that, given "but once," it remains as the Christian's relationship to God despite all the falterings and failings of one's ongoing life. The Arminians spoke of a mutable justification, holding that if faith is lost then justification is lost, with restoration contingent upon the renewal of belief. Puritan theology rejected this, for the covenant is not only conditional, but also absolute. One's personal assurance of justification may fluctuate, influenced by the changing moods of confidence and doubt, but for God's elect justification itself remains secure. Burgess' analogy affirmed that "the Sunne may be in an eclipse, but not removed from its

---

[62]G. Downame, *Certainty of Perseverance*, P. 270.
[63]Burgess, *True Doctrine of Justification*, 2:244.
[64]Bulkeley, *Gospel-Covenant*, p. 358.
[65]G. Downame, *Treatise of Justification*, p. 7.
[66]Burgess, *True Doctrine of Justification*, 1:152.
[67]Preston, *Saints Qualification*, p. 431.

orb."[68] So recurrence of sin does not destroy this fundamental relationship, though one must regularly continue to seek fresh forgiveness, since "there is no pardon of any new sin, without a new act of faith and repentance."[69] Even the loss of faith itself, in the inner struggles to which no person is fully immune, cannot cancel the condition of divine favor, for "justification is an act of God . . . and dependeth upon his eternall counsel. . . . To imagine that our justification is interrupted so oft as the act of faith is interrupted is a dreame."[70]

In the classic *ordo salutis* "justification" is followed by "adoption," again a state of relationship. Ames defined it as "the gracious sentence of God whereby he accepts the faithful for Christ's sake, unto the dignity of Sons." This did not loom large in Puritan theological discussion and was understood essentially as a further enhancement of the relationship established in justification. Ames noted that the faithful have the "title of redemption" by justification and the "title of Son-ship" by adoption. Redemption is the foundation, but adoption, he wrote, "doth ad a certaine manner of excellency and dignity."[71] Both reflect the condition of being in God's favor, the fulfillment of a major promise within the covenant of grace.

COVENANT AND THE MORAL LIFE

The promises of the covenant of grace carry the believer along still farther, however, on the pathway of Christian experience in the journey toward salvation. Next in the *ordo salutis* is "sanctification," and this, like justification, is committed in covenant by God. "Among the greater and more principall promises," wrote Ball, are those "which God hath made concerning our Sanctification . . . that he will enable them that believe, to bring forth fruits of amendment, and perfect the good works done in them day to day. This is the covenant which God hath made with his people."[72] If justification represents a relational change, sanctification represents a real change in the believer. Here sin is not pardoned, but purged. To sanctify is to make holy, to endow with a new character and quality of existence, and particularly so to purify as to bring into and sustain in being a new order of moral life. Ames used for it the term "new Divine creature" because, he said, it is "a new principle of life, communicated by God unto us" and "resembles that highest perfection which is found in God."[73]

In the theological disputes of the sixteenth and seventeenth centuries the charge was sometimes levelled against the more orthodox theologians of

[68]Burgess, *True Doctrine of Justification*, 2:147.
[69]Perkins, "Manner of Predestination," *Works*, 2:634.
[70]G. Downame, *Certainty of Perseverance*, p. 292.
[71]Ames, *Marrow*, pp. 120–21.
[72]Ball, *Treatise of Faith*, p. 62.
[73]Ames, *Marrow*, p. 127.

being unconcerned about the Christian's inner moral condition, to say nothing of outward moral behavior. And in instances of particularly rigid scholasticism this seems in certain measure to have been true. There faith was defined as intellectual assent, and a purely forensic doctrine of justification so emphasized the believer's presence before God clothed in the garment of Christ's righteousness as to leave little interest in the development of the believer's own. But the piety of Puritanism could not live with that view of the Christian Gospel. The "wayfaring and warfaring" were directed above all at the attainment of godliness of life. And this, like the gift of pardon, was to be realized through the covenant of grace. The covenant, said Bulkeley, is not only a consolation, but also "a foundation to all godlinesse and holy walking before God."[74]

Thus Puritan theology was concerned with good works—and was genuinely and consistently so. It is an utter misrepresentation of both Puritan thought and motives to allege, as one critic has done, that "though the Puritan with great scorn and fanfare cast good works out the front door and haughtily refused them any part in the accomplishment of justification, he nevertheless quietly and meekly welcomed their return by the back door to dispel his doubts and to quiet his scruples and to confirm his justification."[75] It is true that good works were in no way contributory to justification, and it is true also that good works were looked upon as one of the many available evidences of one's justification, but there was nothing quiet nor meek nor covert about the Puritan endorsement of them for the Christian's life. Christian experience is simply truncated, even inauthentic, without a vigorous and dedicated moral expression. Though moral works are not "the way" to salvation, they are the manner of the believer's "walking in the way."[76] "We are not saved by good Works," wrote Marshal, "yet we are saved to good Works as fruits and effects of Saving grace."[77] Faith without works is dead, and justifying faith must be a living faith. Where faith is genuine it leads to no quiet withdrawal from the moral scene. "Faith and holiness," said Bulkeley, "can no more be separated, then light can be separated from the Sunne."[78] Daniel Dyke made the observation that "though Faith be alone in justification, yet not in the justified. . . . Faith is a fruitfull Mother of many daughters, and Love is the first borne."[79] So faith must be "incarnated into works, and become flesh as it were,"[80] looking to its model in Christ. With faith thus active and energetic, Sibbes saw the life of

[74]Bulkeley, *Gospel-Covenant*, p. A2.
[75]Reilly, *Elizabethan Puritan's Conception*, p. 29.
[76]E. F., *Marrow*, p. 168.
[77]Marshal, *Gospel Mystery*, p. 148.
[78]Bulkeley, *Gospel-Covenant*, p. 332.
[79]Dyke, *Commentary on Philemon*, p. 103.
[80]Burgess, *Vindiciae Legis*, p. 43.

the Christian as no "idle condition," but as a "busy trade."[81] And Preston's confidence in justifying faith's productive power led to the affirmation that "he that beleeves in the greatest degree the promises of pardon and remission, I dare boldly say, he hath the holiest heart, and the holiest life."[82] Here is no timid "back door" concession. Works of moral worth are a valued and necessary part of total Christian responsiveness. Like Calvin the Puritans maintained that though one is not justified by good works, neither is one justified without them.

Justification and sanctification, therefore, go together. The new relationship to God in faith and the living out of its obligations in faithfulness are each a part of the one total Christian experience provided in the covenant of grace. And the latter part, like the former, is dependent on God's giving. Here, as well, is the fulfillment of covenanted promises and a change in human existence brought about by divine power. The more concrete elaboration of this idea took several forms, even as had its expression in the Scripture itself. From one perspective this is union with Christ, as Paul had affirmed in that "mysticism" which constituted part of his Christian experience and its explication. "We must have Christ as it were borne in us, 'formed in us,'" Sibbes wrote. "Certainly the same Spirit that sanctified Christ doth sanctify every member of Christ; and Christ is in some sort begotten, and conceived, and 'manifested' in every one that is a Christian."[83] Or again, writing in terms specifically related to central covenant conviction, he said, "Whosoever God is a God to, there will be a transforming unto God, a transforming unto Christ, in whom God is our God ... for we are predestinated to be like God incarnate."[84]

Likewise sanctification was understood as the inner working of the Spirit, "a secret and yet sacred blast of the Spirit of God breaking in"[85] and leading to purification and moral endeavor. Cotton affirmed that "the Spirit sanctifying draweth us into an holy confederacy to serve God in Family, Church, and Commonwealth."[86] Still further, the gift of sanctification was interpreted, in much used biblical terminology, as the presence of the Law within, that is, the divine Law now written upon the human heart. To grant this was God's basic covenant promise, and one form of its fulfillment is in the sanctified life. Of the Law Samuel Bolton wrote, "while it is a rule without us: it cannot make us holy, it must be a rule within us." But this has occurred by God's working. So "the law is a principle within us first, and then a patterne without us: we are not made holy by imitation, but by

---

[81]Sibbes, "Art of Contentment," Works, 5:185.
[82]Preston, New Covenant, 2:103.
[83]Sibbes, "Fountain Opened," Works, 5:486.
[84]Sibbes, "Faithful Covenanter," Works, 6:15.
[85]Strong, Discourse of Two Covenants, p. 102.
[86]Cotton, Covenant of Grace, p. 23.

implantation."[87] Here is again the inner path to outward works. "When the law is written on the heart," said Robert Traill, "it is copied out in life."[88]

Puritanism may have had its share, and at times more than its proper share, of moralism and even legal repressiveness. Certainly, at least, it emphasized the importance of disciplined demeanor and conduct under careful self-control. It had its "guides to godliness" and its recommended rules and moral mandates. Its divines knew well how to instruct their parishoners in the details of "walking in the way of the Lord." But the other side of the Puritan coin was its enthusiasm for experience and its sense of the divine redeeming and ennobling power at work in the life of the believer. Preston's ecstacy is expressive of this mood and its theology:

> Christ leads them into his Sellar, as it were, and makes a mans heart glad with Flagons of wine, that is, with the consolations of the Spirit; I say, it quickens him, and makes him zealous, and ready to every good worke, when he hath once tasted of this Wine, his case is like Elihues, he cannot hold it in, but hee must breake forth into good workes, into holinesse of life.[89]

So in sanctification there is at work a divine power, pregnant and productive. When truly experienced, it becomes the motivating and generating ground for the Chistian's behavior. That power, which is God's love, works its wonders within the soul and leads to the soul's own working of wonders in the world. Sibbes wrote, "We have his love first shed abroad in our hearts, inflaming the affections, . . . and then we send back a reflex of love to him. Love is bountiful. All obedience comes from love."[90] Thus experience of God's love leads to new commitment and conduct. Sibbes again put it confidently: "the sense of the love of Christ in pardoning sins will constrain one to a holy violence in the performing of all duties."[91]

Yet such sanctification is also portrayed with a real measure of restraint. Though the change to holiness is genuine in the Christian pilgrim's life, it is by no means complete. The "entire sanctification" which John Wesley was later to affirm as possible for the Christian believer is not anticipated in this Puritan thought. Ames asserted that the perfection of sanctification was not to be found in this life "unlesse in the dreames of some fantastick persons,"[92] an early reference to the type of thinking that led to more full-blown mid-seventeenth century Antinomianism. It is rather that sanctification is a process, and God makes one holy by degrees.

---

[87]S. Bolton, *True Bounds of Christian Freedom*, p. 126.

[88]Robert Traill, "A Vindication of the Protestant Doctrine Concerning Justification," *Works*, 1:278. Quoted in Kevan, *Grace of Law*, p. 208.

[89]Preston, *New Covenant*, 2:177.

[90]Sibbes, "Life of Faith," *Works*, 5:368.

[91]Sibbes, "Salvation Applied," *Works*, 5:399.

[92]Ames, *Marrow*, p. 128.

There is no *simul et semel* for sanctification as is the case for God's works in justification. The gift of new life does not occur all at once, nor is there a once-and-for-all quality attached to it. "The Lord is slow in his works, but sure," explained Harris, "sure but slow." So he counselled his hearers, "That grace which at first was but a sparke ... becomes afterwards a great flame, a shining lamp.... God will doe it, but you must give him time."[93] It is true that the Christian believer is called a "new creature," yet "not because he is perfectly new, but that is the end he lookes to."[94] For this gradual growth in sanctification the analogy of restoration of health was employed: "Sinne is a sicknesse, and God is the Phisitian; a wound and God is the Chirurgian. . . . He cures our sicknesse and sores perfectly: but not suddainely.... He forgives all our iniquity and that is done entirely ... but this is by degrees."[95] Yet though it is slow, it occurs. Said Cotton, "There is growth in grace; this sanctification is not bed-rid."[96] So God "dispelleth the darknesse of sinne and ... doth more and more perfect the light begun, till it come to glorie."[97] For that point of final perfection, however, thought Ames, the language itself might be changed: "In this life we are more properly said to have sanctification then holinesse, and the life to come: holinesse only, and not sanctification."[98]

A major reason for Puritan insistence upon the gradual and growth character of sanctification was its realistic recognition of the continuance of sin in earthly experience. Despite all the divine overpowering of sin in redemption, regeneration, and renewal, there are still the "stubs and reliques" of original corruption that make defective even the deeds of the godly.[99] Greenham was convinced that "wicked motions and affections shall never be out of us as long as we live, for they are almost continually boyling and walloping in us,"[100] and Baynes was aware that such sin "doth fight against the worke of grace, more than water fighteth with the heat of fire."[101] Thus the Christian's life is one of perpetual struggle. The sanctified may well be renewed and "tend unto perfection," but still they must engage in a "spirituall war" and likewise continue to seek "a dayly renewing of repentance."[102] Indeed, the condition of struggle is aggravated by the very fact of renewal, for regeneration brings greater spiritual sensitivity to bear on one's self understanding, and thus "a regenerate man is ... guilty of more known

[93]Harris, *New Covenant*, 1:45.
[94]Preston, *Saints Qualification*, p. 378.
[95]Pemble, *Vindiciae fidei*, p. 74.
[96]Cotton, *Covenant of Grace*, p. 106.
[97]Baynes, *Lords Prayer*, p. 58.
[98]Ames, *Marrow*, p. 127.
[99]Anthony Burgess, *Spiritual Refining*, 1:639. Quoted in Kevan, *Grace of Law*, p. 213.
[100]Richard Greenham, *Works*, p. 307. Quoted in Kevan, *Grace of Law*, p. 93.
[101]Baynes, *Help to true Happinesse*, p. 92.
[102]Ames, *Marrow*, pp. 128–29.

sins than an unregenerate."[103] So though the redeemed life is under grace, it is still in a contrary grasp. Luther's *simul iustus et peccator* was very much reaffirmed in this Puritan thought. In describing the condition of one who has received the "new birth," Dent could say, "The new worke and the old, flesh and spirit, grace and corruption, are so intermingledly joined together in all the faculties of the soule and body, as that the one doth ever fight against the other."[104]

In this fight grace gains a certain upper hand. "In the very first instant of the conversion of a sinner," wrote Perkins, "sinne receiveth his deadly wound in the root, never afterward to be recovered."[105] Sin no longer reigns in the faithful as it does in those untouched by grace. "Sin is pulled downe from his Regency," said Preston, "it may assault thee as a Rebel, but it comes no more as a Lord, as a King."[106] This is what sanctification is all about: through it sin is "broken, subdued, and mortified" and the image of God is so restored in one that "there ariseth a strong tye . . . to be addicted wholly to God and to Christ."[107] But this again is conquest only in the midst of continued struggle. Even the faith of the believer, so crucial for the renewed life, can wax and wane. Dyke noted that it can become "lazie," and "then it is Holy-day and Vacation-time with her till she can recover her selfe again."[108] Sin persists throughout the pilgrimage. Thomas Gouge believed that it "hath so lamed and crippled us, that we shall never perfectly recover our legs while we live; but shall go lame to our graves."[109]

This emphasis upon the continuance of sin in the midst of grace was ground for further theological conflict with Antinomianism. The spiritualizing tendency of the latter, with its claim for the utter domination by Christ over the life of the Christian, lent itself easily to a minimization of sin's presence and power. Major Antinomian expression here had to do with the comprehensiveness of the obliteration of sin through Christ's sacrifice and the imputation of his righteousness. "Now, beloved," affirmed Crisp, "our Scape-Goat hath carried our sins into a land of forgetfulness."[110] By the transfer of the burden to Christ and by the transfer of his righteousness to the saints, the sins of the latter are wiped out completely from God's view. Eaton held that God "made the just a sinner, that he might make sinners just, that is perfectly righteous in the sight of God freely."[111] Or again he urged that

[103]Thomas Goodwin, *Works*, 4:169. Quoted in Kevan, *Grace of Law*, p. 102.

[104]Dent, *Plaine Mans Path-way*, p. 15.

[105]Perkins, "Reformed Catholike," *Works*, 1:562.

[106]Preston, *Saints Qualification*, p. 359.

[107]Ames, *Marrow*, p. 128.

[108]Dyke, *Commentary on Philemon*, p. 134.

[109]Thomas Gouge, *Principles of Christian Religion*, p. 228. Quoted in Kevan, *Grace of Law*, p. 213.

[110]Crisp, *Christ Alone Exalted*, p. 512.

[111]Eaton, *Honey-Combe of Free Justification*, p. 303.

Christ has so prevailed over sin that he has "extinguished" it as is extinguished "a sparke of fire cast into the wide Sea." Thus "God doth cast all the sins of the faithfull, into the bottome of the Sea, . . . that from thenceforth they may never appear before God any more."[112] Then came the further implication, that believers themselves need not be troubled by their shortcomings nor grieve over them in repentance, for they truly have no existence in the awareness of God. It would be a denial of the power of God to be contrite in this manner—and even the petition for forgiveness in the Lord's Prayer is to be seen not as acknowledgement of sinfulness, but as simply the seeking for strengthening of personal assurance of God's ever present favor.[113]

The orthodox objected that God still sees sins in believers. God may not condemn the persons of the faithful, for they have been accepted in covenant, but even in the faithful there is continuing sin needing repentance, and this is subject to the condemnation of God. Eaton, however, had his reply:

> But how comes God to see them in us, after hee hath covered them out of his own sight? These Objectors answer, By looking under the covering. But I would gladly know of them, wherefore did God cover them out of his sight, if hee peepe under the covering to see them againe? Or, I would know of them, whether God so cover our sinnes out of his owne sight, as men cover things with a net, that lie as naked to view as they did before they were covered?[114]

But Burgess had his own response to such argument: "The sinnes of godly men cease not to be sins, though they are justified. We may not say, that in Cain killing of another is murder, but in David it is not."[115]

Such dispute was also aggravated by the tendency in Antinomianism to merge the categories of justification and sanctification, attributing to the latter some of the characteristics of the former. As Ernest Kevan writes,

> The Antinomian authors . . . allowed themselves to be swept away into enthusiastic . . . deductions. From the forensic language of justification, they made inferences about the spiritual condition of those who are justified; from the premise of the believer's perfect standing, they drew the conclusion of the believer's perfect state.[116]

It is not difficult to see this occurring in such an affirmation, for example, as that of Eaton when he declared, "There is no spot left, there remains nothing

[112]Ibid., p. 30.
[113]See Stoever, 'A Faire and Easie Way', p. 140.
[114]Eaton, Honey-Combe of Free Justification, p. 57.
[115]Burgess, True Doctrine of Justification, 1:78.
[116]Kevan, Grace of Law, p. 97.

to be purged in Purgatory."[117] Incidentally, Baxter, whose antagonism to Antinomian perfectionism led him to denounce it as "unsavory stuff," seems to have balanced things in the opposite direction. Kevan observes, "Baxter . . . uses the language of sanctification to expound the doctrine of justification, and, as a result, takes away from justification that perfection which truly belongs to it."[118] But major Puritan divines sought to keep a clear distinction between the two and, once again, were able to affirm, along with God's pardoning and perfecting power, the continuance of sin.

If this led to conflict with Antinomianism, so did the Puritan call for contravening sin with obedience to the Law in the development of the godly life. Antinomians were charged with fixing "their discourses upon the promisory part of the Scriptures, not at the same time attending to the preceptive part."[119] They were "Promise-Preachers, and not duty-Preachers; grace-Preachers, and not repentance-Preachers."[120] Such allegations were valid, for the Antinomian was indeed "against *nomos*," critical of legal prescriptions for obedience, in movement toward manifestation of Christian righteousness. The way to moral life is through the power of the Spirit, inwardly possessed. There must be freedom from constraint, for the Christian life is a life of liberty. Crisp felt that "to be called a Libertine, is the gloriousest Title under Heaven," for a Libertine is "one that is truly free by Christ."[121] As to the Law, this to Saltmarsh was but an "empty, weak means of prevailing against sin, like the mighty sails of a ship, without either winde or tyde. . . . it is Christ crucified, which is the power of all, and in all."[122] But such critique was anathema in major Puritan understanding. James Durham deplored those preachers who "disdain and account it below them to stay a while and talk with Moses at the foot of Mount Sinai, as if they could . . . by one Falcon-flight come at the top of Mount Sion, and there converse with and make use of Jesus Christ."[123]

The Puritan divines did not disdain staying a while to converse with Moses. Without denying the power of the Gospel and its divine promises of grace, these preachers found continuing place for the Law in the proclamation of their message. The Law was not cancelled by the fall and the establishment of the covenant of grace. It can still be preached to Christian believers, both as continuing call to repentance, for sin remains, and as instruction in the ways of covenant obedience. Even Cotton, whose tenden-

[117]Eaton, *Honey-Combe of Free Justification*, p. 32.
[118]Kevan, *Grace of Law*, p. 95.
[119]Burgess, *True Doctrine of Justification*, 1:A3.
[120]Blake, *Vindiciae Foederis*, p. 189.
[121]Tobias Crisp, *Works*, 1:114. Quoted in Kevan, *Grace of Law*, p. 244.
[122]Saltmarsh, *Free-Grace*, p. 68.
[123]Durham, *Exposition of the Ten Commandments*, "To the Christian Reader."

cies were more toward the Antinomian view than were those of any other major New England preacher, could write:

> If any therefore shall accuse the Doctrine of the Covenant of free Grace of Antinomianism, and say, it teacheth men freedome from the Law of Moses; . . . we see how false such an aspersion would be; . . . the children of the Covenant of grace will only tell you, that they are free from the Covenant of the Law but not from the Commandment of it.[124]

Ernest Kevan has proposed this relationship: "The Antinomians held that the Law was abrogated, the Baxterians, that the Law was modified, and the [other] Puritans, that the Law was established."[125] This meant that even in the process of sanctification itself there was abundant place envisaged for Law, duty, and obedience. The Law is a "rule of Sanctification."[126] There is the "necessity of duety, towards God, our Neighbour, Our Selves."[127] And as to obedience, this is obligation both in and out of season: "We must sometimes doe duties out of obedience, although we want both a heart to it, and a heart in it."[128] Indeed, constrained obedience may assist in inflaming the heart, at least so felt Obadiah Sedgwick:

> The ingenuous Scholar will write one line more, and the desirous Archer will make one shot more: So the sincere heart, hee will assay yet more in duty, perhaps frequency in duty (saith he) may breed fervency in duty.[129]

Yet the process of sanctification did not really require that. There was fervency fully furnished by God through the gift and the power of the Spirit. And there was spontaneity. "Good duties," said Sibbes, "come from unsound Christians as fire out of flint; but they flow from the child of God as water out of a spring."[130] So the Puritan understanding of the way of sanctification emphasized both liberty and duty, both spontaneity and obligation. It may be asked finally, then, how these were joined together. One thing to note is that they certainly were not deemed to be contradictory. "The obliging rule, and government of the Law," wrote Rutherfurd, is by no means "contrary to the sweet cords of Gospel-love, by which the Spirit kindly draweth, and gently leadeth the Saints in the way of Sanctification."[131] But the more positive response has to do with the nature of

---

[124]Cotton, *Covenant of Grace*, p. 87.
[125]Kevan, *Grace of Law*, p. 137.
[126]S. Bolton, *True Bounds of Christian Freedom*, p. 98.
[127]G. Downame, *Treatise of Justification*, p. 436.
[128]S. Bolton, *True Bounds of Christian Freedom*, p. 202.
[129]O. Sedgwick, *Doubting Beleever*, p. 166.
[130]Sibbes, "Divine Meditations," *Works*, 7:190.
[131]Rutherfurd, *Spirituall Antichrist*, 2:68.

obedience itself. Some obedience can be that of mere submission, a compliance with law because it is law. It is not that this is to be entirely eschewed, for there may be times when such "legal obedience" is the only possible way. Then, however, God's Law is a "heavy yoake" to be borne. But the obedience of the Christian in the life of grace is more properly an "evangelical obedience," out of such new inward principle as transforms submission into delight. And then "it is naturall to obey," for "we do not obey meerly because it is commanded . . . but out of principles which God hath implanted in us sutable to the commands. . . . The command is the rule . . . but grace is the principle within; the heart and command answer one another."[132]

Rutherfurd felt that "in this new obedience, the spirit so oyleth the wheeles of free will" that obeying "is as free, con-naturall, delightfull, being sweetened with the love of God, as if there were not an awing Law." Then "the beleever obeyes with an Angell-like obedience" as "the Spirit . . . supplyes the Lawes imperious power with the strength and power of love."[133] In the language of the Westminster Confession this was "yielding obedience . . . not out of slavish fear, but a child-like love, and willing mind."[134] Thus the Puritan theologians sought to enunciate a way in which spontaneity and obligation could be conjoined in the manifestation of sanctification in the Christian's life. Their task was to avoid legalism on the one hand and libertinism on the other. What this effort required was an affirmation of responsibility for Christian duty which acknowledged the impulses of Christian liberty. And these emphases they drew and maintained together with remarkable consistency. Samuel Crooke's phrasing comprehended it well:

> From the Commandement, as a rule of life, we are not freed, but contrariwise [we are] enclined and disposed, by [God's] free spirit, to the willing obedience thereof. Thus to the regenerate the Law becommeth as it were Gospell; even a law of liberty.[135]

The final stage in the *ordo salutis* is that of "glorification," the ultimate realization of the destiny toward which the whole process of salvation has been moving. Ames said that it is also called "beatification, blessing, life eternall, glory, the kingdom of our Lord and Savior Jesus Christ, and an immortall inheritance." Actually, when Ames discussed this in the *Marrow* he did not focus primarily on eternity, but viewed it in terms of its anticipations in this life, treating preeminently the question of the believer's personal assurance of the blessings to come. But the state itself is that of life

---

[132]S. Bolton, *True Bounds of Christian Freedom*, pp. 219–20.
[133]Rutherfurd, *Spirituall Antichrist*, 1:318.
[134]"Westminster Confession of Faith," XX,1. Schaff, *Creeds of Christendom*, 3:643.
[135]Crooke, *True Blessednesse*, p. 85.

in eternity, when "Perfect Glorification is the taking away all imperfection from soule and body, and communication of all perfection."[136] As thus portrayed, glorification is a completion of sanctification, the culmination of the progress in holiness. Burgess saw it as a state in which justification itself, with its imputation, would then cease, "for having perfect righteousness inherent in ourselves, we shall need no covering."[137] Drawing upon an idea from Augustine, Perkins spoke also about the immutability of this perfection, saying that "In this estate the liberty of wil is a certain freedome, only to will that which is good, and pleasing to God. . . . perfect liberty . . . cannot will that which is evill."[138] Here, in Puritan faith, is the culmination of the whole process of human renewal under God's covenanting care, the final fulfillment of the promises of the covenant of grace.

[136]Ames, *Marrow*, pp. 129–33.
[137]Burgess, *True Doctrine of Justification*, 1:284.
[138]Perkins, "Gods Free-grace and Mans free-will," *Works*, 1:739.

Chapter 5

COVENANT AND PREDESTINATION

English Protestantism from its very outset, and in keeping with one of the themes of the Protestant Reformation generally, gave prominent place to the doctrine of predestination.[1] Article XVII of the "Articles of Religion," prepared first in the reign of Edward VI and then confirmed under Elizabeth I, read in part:

> Predestination to life is the everlasting purpose of God, whereby (before the foundations of the world were laid) he hath constantly decreed by his counsel secret to us, to deliver from curse and damnation those whom he hath chosen in Christ out of mankind, and to bring them by Christ to everlasting salvation, as vessels made to honour. Wherefore, they ... be called according to God's purpose by his Spirit working in due season: they through Grace obey the calling: they be justified freely: they be made sons of God by adoption: they be made like the image of his only-begotten Son Jesus Christ: they walk religiously in good works, and at length, by God's mercy, they attain to everlasting felicity.[2]

Here one's progress through the *ordo salutis* itself is seen within the context of God's predestining act, a construction based on Paul's affirmation in his Letter to the Romans that those whom God knew to be "his own before ever they were" and has predestined to be "shaped to the likeness of his Son" have now been called to be effectually led by God through the Christian pilgrimage to its ultimate fulfillment.[3]

This connection with the *ordo salutis* is especially important because in early Protestant theology predestination was viewed chiefly in terms of its soteriological significance. The doctrine of predestination was not developed in the early sixteenth century as a theory for the explaining of God's operation of the universe, or as an organizing principle for a theological

---

[1]See Wallace, *Puritans and Predestination*, chaps. 2–4, for an examination of this issue in English Protestant theology throughout the sixteenth and early seventeenth centuries. This presentation of the general English emphasis on the sovereignty of grace has special importance as context for understanding Puritan covenant thought throughout that period. Also see his earlier article, "Doctrine of Predestination," pp. 201–15.

[2]"The Thirty Nine Articles of Religion of the Church of England," XVII. Schaff, *Creeds of Christendom*, 3:497.

[3]Romans 8:29–30.

system. These usages of the doctrine were to emerge especially within late sixteenth and early seventeenth century Reformed scholasticism, and their influence was then to be felt to some extent in Puritan thought. Perkins, for example, showed some of this impact, drawing in part upon Beza and Zanchius in his approach to predestination. But for the most part the speculative and rationalistic elements were muted in the earliest Protestant handling of the predestination idea, and this continued by and large as characteristic of Puritan theology. Rather, predestination was seen mainly in relation to salvation. In Calvin and Bucer, much read by the Puritans, it became chiefly the guarantor that the steps in the *ordo salutis* can occur, the certification that despite human weakness and sin God will justify and sanctify. Salvation does not depend upon the uncertain and frail response of the human person, but is much more certainly in the invincible action of God.

With this assurance the doctrine of predestination was seen to contribute to the comfort of the Christian. Early in the English Reformation John Bradford, chaplain to Bishop Ridley of London, wrote of predestination as a source of comfort: "It overthroweth the most pestilent papistical poison of doubting God's favour.... It setteth up Christ's kingdom, and utterly overthroweth the wisdom, power, ableness, and choice of man, that all glory may be given only to God."[4] And Article XVII of the Church of England could add that "godly consideration of Predestination, and our Election in Christ, is full of sweet, pleasant, and unspeakable comfort ... [and] doth greatly establish and confirm ... faith of eternal Salvation to be enjoyed through Christ."[5]

It is against this background that the Puritan handling of the predestination idea must be viewed, as also with the awareness that it was incorporated fully into Puritan covenant theology. During the reign of Mary a "Freewill" movement arose, and its leader, Henry Hart, published a tract entitled "The Enormities Proceeding of the Opinion that Predestination, Calling, and Election Is Absolute in Man as it Is in God." Among the "enormities" was this: it "pulleth away the covenant between God and man." This hampering is "partly on God's part" through the imposition of a view of limited atonement impeding God's action, but "altogether on man's part; for it taketh all the power and ableness, which God hath before given, from him."[6] Puritan theologians, however, would have strongly rejected that conclusion. The doctrine of predestination, they would affirm, can be thoroughly integrated into the idea of covenant. For one thing, predestination does not abolish human action, but enhances it, for the divine and the

---

[4]*The Writings of John Bradford*, p. 308. Quoted in Wallace, "Doctrine of Predestination," p. 214.

[5]"The Thirty Nine Articles of Religion of the Church of England," XVII. Schaff, *Creeds of Christendom*, 3:497.

[6]Quoted in Hargrave, "Freewillers in English Reformation," p. 275.

human must go together in fulfillment of covenant conditions. But further, the covenant, in the last analysis, is also more than a conditional matter. Its fulfillment rests in a still prior sense upon election by God, for the covenant likewise is absolute.

ETERNAL DECREES

When Ames discussed predestination in his *Marrow* he did so not in the first chapter, but in the twenty-fifth, introducing it after having considered the saving work of Christ and its mode of application to humanity through the covenant, just prior to his exploration of the nature of the Christian pilgrimage itself. This is indicative of the soteriological weight put upon it, for predestination was made a transitional theme between the objective saving action of God and its subjective appropriation in the life of the believer. It was a way of assuring that this new life can indeed occur. But predestination itself, as a divine determination, was viewed as having occurred far prior to the time of the saving process. Its own locus, Ames strongly affirmed, is in the counsels of God which have pre-existed from all eternity. In its initiation it transcends the history that it later effects. So predestination, which has to do solely with human destiny, is one of the eternal decrees by which God's total government is carried out in accordance with an eternal plan.[7] In the words of John Ball, "God doth nothing in time, which he decreed not to do from all eternity. Whosoever, therefore, is called in time, he was predestined from eternity. . . . The execution cannot vary from the decree, but that the note of changeableness must be ascribed to God."[8]

Predestination, moreover, in this Puritan understanding, rested entirely upon the free choice of God. It is in fact, declared Ames, a double decree, selecting from eternity some persons for the grace of salvation and leaving others in the judgment of damnation, with the distinguishing of the elect from the reprobate depending "upon no cause, reason or outward condition," but simply on "the will of him that predestineth." This means "that the difference of the decree doth not depend upon man, but that difference, which is found in men, doth follow upon the decree."[9] Further, since the end of all God's eternal counsel is "the glory of God himselfe, that is, the goodnesse, or perfection of God which is made manifest by his Efficiency, and shines forth in his works,"[10] this decree and its operation serve that purpose. There are also other divine motives to be identified. Election of some to grace and salvation is an act of love, whereas the reprobating of

[7]Ames' discussion of God's total governance of the universe by eternal decree is found in his *Marrow*, chap. 7.

[8]Ball, *Covenant of Grace*, p. 345.

[9]Ames, *Marrow*, p. 105.

[10]Ibid., p. 24.

others is an act of justice in the light of the magnitude of human sin. But these both partake of that more comprehensive and ultimate end, and predestination, therefore, Ames urged, "is the decree of God manifesting his special glory in the eternall condition of men."[11] Puritan theology shared fully in this basic emphasis on God's glory, a theme stemming from Calvin and permeating the whole of the Reformed tradition. It may well be, as John Eusden has suggested, that the reprobation aspect of God's work was minimized by some in this period,[12] but still God's sovereign action governs all.

There were, however, theological differences in the interpretation of the decrees themselves, and these were intensified by the Arminian controversy. Among the major Puritan divines the question of the order of the decrees came in for some debate. A supralapsarian view posited the following pattern: decrees (1) to create a human race, (2) to elect some to eternal life and to reprobate others to eternal death, (3) to permit sin to enter human history that the reprobate might in justice be condemned, (4) to send Christ to save from sin those who are elect. The crucial matter here is that the decree to elect or reprobate antedates permission of the fall. Perkins defended this view on the ground of the distinction between end and means, holding that the end is the first thing in the intention of an agent. But the entrance of sin through the fall is one of the means for achieving the ultimate end of God's decree, namely, "the manifestation of his glory in saving some, and condemning others," and therefore is subsequent to the latter.[13]

An infralapsarian view, more commonly held within Puritan circles, reversed the order of the decrees to elect or to reprobate, on the one hand, and to permit sin, on the other. It was "out of Mankinde seen fallen in sinne and misery" that God chose to redeem some and to reject others.[14] Such a pattern did not diminish the glory of God in free election and in the setting of human destiny, but it did absolve God of the charges of necessitating sin and of naming for both salvation and condemnation those who were not yet evil. For Ames, however, the effort to make this distinction was far less important than the ultimate meaning of predestination itself. In his controversy with the Dutch Arminians he encountered a contrasting of the supralapsarian and the infralapsarian views in one of their writings and responded: "We can explain this simple yet infinite matter only in an imperfect manner and with various interpretations, ... but all agree that the source of predestination is in God alone, in his own good pleasure."[15] Dent simplified matters by listing all the decrees, including that of permission of

[11]Ibid., p. 103.

[12]Eusden, *Puritans, Lawyers, and Politics*, p. 21, n. 16.

[13]Perkins, "Golden Chaine," *Works*, 1:112–13.

[14]Plaifere, *Appello Evangelium*, p. 17.

[15]Quoted in Visscher, "William Ames." Douglas Horton, ed., *William Ames*, p. 92.

the fall, and by saying that in these "God decreed with himselfe, *uno actu*, at once."[16]

The major dispute concerning the decrees, however, came in the Arminian controversy, for among the several contested issues which it produced was the question of the freedom of God's ultimate choice. In 1610 the Dutch Arminians urged in their *Remonstrance* that God's eternal decree of election and reprobation was one to elect for salvation from fallen humanity those who, through God's assisting grace, believe in Jesus Christ and persevere in faith and obedience, and to reject correspondingly those who fail to fulfill this condition.[17] This was conditional predestination, with God's final choice conditioned upon human response. In this theology sufficient grace to believe and to persevere is seen as made available to all by God's graciousness, but that grace's efficiency depends upon its being accepted and employed.

Though orthodox Calvinism triumphed over Arminianism at the Synod of Dort in 1619 and established as the first of its "five points" the doctrine of unconditional predestination, this rejected outlook still found considerable support in England. John Goodwin was one of its chief advocates. A part of Goodwin's criticism was aimed at the doctrine of absolute reprobation. "We hold," he wrote, "that God hath not decreed from Eternity the Reprobation of any person . . . who may not very possibly be saved."[18] Or again, "Though it not be denied, but that God hath an absolute Sovereignty and Lordship over his Creature, . . . yet it is an horrible indignity and affront put upon him . . . to affirm that he exerciseth or administreth this Soveraignty and power, upon the hardest terms."[19] To Resbury's claim that the doctrine of absolute reprobation could be found in Romans 9, Goodwin replied, "You may as soon discover the element of fire at the bottom of the sea, as such a Reprobation in that Chapter, or in any other quarter of the Scripture."[20]

Even much earlier than the time of Goodwin there had been some joining of this issue. In the late sixteenth century one liberal preacher, Samuel Harsnet, had declared that though at creation God had said, "Let us make man," the decree of absolute reprobation necessitating the fall "would faine alter the case, and put it thus: Let us mar man." He contended that the decree likens the actions of God to "the abominations of Queen Jezebel," who set up Naboth among the princes so that "he might have a greater fall." God "planted man in Paradise . . . and honoured him with all the Soveraignty over all the Creatures," but this was certainly not done so that

[16]Dent, *Plaine Mans Path-way*, p. 283.

[17]Harrison, *Beginnings of Arminianism*, p. 150.

[18]J. Goodwin, *Agreement and Distance*, p. 2.

[19]J. Goodwin, *Redemption Redeemed*, p. 68.

[20]John Goodwin, "Letter of October 15, 1651 to Richard Resbury." Quoted in Jackson, *Life of John Goodwin*, p. 276.

"he could ... pass a Decree from all eternity against him and throw him down headlong into Hell: for God is not a Jezebel."[21]

As to election to salvation, it was equally urged by these English liberals that arbitrariness must be replaced by conditional choice. Goodwin wrote, "We hold and teach, that God hath not decreed from Eternity to Elect any person of Mankinde, upon any terms, but that, in case he liveth to years of discretion, he may very possibly perish, notwithstanding any such Decree."[22] At this point, however, Goodwin's positive view finally took a different form from that of the Arminianism which had so influenced him. In the latter God's decrees continued to be of the election or reprobation of particular persons, though these persons were those whom God had foreseen in infinite wisdom respectively to persevere in belief or to fall away. For Goodwin, however, the eternal decree of election was not of particular persons at all, but of a species or class, that is, of any and every one who could conform to the condition. "The only Decree of Election," he wrote, "is this, ... Whosoever believeth, shall be saved; and the onely Decree of Reprobation, this, Whosoever beleeveth not, shall be damned."[23] Thus properly speaking, in Goodwin's view, predestination of given persons either to life or to death takes place not in eternity, but in time. The setting of the condition is an eternal act in God's counsel, and the promise to a "species" is God's eternal decree, but God's election of any specific persons to life is only when God actually "prevailes" upon them "by his Word and Spirit ... to believe," even as personal reprobation also has its origin in the arena of human history.[24] There are none named by name, so Goodwin urged, in God's eternal decrees.

Puritan orthodoxy, however, be it supralapsarian or infralapsarian, could in no way countenance these tamperings with the decrees and the free act of predestination which they enshrined. In fact such liberalization seemed to make this a matter of post-destination, if God's choice is contingent upon foreseen or prior human act. This would say that election follows faith and perseverance, rather than being their source. But one believes, it was affirmed, because one is predestined, rather than is pre(or post)-destined because one believes.[25] Such modification really takes one back, so it was felt, to the circumstances of the first covenant at history's beginning. Arminians, said Cotton, "look at no gift of God, but meerly upon the Faith, or Works of the creature foreseen ... they hold forth no more but a Covenant of Works."[26] And this conjured up all the old difficulties connected with a

[21]Harsnet, A Sermon, pp. 137–38.

[22]J. Goodwin, Agreement and Distance, p. 2.

[23]Ibid.

[24]J. Goodwin, Redemption Redeemed, p. 62.

[25]Reuter, "William Ames." Douglas Horton, ed., William Ames, p. 250. See also Dent, Plaine Mans Path-way, p. 288.

[26]Cotton, Covenant of Grace, p. 33.

program of self-reliance. Francis Taylor put his finger on what was certainly the heart of the problem: "Consider the corrupt estate of all men by nature, and see if any man can come to God without election. We are the best of us too much corrupted by nature to repent of our selves. Gods choice therefore must make the difference."[27] Arminianism was a new Pelagianism, so it was charged, and like the Pelagianism of old could provide no certainty of the fulfillment of God's purposes. Jenison was aghast at the thought that if election were only conditional, all might be reprobated, Christ's church fail on earth, and therefore he not be its Head because it would have no members![28] And Ames wondered how it could be possible for Christ himself to be predestined to die for human redemption without certainty that any good would come from the act.[29]

If such tampering with the decrees posed problems because of the fact of human sinfulness, this was also to be condemned, however, as an affront to the divine majesty. God is sovereign, and sovereignty is not to be hampered by conditions that frustrate its full realization. Rutherfurd charged that such a circumstance prevails in Arminian conditional predestination, for it includes an implied antecedent desire of God that all persons be saved. This desire, however, is not fulfilled, and God's sovereignty is frustrated. And such a frustration, so went his sweeping condemnation still further, is of a piece with other portrayals of God's frustrated power, as in the Talmud where God is portrayed as sorrowing, in the "Alcoran" where God's wish to free Mahomet from death cannot be realized, and among the heathen where Jupiter can only deplore the destinies he cannot amend![30] If *soli deo gloria* is to be the watchword, there can be no contradiction between desire and decree, nor between counsel and consequence. But it is in unconditional predestination, the orthodox declared, that God's desire, decree and deed are one, as by God's own will and purpose some are selected for life and others are passed by for death. In no way can the causes for such selection be humanly discerned. But though "the reason for this separation lieth hid," wrote Sutton in quoting Ambrose, "the separation it selfe lieth not hid."[31] And it is an act of divine omnipotence. Beyond all considerations of divine love and justice that may be involved, God's eternal decrees of predestination are established that "his glorie might be manifested."[32]

For those chosen for life the decree of election also includes the promise of perseverance. It is God's eternal intention that those elected to be God's people be sustained throughout their pilgrimage in all things needed to bring this to fulfillment. God elects in eternity and acts in time, but the

[27]F. Taylor, *Gods Choise and Mans diligence*, p. 169.
[28]Jenison, *Concerning Gods Certaine Performance*, p. 50.
[29]Visscher, "William Ames." Douglas Horton, ed., *William Ames*, p. 90.
[30]Rutherfurd, *Covenant of Life*, pp. 56–57.
[31]Sutton, *Lectures on Romans*, p. 71.
[32]Ibid., p. 50.

actions in time are themselves decreed in God's eternal counsels. Were such perseverance not committed and provided, God would again be at the mercy of the frailty of human choice, and God's sovereignty would be frustrated by the resistance of human sin. Baynes declared:

> God's calling is sure and permanent. Can no man or woman fall away; when once they are effectually called? why, are they not weake, and have many corruptions and infirmities abiding within them? True, but the question is not what we are, but what God is: Is He weake, or can Hee grow weary? So that all our safety stands in GOD's everlasting purpose, not in our power.[33]

And Sibbes wrote that "to hold that an elect Christian may fall away is to pull Christ out of heaven, [for] we are in heaven already in Christ."[34] Arminianism, however, argued for a contrary view. The Arminian position leading to the Synod of Dort unequivocally affirmed that it was possible for persons of true faith, entirely by their own fault, so to lose their faith as ultimately to fall away.[35]

Though Dort rejected this position and established as the fifth of the "five points" of Calvinism a doctrine of the "perseverance of the saints," its continuation became a major matter in liberal circles, with John Goodwin especially representing it in Puritanism's left wing of the mid-seventeenth century. In 1652 Goodwin published a document entitled *The Agreement and Distance of Brethren* in which he analyzed in detail his agreements and disagreements with orthodox Puritan divines on each of the five points on which Dort had declared. Written in a tone intended to achieve as much conciliation as possible, Goodwin identified places on which he found a common mind with his brethren, as well as points of dispute. On the issue of perseverance, then, there were agreements such as these: (1) "God hath promised unto true Beleevers ... supplies of his good spirit ... which are abundantly sufficient to preserve them from falling away" and even (2) the affirmation "that it doth not spring ... from regenerate men themselves, or from their will, that they fall not wholly away, ... but from the special love of God, and his operation in them, together with the intercession and safe-keeping of Christ." But then he added the one point of "distance" separating his position from theirs: "They hold, that persons once true Beleevers, and truly justified, can never fall away from their Faith, either totally or finally: we hold, that even such persons may fall away in both considerations."[36]

His assessment was indeed sound. Perkins had earlier observed that if

---

[33]Baynes, *Commentarie upon Colossians*, p. 268.
[34]Richard Sibbes, *Saints Cordialls*, p. 105. Quoted in I. Morgan, *Puritan Spirituality*, p. 27.
[35]Harrison, *Beginnings of Arminianism*, p. 151.
[36]J. Goodwin, *Agreement and Distance*, pp. 64–67.

the elect could wholly fall from grace, "then there must be a second insition or ingrafting into the mysticall bodie of Christ, and therefore a second Baptisme: nay, for every fall a new insition, and a new Baptisme." But this was in no way to be granted. So his conclusion, on these as well as other grounds, was the unqualified assertion that "they which are predestinate to be in the state of grace, are also predestinate to persevere in the same to the end."[37] And for the theologically orthodox that conviction remained consistent throughout. Even such a separatist in church polity as Henry Ainsworth put the conviction in this manner: "Though they [the elect] through their weaknesse sinne and fall . . . they cannot sin unto death because they are borne of God."[38]

Such assurance was not free, however, from certain continuing problems, especially as related to pastoral practice. One was simply the fact that confidence in predestination could be turned into an occasion for license. Perkins spoke of the "belly-gods of this world" who reason that "if we be predestinate to eternall life and our predestination be certain and unchangeable, what need we endeavour our selves, beleeve or doe good works?"[39] John Goodwin argued that a view of "conditional perseverance" would discourage that disposition, for teaching that there can be an "apostatizing to Perdition" provides deterrent to sin, giving "a sharp bit and bridle" of restraint.[40] But the orthodox found sufficient positive considerations on which to rely. One should rather reason with oneself in this manner, remarked Sutton: "If I belong to God's selection, then shall I use the meanes to come into glorie: I will therefore use all holy and godly courses, that I may get my election sure and sealed."[41] God's election of some to life is also an election to use of the means that lead to life. In the process of salvation the end cannot be separated from the means by which it is attained. So Perkins could deplore those who find predestination an excuse for license, "as though God did glorifie them who he did predestinate, before he called and justified them: yea, and before they can beleeve, and shew their quicke and lively faith by works."[42] Predestination, with its perseverance, is in no way detached from the *ordo salutis* and its requirements for the Christian's pilgrimage toward the end which is itself decreed by God.

Indeed, it was urged, the awareness of one's own election actually can contribute to increased moral endeavor. Experiential considerations were important here, in addition to the purely theological, with the result that

[37]Perkins, "Estate of Damnation," *Works*, 1:417.

[38]Ainsworth, *Seasonable Discourse*, p. 18.

[39]Perkins, "Brief Discourse out of Zanchius," *Works*, 1:438. This is in fact an observation of Zanchius which Perkins endorsed.

[40]J. Goodwin, *Redemption Redeemed*, p. 167.

[41]Sutton, *Lectures on Romans*, p. 54.

[42]Perkins, "Brief Discourse out of Zanchius," *Works*, 1:438. Again an observation of Zanchius endorsed by Perkins.

predestination's affirmation was then buoyed by its morally compelling consequences. Of the knowledge of one's election Dent wrote, "How it doth ravish the hearts with the love of him! . . . For it is the persuasion and feeling of Gods love toward us, that draweth up our love to him againe."[43] And George Downame added his observation that "the more a man is perswaded or assured of Gods eternall love towards him, the more fervently he will love the Lord and carefully obey him."[44]

This leads, however, to the second problem in pastoral practice accompanying the affirmation of a doctrine of unconditional predestination, namely, the problem of despair, the fear that one may not be among those elect who are chosen by God. Perkins saw this as the greatest of all "cases of conscience" and, as did many others, devoted major attention to it. The problem of personal "assurance" thus became a matter of central concern among the orthodox brethren, and the effort to counter despair developed into a major task for both theological writing and pastoral ministry. For some it could seem as though life were simply what might be called "God's Lottery"[45] in which one was no more than a victim of chance. One liberal attack on this view of predestination put the issue in particularly graphic fashion: even when among the apostles "the odds were eleven to one on the innocent parties side," it "raised so much scruple and suspicion in their bosoms, as made them very anxious and inquisitive, Master is it I?"[46]

But the "physicians of the soul" had many responses, both theoretical and practical, to the questions of anxiety, and the leading of persons from despair to confidence was the practice of their profession. It will be our task to examine these responses and their prescriptions in the final chapter of this study and to take note of how the generating of assurance was itself an aspect of covenant thought. For the moment, however, it may suffice to note that the possibility of such assurance was strongly affirmed and the obligation to seek it was earnestly urged as one of the Christian's major duties. A favorite text was II Peter 1:10, which spoke of the need to "make one's calling and election sure," and dedication to that task became a central characteristic of the Puritan movement. Moreover, in this effort the idea of God's sovereignty in divine decree served not only as cause for anxiety, but also as cure. The decrees are from a God who can implement them, and the promises are from a God who can fulfill them. Election is not conditioned upon the frailty of human response, but reposes in the invincibility of the divine. Baynes declared, "The Scripture could not say, that hee that beleeveth hath an everlasting life . . . did it not take our faith and the fruits of it to be such, from which we should never fall, through the power of God."[47]

[43]Dent, Plaine Mans Path-way, p. 299.

[44]G. Downame, Certainty of Perseverance, p. 410.

[45]This is Thomas Goodwin's phrase. Quoted in Greaves, John Bunyan, p. 65.

[46]Womock, Examination of Tilenus, p. 314.

[47]Baynes, Commentary Upon Ephesians, p. 121.

So there is comfort in predestination, this awareness of being "begotten in the Womb of Eternal Election."[48] Ames believed that "the beginning and fountaine of all our happiness and consolation consists in this, that we are the elect of God."[49] And this is to be seen particularly as a feature of Puritan covenant understanding. Perkins, we may recall, viewed the covenant as the instrument utilized by God for the carrying out of the divine decree of election.[50] The conditional covenant is employed for purposes that are themselves absolute. Election and the conditional covenant are not in conflict. Because the Arminians do not accept this final dimension of God's sovereignty in covenant action, envisaging even the possibility of the true believer falling away, "they know not," wrote Bulkeley, "the difference between the covenant of workes and the covenant of grace."[51] But there is a vast difference, from this Puritan perspective, and the decisive factor is God's guarantee of the covenant's completion. George Downame identified it by saying of the two covenants that "in the former the Lord requireth perseverance to be performed by us, . . . but in the latter . . . he promiseth to give it to us."[52] So election and perseverance themselves are a part of God's covenanting, and here is the firmest ground for comfort. Prynne put it confidently:

> Those whom God hath chosen for to be his people, and hath likewise caused them to choose him for their God, and to Joyne themselves unto him in such an everlasting covenant as shall never be forgotten, it is impossible that they should ever finally or totally fall from grace.[53]

It is at this point that Puritan thought provided the connective between the theological requirements drawn from both its piety and its predestination, and it did so through its understanding of the covenant of grace. The covenant is conditional, but for the elect the fulfillment of its conditions is guaranteed. The covenant is also absolute.

UNIVERSALISM AND PARTICULARISM

This connection between the conditional and the absolute in Puritan covenant thought, as well as the tension it represented, now must be examined more fully. Here is the point where Puritan theology probably faced its greatest challenge and pastoral practice encountered its most important task. At any rate, neither from the theoretical perspective, nor from

[48]T. Goodwin, *Works*, 3:37.
[49]Ames, *Analytical Exposition of Peter*, p. 3.
[50]Perkins, "Golden Chaine," *Works*, 1:32.
[51]Bulkeley, *Gospel-Covenant*, p. 275.
[52]G. Downame, *Certainty of Perseverance*, p. 304.
[53]Prynne, *Regenerate Mans Estate*, p. 111.

the practical perspective, could the conjunction of these two aspects of covenant understanding be ignored. Dealing with them was therefore a necessity imposed upon Puritan divines, as implications of both the conditional and the absolute covenant were not only utilized in pastoral counsel, but also theologically expounded as parts of a twofold emphasis within the biblical message itself. It was from the Scripture that Puritanism found the ground for both evangelicalism ànd election, both piety and predestination. Thus the relations of the two need to be examined as part of the effort for a total biblical understanding with its implications for the exercise of the spiritual life.

One approach to this matter on the exegetical, and theological, level was to note the stress on both universalism and particularism in the biblical Gospel. Clearly the Scriptural mandate was, on the one hand, that the promises of God of salvation in Christ be broadly, indeed universally, proclaimed. The Christian evangelist is to go forth into all the world, to speak everywhere of God's love, to summon all persons to repentance and faith. When Preston spoke to those not yet in covenant he declared, "Now you must know that the Lord offer him [Christ] to you, he is exposed to you if you will but take him."[54] Or again he urged, "For you that are without, to you I say, you may, if you will consider it, come to the assurance of his love towards you. . . . The Lord has made knowne his owne willingnesse to take you to marriage. . . . What is required now? Nothing at all but thy consent."[55] Even more forcefully was this put forth by Jenison who, like Preston, held strongly to a doctrine of predestination:

> If I were among the Barbarous heathen, among Jewes, Turks and Infidells, I . . . would first endeavour to let them know Christ and his benefits, and then I would seriously invite them all to beleeve on him, yea and would assuredly in Christ's name, promise unto all true penitents and beleevers among them, pardon of sinne and life eternall.[56]

The universal offering of the Gospel rests, moreover, upon the general character of the Scriptural promises themselves. There is nothing exclusive about them, for they are portrayed as offered to all without arbitrary restriction. "Note the goodness of God," said Baynes, "who would have everie man taught that he might be saved . . . and therefore offereth salvation to all men."[57] Preston put it even more explicitly: "Scripture makes no particular promise to any man; it saith not, thou Thomas, or thou John shalt be saved, but it saith, whosoever will, let him come and drinke freely of the

---

[54]Preston, *Saints Qualification*, p. 438.
[55]Preston, *Breast-Plate of Faith and Love*, 3:144.
[56]Jenison, *Christs death and love*, p. 216.
[57]Baynes, *Commentarie upon Colossians*, p. 165.

water of life."[58] Indeed, still further, the universal offer also carries with it a divine mandate for affirmative response. Culverwell wrote, "God doth proclaime in the Gospell his Sonne Christ, and all his benefits generally to all, and every Soule, to whom the Gospell comes: so that every one who heareth the Gospell, ought to beleeve."[59]

Yet when Culverwell declared this Gospel mandate upon all to believe, he immediately added the qualification, "which none can without speciall grace." Here is the other side of the biblical story. It is by God's special act that a people are chosen, that saints are selected, that faith itself comes to be. "To believe," said Sutton, "is a gift proper to the Elect alone. Acts 13.48."[60] This theme of the particularizing of the receiving of the promises by God's sovereign choice thus steadily accompanied in Puritan thought the theme of the universality of God's offer, often to the point of placing severe constrictions upon the latter. One prominent exegetical instance relates to the meaning of the word "all" in biblical passages, such as I Timothy 2:4, asserting that God's desire is for all to come to salvation. Puritan theologians did not hesitate, when moved by particularistic concerns, to interpret this term of inclusion in a manner implying a measure of exclusion. It could refer simply to "all the elect,"[61] excluding the non-elect. Or it could mean that some, but not everyone, of "all sorts" of persons will be saved. Dent explained that this would include, for example, "some Jewes, some Gentiles, some rich, some poore, some high, some low."[62] Another added, "some Italians, some English,"[63] in expanding the "all sorts" who were to be represented! John Goodwin's reply was, in effect, that the biblical declarations must be taken actually to mean what they literally say and that God's intention, therefore, is that all, in its full inclusive sense, be saved. Not all are, but God's "antecedent" intention is that they be, even though the divine "consequent" intention limits this to those who believe.[64]

Another instance of exegetical endeavor to qualify the universal by emphasis on the particular came in interpretation of John 3:16, a text proclaiming that "God so loved the world that he gave his only begotten Son that whosoever believeth on him would not perish but have everlasting life." The question was, "What was the 'world' that God so loved?" When particularism dominated dogma, this "world" was restricted to the elect. Liberals, however, had a ready reply. Samuel Hoard pointed out that if the text meant "God so loved the Elect," and the remainder of it implying a division were to be considered, then "this would follow, there are two sorts

[58]Preston, *Liveless Life*, p. 56.
[59]Culverwell, *Treatise of Faith*, p. 154.
[60]Sutton, *Lectures on Romans*, p. 447.
[61]Ibid., p. 444.
[62]Dent, *Plaine Mans Path-way*, p. 264.
[63]Milbournes, *Wisdom Crying out*, p. 18.
[64]J. Goodwin, *Redemption Redeemed*, pp. 448–50.

of the Elect, some that believe, and shall be saved; others that doe not believe, and shall be damned, which is a . . . distinction unknown in Divinity." It is rather, added Hoard, that when "God so loved the world," this was a love for "the whole lump of Mankind."[65] But Puritan particularism insisted on the restriction and, for the orthodox, continued to be in tension with the universalism which the divines equally found in the biblical Gospel's mandate for a proclamation of God's promises to every person.

A place of special importance where these diverse perspectives converged was in the interpretation of the scope of the atoning work of Christ. There was no dispute as to the fact of this work through Christ's death upon the cross. Such doctrine was standard in any repertory. But the questions were "for whom?" and "to what extent?" When John Goodwin analyzed this matter in his *Agreement and Distance of Brethren*, he listed among the agreements the convictions that "Christ died sufficiently for all men, without exception" and that salvation is "to be offered in the Ministry of the Gospel, freely unto all Men . . . without exception, upon the account of the death of Christ." The major difference between the orthodox and himself was in their maintaining "that Christ according to the Counsel and intentions of God, died only for the salvation of a certain determinate number of men . . . whom they call the Elect."[66] This stated the matter plainly and accurately, also lifting up the dual emphasis found in the thought of the orthodox brethren. On the one hand, so Goodwin noted, they affirmed that "Christ died sufficiently for all men." Here is the pull of universalism which draws the doctrine of atonement itself into the broad compass of relevance to all humanity, even as the Gospel promises of forgiveness are offered to all. Ames wrote, "in respect of that sufficiency which is the mediation of Christ, it may be rightly said . . . Christ satisfied for all, or every one," and then he added, in discussing the offer of Christ, "those promises . . . are propounded to all without difference, together with a command to believe them."[67] Others likewise spoke of this universal "sufficiency," meaning that the worth and value of Christ's death was sufficient to serve as sacrifice for the sins of all humanity. Should it be God's plan, there is adequacy in that atoning act for a universal redemption.

Yet the redemptive act, so these orthodox maintained, was not for all humanity, for sovereign selection by God entered even into this act of sacrificial love and limited its scope to the chosen. John Goodwin was quite right in saying that for these brethren Christ "died only for the salvation of a certain determinate number of men . . . whom they call the Elect." The universality of "sufficiency" is qualified by the particularism of "efficiency" which itself is rooted in the intention of God. Ames could thus add

---

[65]Quoted in Twisse, *Riches of Gods Love*, p. 108.

[66]J. Goodwin, *Agreement and Distance*, pp. 18–19.

[67]Ames, *Marrow*, pp. 100, 111.

concerning the atonement: "It is rightly said: Christ did only satisfy for those that are saved by him ... we may not pronounce of all together collectively that Christ did equally plead their cause before God." And of those promises universally proclaimed he could further write, "as touching the propriety of the things promised, which depends on the intention of him that promiseth, they belong only to the elect."[68] Dent put it equally directly: "Christ died for all in the sufficiency of his death, but not in efficacie unto life," for by his death "only the Elect shall be saved."[69] All of this was doctrine fully in accord with the conclusions of the Synod of Dort and constituted a view of "limited atonement." The orthodox in the Puritan movement, with but rare and tentative exception, did not break with this classic conviction within the Reformed tradition.

One such exception, however, gave impetus to a significant movement on the continent that in its effort to modify scholastic Calvinism also had impact on covenant theology. This was found in the thought of John Cameron, Scottish Puritan of the early seventeenth century, and then more fully in that of Moses Amyraut whom he influenced and who developed the theology of the French Huguenot school at Saumur.[70] Examination of their point of view can, moreover, enable us to understand the Puritan position more clearly. A major matter in the thought of both Cameron and Amyraut was the "unlimited" nature of Christ's atonement. Cameron objected to the "sham explanation of the divines" in their interpolation of the term "elect" after each statement in Scripture that Christ died for all. It is rather that "Christ is given for ... every creature, all flesh, the world."[71] It is true that the condition is attached making this efficacious only for those who believe in him, and further that faith is itself God's gift granted to the elect. But the crucial matter at this point is the universality of the atoning act itself and the attempt truly to be faithful to the Scriptural affirmation that "Christ died for all."

In Amyraut there is similar rejection of the idea of limited atonement and a universalizing of the scope of the redemptive act. Brian Armstrong observes that in him "we see not only that the sacrifice of Christ is a sufficient price for the sins of the whole world, a statement which most of the orthodox would have endorsed, but also that He *intended* to die for all men, a position wholly untenable for the orthodox."[72] So here is substantial theological ground, in Amyraut's understanding, for the conditional or evangelical covenant which God has established. As Christ has died for all, he can be

[68]Ibid., pp. 100–101, 111.

[69]Dent, *Plaine Mans Path-way*, p. 264.

[70]For an analysis of this movement and its relation to covenant theology see Armstrong, *Calvinism and the Amyraut Heresy*, especially chaps. 4–7.

[71]John Cameron, "Letter of December, 1610," *Opera*, p. 531. Quoted in Armstrong, *Calvinism and the Amyraut Heresy*, p. 57.

[72]Armstrong, *Calvinism and the Amyraut Heresy*, p. 211.

offered to all in the Gospel proclamation. All persons can properly be invited to believe, for the benefits of his atonement are actually available to any who will receive.

Yet cutting across this universalism in Amyraut's thought, as in Cameron's and indeed in all of Calvinism, was the other note of God's sovereign choice. From that perspective the application of the unlimited atonement becomes limited by God's own selective decree, and those who believe and receive are the elect. Amyraut was not an Arminian, and absolute predestination was a part of his theological system. Thus for him the covenant, which was truly conditional, was also truly absolute, and the two purposes of God stood in dialectical tension with one another. Neither is to be denied, though their conjunction cannot be rationalized. Reason must bow before revelation in the face of this contradiction. Yet for purposes of pastoral practice emphasis must be accorded to the conditional factor. Election is a part of God's secret will and falls outside the range of the evangelical covenant. There is little one can know about election, and speculation is to be avoided. Within the work of both theology and the ministry, Amyraut urged, attention should be directed to the conditional covenant promises of God.

There is much common ground between Amyraut and his Puritan contemporaries. Yet there is also an important point of difference which establishes the Puritan dialectic of the conditional and the absolute on a different basis from that of the French Huguenot. This is found in their interpretations of the scope of Christ's atonement, a difference that led Puritanism to a somewhat less theologically and a somewhat more psychologically influenced handling of the tension between evangel and election. On the theological front there was Puritan rejection of genuine universalism in Christ's redemption. Beyond its fundamental acceptance of the idea of "limited atonement" as part of its doctrinal inheritance, Puritanism was wary of the dangers of Arminianism inherent in any modification. "Unlimited atonement" could open the door to a view, as Arminians affirmed, that the covenant of grace was actually made with all, an aberration quite unacceptable in orthodox Puritan understanding. With the emphasis on exclusiveness that can all too easily prevail in a closed system, Rutherfurd protested the thought of Christ's atoning benefits being potentially applicable to "Pharoah, Cain, Aegyptians, Syrians, Persians, Chaldeans,"[73] and then also added "Indians and all wild Savages"[74] to bring it up to date! Amyraut could hardly have said that.

Yet Amyraut, with his vote for unlimited atonement, was still not an Arminian, and his disagreement with that view concerning human freedom

---

[73]Rutherfurd, *Covenant of Life*, p. 327.
[74]Ibid., p. 119.

points to still another conviction on which the Hugeunot and the Puritan concur, namely, the irresistibility of grace. So among the theological positions we are viewing there were three different conceptions. Arminianism spoke for an unlimited atonement and resistible grace. Christ's redemptive act includes all, but the grace given to appropriate it could be accepted or rejected. Amyraut spoke for an unlimited atonement and irresistible grace. Christ's atoning work comprehends all, but its applied benefits are for the elect who are chosen for it by God without possibility of deviation. Puritanism, however, spoke for a limited atonement and an irresistible grace. Christ's redemption is for those whom God has elected and who have then been brought by sovereign power to its benefits.

There is at this point in Puritan thought and practice, however, a huge "and yet." The "and yet" notes that there is a conditional covenant, that this covenant is based upon divine promises, and that the Scripture urges the promises be extended to all. It is not, as in Amyraut, that the death of Christ is dogmatically defined to be for everyone. "And yet" Christ is to be offered to all, for this is the Gospel obligation. So on the basis of Scriptural mandate, with its consequent component of psychological desirability, there was a Puritan universalism. Preston said, "when the pardon is generall, and offered to all, then I can beleeve that the pardon belongs to me."[75] This could not happen, he added, if it were to be offered only to the elect. Though this is not a theological universalism, it is a practical universalism as ground for Puritan proclamation, sanctioned as well by Scriptural stipulation. And it, in its own manner, provided the dialectical tension more dogmatically defined by Amyraut. Jenison said, "Here then is the mystery: Though God invite all, and promise life to all upon the condition of faith, . . . yet the fruit of Christ's death doth actually belong . . . to the Elect only."[76] And Preston added, "Though Christ be offered and freely given to all, God intends him onely for the Elect . . . the gift of faith is the fruit of Election."[77] Still, the practical policy commended by Amyraut had its counterpart in Puritan pastoral psychology. Preston brought the mystery and the method together:

> When Christ was offered, freely to every man, and one received him, another rejected him, then the Mystery of Election and reprobation was revealed; the reason why some received being because GOD gave them a heart, which to the rest hee gave not; but in point of offering Christ, we must be general without having respect to Election.[78]

[75]Preston, *Breast-Plate of Faith and Love*, 1:12.
[76]Jenison, *Christs death and love*, p. 232.
[77]Preston, *Breast-Plate of Faith and Love*, 1:11.
[78]Ibid., 1:10.

GOD'S HIDDEN AND REVEALED WILLS

There was a still more profound dimension, however, to this tension between the conditional and the absolute. In the last analysis it could also be identified as representing two wills in God. This view was central in the thought of Amyraut, who supported his affirmation by finding this designation in Calvin. It likewise became a fundamental factor in Puritan theology itself. On the one hand there is God's commanding and forbidding will. This is God's declaring will or God's will of precept. It is the will of God as known in God's Word, the will that prescribes and promises. It is God's signifying will which shows what God proposes to do for one by way of grace and what one is obligated to do for God by way of duty. It is thus the known will, the will of the conditional covenant, the revealed will of God.

On the other hand, there is the will of God's good pleasure. This is God's decreeing will by which the judgments in God's eternal counsels come to be. This is the will of God's sovereignty and ultimate power, the will in which God "willeth . . . what he wil, when he wil, and how he will." In this "we are at Gods pleasure, as clay is at the pleasure of the potter."[79] This is the predestining will, the will of God's private purpose. It is the will of the absolute covenant, the will by which the elect are chosen and then incorporated into the covenant of grace. It is the secret will or the hidden will of God.

To show the contrast Rutherfurd wrote:

> God decrees, if Judas repent and beleeve, he shall be saved according to the will of precept, and yet according to the Lord's will of purpose, neither did the Lord decree or intend the repenting and saving beleeving of Judas, nor was grace to beleeve and repent purchased by the death of Christ for Judas.[80]

Though salvation is promised in God's revealed will upon the fulfillment of certain conditions, its actual realization through the fulfillment of those conditions is dependent upon the decree in the hidden will of God. Here for Puritanism as for Amyraut, though with not precisely the same theological grounding, is the tension between the conditional and the absolute. There are promises of salvation which point to the evangelical covenant, even as the doctrine of the decrees indicates God's ultimate sovereign choice.

It is not, however, that this posed for Puritans a conflict or a contradiction within God. The ultimate unity of God's will had been affirmed by Calvin and Amyraut, and Puritans agreed. Jenison said, "If God . . . reveales part of his will and conceales part, this is neither to contradict himselfe, nor to deale doubly and deceitfully with his creature. He speaks not one thing and

---

[79]Perkins, "Gods Free-grace and Mans free-will," *Works*, 1:723.
[80]Rutherfurd, *Covenant of Life*, p. 244.

meanes another." It is rather, he continued, simply that "the Conditionall part of Gods will is set downe in his word; But what he hath set downe absolutely, and whom in particular he will save . . . he hath reserved to himselfe, (as not being bound to reveale it till the event show it) onely that there is such an absolute will is revealed."[81] Yet if there is no ultimate theological contradiction in the two wills of God, there is still the psychological problem of how one relates to them. But here Puritan divines spoke strongly, even as did Amyraut, for dealing with the known and the promised. And this became a major feature of Puritan pastoral practice. "I see it is an over curious pride," said Timothy Rogers, "for mee to goe about to prie into the secret and hidden councell of God, any otherwise then as hee hath revealed the same to mee, for secret things belong to God, but things revealed to us."[82] And what Rogers prescribed for himself was also seen as good fare for others.

One word of counsel, therefore, in this practical theology was to urge avoiding the attempt to probe the decrees in an effort to determine one's destiny. This is fruitless speculation and can lead only to increased puzzlement and despair. Speaking in terms similar to those used by Calvin a century earlier, Sutton observed, "They that in this have beene inquisitive and curious, have plunged themselves into such inextricable labyrinths and mazes that they have never been able to come out of them." And the labyrinths are truly complex, he said, for in them God has even "hidden contraries under contraries."[83] The anonymous author of *The Marrow of Modern Divinity* advised against "meddling with God's secrets."[84] And Dent could urge, "Let no man climbe up to the cloudes, to search whether hee bee inrolled in the secret councell of GOD, nor let him busie himselfe with many curious speculations below."[85] This is not a knowledge one can obtain, nor is it then proper or profitable to seek to obtain it. Jenison said that "if wee will needs pry into the arke, we shall be destroyed, with those of Bethshemesh; if wee will search and gaze upon the majesty of God and dive into those depths we shall be overwhelmed with his glory, and perhaps, come into the bottomlesse depth of all." Thus we should not speculate on God's hidden reasons and should "deny our owne reason where God denies to give us a reason."[86] The specific workings of God in the absolute covenant are not to be explored, for they are beyond finding out.

Rather, one should turn from the hidden will to the revealed will of God. Here should be adequate satisfaction, for this is the disclosure of God's enacted goodness and determined way. Here is the revelation of divine

[81]Jenison, *Concerning Gods Certaine Performance*, pp. 55–56.

[82]T. Rogers, *Righteous Mans Evidences*, p. 199.

[83]Sutton, *Lectures on Romans*, pp. 460, 459.

[84]E. F., *Marrow*, p. 120.

[85]Dent, *Opening Heavens gates*, p. 86.

[86]Jenison, *Christs death and love*, pp. 262–63.

purpose and promise. Here is the covenant of grace, with its conditions and consequences. Here is the Word, with its Christ of mercy freely offered. And here is abundant "employment," wrote Sutton, "sufficient for our soules health to busie our mindes all the dayes of our life, in searching out, in musing upon, in bringing into practice the lessons of God's revealed will and word." Indeed, he added, "to know and practice such things as concern our faith, the sanctification of our life, and the salvation of our soules, this will find employment enough, though we were as wise as Salomon and could live as long as Methusalem."[87]

This is the way, then, to that knowledge of God's working which can bring desired consolation and confidence. To those whose belief faltered because of uncertainty of whether or not they were under God's pardon Culverwell declared, "I . . . advise every one who is kept from beleeving by this, . . . not to looke to Gods secret will, but to attend to Gods revealed will in his Word, wherein it is expressly said, that God would have no man perish, but would have all come to repentance . . . that hereby he might be moved to seeke and hope for that mercy, which God is so willing to bestow."[88] And Ball was equally explicit in urging a turning of concern and attention from the hidden to the revealed will of God. He wrote:

> The decree of God which is secret in the bosome of the most High is not the rule according to which we must walke, but the word of life, revealed in the holy Scriptures, we must take for our direction. If God make offer of mercy and forgiveness unto us in the ministery of the Gospel, which is the Word of truth, the Word of salvation, we are bound to receive it, without looking into the booke of his election: and if we receive them truely, we shall be saved, as the Lord hath spoken.[89]

The author of the modern *Marrow* declared in even stronger language that when one puts aside prying into God's hidden counsel and turns instead to God's revealed will, complying with its requirements for a believing on Christ, then "you may put it out of the question, and be sure that you are one of God's Elect."[90]

The pastoral recommendations that direct attention from the hidden will to the revealed will of God go, however, still one step further. It is not simply that one should rely on the revealed will, but also one should turn more inwardly to the conditions of one's heart and one's life to determine the reality of that reliance. Here we are moving into the area of subjective assurances which will be explored in our final chapter. But it is important at the moment to see how these also are connected with the issue of anxiety

[87]Sutton, *Lectures on Romans*, p. 461.
[88]Culverwell, *Treatise of Faith*, p. 185.
[89]Ball, *Treatise of Faith*, p. 166.
[90]E. F., *Marrow*, p. 120.

over predestination. Perkins was much interested in this matter. A thorough-going supralapsarian predestinarian, he likewise had pastoral concern for the afflictions of conscience. And his recommendation was that one turn from the heights to the heart. There are two ways, he noted, to seek knowledge of one's election:

> The one, is by ascending up as it were into heaven, there to search the counsell of God, and afterward, to come downe to our selves. The second, by descending into our owne hearts to goe up from our selves, as it were by Jacob's ladder, to God's eternal counsell. . . . The first way is dangerous, and not to be attempted. For the waies of God are unsearchable and past finding out. The second way alone is to be followed . . . [for it] teacheth us by signes and testimonies in our selves, to gather what was the eternall counsel of God concerning our salvation.[91]

There is concurrence in this process by Sibbes who likewise would probe the heart for signs of election. Consideration of one's eternal predestination must be pursued on the more accessible grounds of one's spiritual condition. "Look to thy heart," he said, "whether God hath taught it to love or no, and to relish heavenly things. If he hath, thy state is good. And then thou mayest ascend to those great matters of predestination and election." But the sequence is important: "Go first to thine heart, and then to these deep mysteries afterwards."[92]

Although the ideas of predestination and the absolute will of God could stimulate anxiety and uncertainty, practical counsel was to focus on God's revealed will and the evidence of its realization in one's life. It means, as Amyraut had stated, that God's predestination does not fall within the compass of the evangelical covenant. God's action in the absolute covenant is indeed the guarantee of the fulfillment of the gospel conditions. But one's knowledge, one's life, and ultimately one's confidence must relate primarily to the conditional covenant itself. Perhaps Dent expressed it as well as any when, after urging that no one climb up to the clouds to seek evidence of predestination, he concluded, "but let him . . . enter into him selfe, and consider how his faith doth stand in Christ . . . [and] thereupon let him rest, wrapping his whole bodie and soule under his promise."[93]

[91]Perkins, "Exposition of the Creed," *Works*, 1:284.
[92]Sibbes, "Glance at Heaven," *Works*, 4:182.
[93]Dent, *Opening Heavens gates*, p. 86.

Chapter 6

THE AGENTS OF THE COVENANT

A major issue involved in all theology of divine-human relationship, but particularly urgent for Puritan theology with its dual view of the covenant, is the question of "agency." Issues connected with it have been implied in earlier discussion, but now they must be more specifically explored. The covenant's mutuality requires human participation or agency in covenant action. As the covenant is conditional, the conditions are fulfilled in and through the faith and faithful work of human persons. Life in the covenant is not divinely sterilized against human endeavor. And yet, there is likewise the divine agency, the work of God so central and crucial to covenant completion. In part this divine work is necessitated by the frailty of human effort. Only through such remedy to sin can the conditions of the covenant be fulfilled. But equally, this fulfillment is necessitated by the nature and intention of divine sovereignty. God's rule is total, God's control is complete. Thus God's decrees of eternal election will be unfailingly executed in the passage of time. Predestination itself, therefore, requires God's participation as an agent in covenant action. The conditional covenant is also absolute.

VIEWS OF AGENCY

Antinomianism sought to minimize the role of human effort and to maximize the role of the divine. At the beginning of the whole covenant process, for example, God is understood to act so exclusively as to compel unwilling subjects to receive the saving grace. It is not simply, as Tobias Crisp put it at one point, "that the very Motion of our coming to Christ, is from Christ himself, and from Christ's coming to us before we do so much as move." It is also that "the Father doth force open the Spirit of that person and pours in his Son in spight of the Receiver." The analogy used is that of the physician forcing a bitter medication into the closed mouth of a patient, though for the patient's own good. It is only through such drastic action that the human spirit is "broken" and "tamed" and then begins to "embrace Christ." The work of conversion, therefore, is God's, and the human role is purely passive. Crisp said, "Though men have no hands to take Christ, yet may they receive him."[1]

---

[1]Crisp, *Christ Alone Exalted*, p. 204.

Similarly, the continuing work of the Christian's life is viewed essentially as a divine act. Thomas Welde pointed to the Antinomian belief that "in the conversion of a sinner ... the faculties of the soule ... in things pertaining to God, are destroyed and made to cease," and "instead of them, the Holy Ghost doth come and take place, and doth all the works."[2] It is not that all Antinomians blinded their eyes completely to some human role. Powell spoke of Christian believers who at the outset were "meer passives" becoming "co-workers" with God. But then he needed immediately to add, "herein we must also know that it is not enough for God to tune the instrument of the soule, but he must also play thereon himselfe (otherwise the Musicke cannot be melodious)." Though God gives "habits of grace," God must also "incite, exercise and act through those infused or created habits."[3] In general, then, the Antinomian position was that the good works of the Christian's life were the activity of the Holy Spirit in which the believer took little or no part. Robert Towne spoke of the obedience of Christians as "the work of the Spirit in them; so its passive to them."[4]

Orthodox Puritans rejected emphatically these views which so disparaged the presence of human decision and participation in the process of salvation. As to coerced conversion, Burgess responded that it is "impossible that a man should beleeve unwillingly."[5] And Shepard complained that downplaying the human role in further good works left the Christian "like a weathercock which hath not power at all to move, but as the wind blows it."[6] In fact, the human factor is so denied in this conception that "the Lord makes his music without any strings."[7] Despite their emphasis on the power of God's working, the Puritan divines insisted on the responsible involvement of the human creature.[8]

Arminianism provided a quite opposite view, for its affirmation of the will's liberty and capacity led to an unqualified rejection of any portrayal making grace irresistible in conversion or in the covenant's continuation. In the mid-seventeenth century Laurence Womock wrote a fanciful dialogue from an essentially Arminian perspective reporting the presumed examination of a liberal candidate for the office of public preacher in the commonwealth of Utopia. The situation was not exactly utopian, however, for the

[2]Welde, *Rise, reign and ruine*, p. 1.

[3]Powell, *Christ and Moses*, pp. 59–60.

[4]Robert Towne, *The Assertion of Grace*, p. 23. Quoted in Kevan, *Grace of Law*, p. 220.

[5]Burgess, *Vindiciae Legis*, p. 98.

[6]Shepard, *Works*, 2:332.

[7]Ibid.

[8]For a discussion of the manner in which Reformed theology as a whole, and Puritan theology in particular, stressed human participation within the context of divine sovereignty see Stoever, 'A Faire and Easie Way to Heaven'. His major point is that "the ontological and moral orders established at creation were not violated by God's omnipotence," p. 8.

examining committee was made up of predestinarian Calvinists, among them Mr. Fatality, Mr. Narrow-grace, Mr. Efficax, Mr. Indefectible, Dr. Dam-man, and the chairman, Dr. Absolute! At one point Mr. Efficax said, "You speak as if the Grace of conversion were resistible; and so you would make man stronger than God ... [But] the Apostle saith, It is God which worketh in you, both to will and to do his good Pleasure." The candidate replied, "Speaking of his absolute Power, God can compel and necessitate the Will of Man, and so we do not make him stronger than God; ... yet he will not, because he will not violate that order which he hath set in our Creation. He made Man after his own Image, ... therefore God deals with Man as a free Agent." Mr. Narrow-grace interposed that the Apostle spoke, however, about doing all things "thro' Christ strengthning me; for without Christ we can do nothing." The candidate replied, "Observe, 'tis not thro' Christ forcing, but thro' Christ strengthning me. The Grace and Ability is from Christ, but it is our part and duty to actuate that Ability, and cooperate with that Grace."[9]

Similar sentiments are found in Thomas Goad, who had been one of the English Calvinists at the Synod of Dort, but who changed his mind on the issues after his return and wrote a tract critical of the orthodox view of predestination and the eternal decrees. Among other allegations he charged that the prevailing interpretation "makes a Man to operate with no more freedom than a Stock or Stone." It is "more wonderful" and "admirable" to see God's action in eternity based on a divine "Fore-knowing whatsoever his Creatures would do, or not do," than on an absolute fore-ordaining bringing unyielding necessity into human life.[10]

A major spokesman, however, for this liberal position in mid-seventeenth century England was once again John Goodwin. Much controversy swirled around Goodwin's view of grace, and he was charged at this point, as in his strong affirmation of human freedom, with representing a new Pelagianism. Goodwin himself, however, often stressed his honoring of grace in many of its traditional aspects and his agreements thereby with the orthodox brethren. He wrote that he shared with them the convictions that "the first and primary cause" of salvation is "the free grace, and good pleasure of God," that "it is from the free and undeserved Grace of God that any person ... hath power and means ... sufficient to enable him to believe," and that "not only the power of converting and believing, but the acts themselves are the effects and fruits of ... the free Grace of God."[11] Or again on another occasion he wrote that "the whole plot and counsel of God concerning the salvation of the world, is of free grace," and then he went on

[9]Womock, *Examination of Tilenus*, pp. 274–80.
[10]Goad, *Necessity and Contingency*, pp. 371–75.
[11]J. Goodwin, *Agreement and Distance*, pp. 29–32.

to identify its work in the gift of Christ, the gift of justification, the gift of the power of believing, and the gift of assistance itself in that belief."[12]

Yet there was also great "distance" from the brethren, basically on two grounds: (1) rather than holding grace to be limited only to some, "we contrarily judg it to be diffusive . . . throughout all mankind," and (2) rather than maintaining it to be irresistibly coercive, "our sence . . . is, that no man is so constrained, or necessitated, . . . but that he may possibly, through his voluntary negligence and obdurateness of heart, remain finally unconverted, and unbelieving."[13] Grace is thus universal, all persons being restored from sin and given "a good capacity of Salvation."[14] But grace is also resistible, for "no act of God . . . imposeth any necessity upon any free-working cause."[15]

For Goodwin, as for all in this liberal tradition, conversion comes back finally to free human choice. "God is not only Omnipotent," he said, "but also Omniprudent." God therefore does not act "in opposition to those natural and essential Properties and Principles" implanted in the human creature. So an "interposition of grace" will "well consist with the natural and essential freedom and liberty of [the human] will." Goodwin affirmed this to be true in even such a miraculous conversion as that of Paul, though that event was effected "with as high a hand of means, as ever was lifted up by God for the conversion of a man."[16] It is not, however, so Goodwin insisted, that large control of conversion must be attributed to human act. At one point he claimed that in the act of believing 999 out of 1000 parts can be ascribed to grace, with only the one remaining to human effort.[17] This is reminiscent of Erasmus' defense of himself against Luther on this same issue. He too would ascribe much to grace, but fervently protested that "not nothing" be attributed to independent human action.

Yet as Luther found this unacceptable, neither could the Puritan divines accept Goodwin's view, nor any related Arminian conception relying on the will's free act. Not only was this outlook inconsistent with the doctrine of human impotence, it was also out of accord with the belief in the absoluteness of divine sovereignty. For Preston an emphasis on independent human action, whether large or small, was ground for holding that Arminianism was actually more destructive of grace than was the view of the other major "heresy" on human ability, that of the Jesuits. Though Jesuits, like Goodwin, spoke only of moral persuasion as the way of conversion, they developed a doctrine which so emphasized God's foreknowledge of the possible effects of persuasion under various circumstances which God can freely control, as

[12]John Goodwin, *The Remedy of Unreasonableness*. Quoted in Jackson, *Life of John Goodwin*, p. 225.

[13]J. Goodwin, *Agreement and Distance*, pp. 31–32.

[14]Ibid., p. 58.

[15]J. Goodwin, *Redemption Redeemed*, p. 53.

[16]Ibid., pp. 426–28.

[17]Ibid., p. C2.

to lead in effect to God's infallible determination of destinies, through selection of appropriate circumstances, despite the reality of free human choice. Thus the Jesuits could in this sense be said to attribute conversion to the good pleasure of God and see it as the irresistible calling of the elect. In Arminianism, however, there was explicit affirmation that grace could be rejected, even though God's desire and labor are for one's conversion. So Arminian views are more derogatory and damaging to grace than are those of the Jesuits.[18] And it all rested back on the Arminian interpretation of the human will, for the implications of freedom of choice and act are immense. On the practical or psychological level alone it is disabling. Preston said that if one seeks to live by that conviction, one will "goe about a worke without strength," attempting "to leape over a great ditch with a short staffe."[19] And in the theological realm it is catastrophic. Dent summarized it simply: "Therefore to give free will his packing penny, we may baldly say, that if free wil be, God's providence is not."[20]

<h2 style="text-align:center">THE AGENTS OF CONVERSION</h2>

Turning now to the Puritan attempt to identify and define its own positive understanding on the subject of "agency," between the poles of Antinomianism and Arminianism, we may see it successively in relation to major stages in the *ordo salutis*. Throughout the entirety of the Christian's spiritual life, from its birth to its culmination, there is the participation and the intertwining of the divine and the human. So we start with "calling." Here the Christian's life begins through effective introduction into a new form of existence, the translation from a state dominated by sin to a state enveloped by grace. This is the place, as Ames had indicated, of the Christian's regeneration or conversion. It is in "calling" that the "new being" comes to be. Anticipatory preparations may indeed clear the way, but the effective beginning point of the Christian's new spiritual condition is in conversion itself.

When John Bunyan portrayed this commencement of spiritual life in his *Book for Boys and Girls*, he included the couplet:

NOR can a man his Soul with Grace inspire,
More than can Candles set themselves on fire.[21]

This expressed emphatically the fact of human impotence in conversion's initiation. Among Puritan divines the universally acclaimed view was that the origin of the soul's turning is to be found alone in God. The fallen human

---

[18]Preston, *Irresistibleness of Converting Grace*, pp. 1–4.

[19]Preston, *Saints Qualification*, p. 413.

[20]Dent, *Opening of Heavens gates*, p. 47.

[21]John Bunyan, *A Book for Boys and Girls*, p. 14. Quoted in Greaves, *John Bunyan*, p. 61.

will has no capacity to initiate this or even, unturned, to accept it. It is dead to such life in its "thralldome to sin."[22] Even the desire to be converted, said Perkins, depends on God's work of regeneration which comes through the sovereign divine act of providing a new heart.[23] Thus the human person is completely passive at the beginning of the new spiritual life.

Ames spoke of the first receiving of Christ as a "passive receiving" in which a "spirituall principle of grace is begotten in the will of a man."[24] Cotton reiterated the need for this passivity in his portrayal of conversion. "If any man will come unto Christ," he wrote, "he must deny himself, even all his own gifts . . . until there be nothing left of which a man can say, This I am able to do." Only then, when one "is left utterly void, . . . doth the Lord take possession, and fill the empty soul."[25] Harris noted that the soul at the outset of its pilgrimage is like the infant naked at birth which cannot clothe itself.[26] The beginning of conversion is the work of another. Indeed, said Preston, "till GOD come and drawe a man, and change his will the worke is not done."[27] This sounds, of course, suspiciously like Antinomianism, but Puritan theologians, both to guard against Arminianism and to hazard in no way a relinquishing of divine sovereignty, spoke in these terms with fervor and frequency. The covenant promises were for the granting of the new heart, and this is by God's own doing. Only God can create the new being. Perkins wrote that it was not "til God once againe create in them a new qualitie or property of holinesse, that the minde in thinking may thinke well, and the will in willing may will well."[28] There is an unconditioned beginning of the conversion process in the recreating action of God.

Yet there was also at the same time another side to this Puritan understanding and affirmation. It was to insist that in the very act of God's recreating the will there is a consenting of the will itself to the act of recreation. The Antinomian conception of coercion was explicitly and soundly rejected. There is no "forced feeding" in this gift of divine renewing. And a major reason for this conviction parallels the Arminian view that the human person is not a "block or stock,"[29] but a living subject created with capabilities of mind and will in the image of God. "Reason, or the light of Nature," wrote Burgess, "makes man in a passive capacity fit for grace, although he hath no active ability for it."[30] But that passive capacity can be activated by God's initiative. Then the will itself is made willing, so that it

[22]Dent, *Plaine Mans Path-way*, p. 13.

[23]Perkins, "Gods Free-grace and Mans free-will," *Works*, 1:734.

[24]Ames, *Marrow*, pp. 112–13.

[25]Cotton, *Covenant of Grace*, p. 23.

[26]Harris, *New Covenant*, 1:29.

[27]Preston, *Breast-Plate of Faith and Love*, 1:58.

[28]Perkins, "Gods Free-grace and Mans free-will," *Works*, 1:734.

[29]Jenison, *Concerning Gods Certaine Performance*, p. 104.

[30]Burgess, *Vindiciae Legis*, p. 72.

willingly accepts the regenerating renovation which God provides. Harris
wrote, "True it is that man cannot make himself a new heart; but it is true
also, that hee concurre, not as a cause or agent in this work, yet he must
concurre as a subject capable of being renewed."[31] Perkins defined more
precisely this view in his "Treatise of God's Free-grace and Mans free-will:"

> The first act of will; whereby the will in his regeneration begins to
> assent unto God, and begins to will to be converted, is indeed the worke
> of the will, (because it is the will that willeth) yet doth it not arise of the
> natural strength of the wil, but from the grace of God that renueth it. . . .
> If any man thinke that by this doctrine, men are regenerate against their
> wills: I answer, when God begins to regenerate us, he makes us then
> willing, being otherwise by nature unwilling: and thus he regenerates
> us not against our wills: yet so, as the willingnesse to be regenerate is not
> of us, but of God.[32]

Here is the theological effort to say two things, both of which Puritan
theologians felt truly to be pertinent in any analysis of the beginning of
conversion to the Christian life. On the one hand, this is an act of God and,
even more, of God's sovereignty. And, on the other hand, it is an act in which
the human person participates as a willing and concurring subject. So there
must be freedom for both in this conjunction. Neither divine coercion nor
human coercion will do. Perkins, in "A Golden Chaine," put the two
together in the actual language of agency. "The will both in it selfe and of it
selfe," he wrote, "is a meere patient in her first conversion unto God; but if
it be considered as it is moved by the spirit of God, it is an agent. For being
moved, it moveth. It is not therefore compelled, but of a nilling will, is made
a willing will."[33]

Preston, likewise, sought to find a form for such a duality of causation,
though, in the last analysis, priority is pictured as God's. He wrote first, in his
discussion, about the will's new power:

> men are free Agents, and therefore have a power by vertue of which they
> act, being acted by God, and therefore may be said truly to act, and turn
> themselves; for the will being changed from evill unto good, and of
> unwilling made willing, hath in itself an inward principle of willing
> well; from whence the dominion of its owne act, whereby it turnes to
> God.

But if this new will in conversion is a principle "which worketh," the grace
of God is the principle "by which" the good turning occurs. So priority is to
be noted within the order of causation. God is first and efficient cause, while

---

[31]Harris, *New Covenant*, 2:5.
[32]Perkins, "Gods Free-grace and Mans free-will," *Works*, 1:734.
[33]Perkins, "Golden Chaine," *Works*, 1:101.

the human will is secondary and "next efficient cause." Thus Preston can conclude, in refining his description of the role of the will:

> as the effects are wont to be attributed unto second and created causes, although they act by vertue of the first cause, so conversion is most properly to be attributed to the Will, although it act wholly in the strength of God and converting Grace.[34]

Perkins, too, ended up with a recognition of God's priority in this duality of wills at work in a person's "first conversion," though his retention of human participation remains strong. One interesting handling of the issue appeared in "A Reformed Catholike" where, in disputing the idea of a natural human will being a partner in conversion, he urged the role of the will renewed by grace. There is, however, he noted, no temporal precedence to be given to God's act of renewal. Of the human person's conversion he wrote, "at the very time when he is converted by God's grace he wils his conversion." But, he quickly added, "howsoever in respect of time the working of grace by Gods spirit, and the willing of it in man goe together: yet in regard of order, grace is first wrought, and mans will must first of all bee acted and moved by grace, and then it also acteth, willeth, and moveth it selfe." Thus "we say that mans will worketh with grace in the first conversion: yet not of it selfe, but by grace."[35]

An issue discussed in further explication of God's working in conversion had to do with the manner of God's effecting this change in the human will. Two general positions emerged. One portrayed the divine transforming of the will as occurring in a direct and miraculous manner. This was a "physical regeneration," as was sometimes said. God transformed the will by altering its loyalties and affections. The new life effected by grace was based on a new direction given to the will through the infusion of a new quality of being, the gift of a new heart. The other spoke of God's action in changing the will in terms of the power of persuasion. God's "arguments" were so strong as to convince the soul and thus lead to its turning. The first of these interpretations pointed in the direction of Antinomianism, and the second in the direction of Arminianism. Puritan orthodoxy, without capitulating to either extreme, moved toward one or the other of the views, or more generally toward both in combination. There was much variety in the discussion of this issue.

Jenison argued for the first of these positions, saying that grace acting through persuasion is inadequate "unless God first create in us spirituall life, whereby we may heare and yeeld to his motives," and the reason for this is that "where there is no Life, swasion can take no place, no more than if

---

[34]Preston, *Irresistibleness of Converting Grace*, p. 9.
[35]Perkins, "A Reformed Catholike," *Works*, 1:558–59. See also Perkins, "Gods Free-grace and Mans free-will," *Works*, 1:737.

Cicero with his eloquence should seeke to move the affections of a dead man."[36] Here was a scepticism about the effectiveness of even God's persuasion unless accompanied by spiritual renewal. Conversion must involve rebirth. But that is what God has promised, the removal of the "stony heart," the giving of the "heart of flesh," the redirecting of life's love and loyalty through the gift of "new being." There is an ontological dimension, therefore, to the work of grace. It provides not only a new power, but also a new person. And without this the distinctive divine act in conversion does not exist. Harris exclaimed, "If God onely persuade, what's his work more . . . than the ministers?"[37] Thus there is need for "such a grace as gives to the Soule a spirituall and divine being, which is to the Soule as health to the body."[38] It is not a grace which compels, for "of unwilling he makes them willing." But it is a grace of effective action, for, said Ball, as persons "are gathered into the Kingdome of Christ by effectuall holy vocation, . . . Christ doth not only invite them . . . but by his Spirit doth assuredly bring them unto himselfe, or unto participation in the Covenant of mercy."[39]

The divine turning of the will in the act of conversion was particularly important to Ames who viewed the will as the commanding and effecting center of the human person. He noted, "The will is the most proper and prime subject of grace, because the conversion of the will is an effectuall principle of the conversion of the whole man." But that conversion of the will, he affirmed, occurs as "a spirituall principle of grace is begotten" within it. "The enlightening of the mind," he pointed out, "is not sufficient to produce the effect." The reasons are important. On the one hand, enlightenment does not remove the will's corruption. And, on the other hand, it does not communicate to the will "any new supernaturall principle" by means of which the will "may convert it selfe."[40] So the will must be both purified and empowered in order that it might turn to God. Rebirth to Christian life is the fruit of the invasion of living divine reality, a change in the very nature of one's being. It is not that God ignores the mind. Ames also spoke about "moral perswasions" being involved in our "calling."[41] But the change in the will is the core of conversion.

Baxter took a quite different approach and was critical of any portraying of converting grace as "physical regeneration," rather than as "moral suasion." He deplored those who "talk of God's work of grace in the soul, as if there were no more in it very honourable than a physical Motion, and God converted souls as Boys whip their Tops, or Women turn their Wheels." Then he went on to characterize those divines as "Cartesian blind

---

[36]Jenison, *Concerning Gods Certaine Performance*, pp. 132–33.
[37]Harris, *New Covenant*, 2:111–12.
[38]Jenison, *Concerning Gods Certaine Performance*, p. 133.
[39]Ball, *Covenant of Grace*, p. 324.
[40]Ames, *Marrow*, pp. 112–13.
[41]Ames, *Analytical Exposition of Peter*, p. 163.

Theologues . . . fitter mechanically to treat or deal with Stones, or Bricks, or Timber, than Men, being unfit to treat of humane Government, much more of Divine."[42] The "Cartesian" designation is revealing, for it is indicative of a basis for Baxter's immense hostility. The metaphysical context of Baxter's thought was drawn from Descartes for whom there were two types of substance, thinking and non-thinking, and two corresponding types of causation, moral and physical. Since Baxter interpreted these as mutually exclusive of one another, he became convinced that those who spoke for "physical regeneration" of the will necessarily ruled out moral causation, thereby implying that God did not treat the human person in conversion as a living, thinking subject. Orthodox divines were unable to persuade Baxter that this was an improper opposition of what were in their judgment two complementary forms of causation, persuasion by the Spirit through the Word and the direct implanting in the will of the spiritual capacity to respond in faith and obedience. His continued insistence was that if the influence were "physical," then it could not be "persuasive," but it is the latter that characterizes God's saving work with human persons. God gives high honor to human consent, and this means divine appeal to the mind and the conscience in the conversion process.

At this point, however, Baxter differed from other theologians who likewise urged the importance of "moral suasion," in that he rejected both the "intellectualism" commonly involved and any necessitarianism that might be implied. A major example of such unacceptable outlook is found in the position of John Cameron at Saumur, subsequently also adopted by Moses Amyraut—and this rejection was despite the fact that Baxter agreed in other fundamental respects with the Salmurian theology. In Amyraut's view human nature is such that the will invariably follows the lead of the intellect, as the intellect presents to the will what it deems to be good. Sin, however, has darkened the mind, confusing its understanding of the good and leading to life's evil. God's work of conversion, then, comes through the illumination of the intellect by the Holy Spirit so that it can see clearly the truth of the Gospel and its proffered benefits. This illumination, moreover, is an act of God's sovereignty and cannot be resisted. The mind is led necessarily to this truth, which the will then obediently embraces. For Baxter, however, the will has greater independence, and "moral suasion" must call forth its free acts. He objected to the will's being coerced by the mind and to both being coerced by God. By affirming that God gives differing degrees of grace and by denying that every person always has sufficient grace, Baxter was able to reject the charge of Arminianism raised against him. But "moral suasion" freely responded to was central for his thought, as he urged that the Spirit

---

[42]Richard Baxter, *Catholick Theologie.* Quoted in Packer, *Redemption and Restoration*, p. 386.

acts by "exciting and using reason and conscience, as the instruments to persuade the will."[43]

Generally speaking, however, views of "moral suasion" were so formulated as to include a more prominent role for the intellect, even as they were also held in combination with affirmation of the will's "physical regeneration." Both Ames' and Baxter's voluntarisms, though differing from each other in relation to God's work of conversion, were themselves uncharacteristic of the prevailing Puritan conception of human nature. Orthodoxy by and large found a more significant place for the intellect and correspondingly for the mind's enlightenment in the conversion process. Ball said that in producing faith "first God bestoweth upon man the gift of understanding and spirituall wisdome, opening and illuminating the eyes of his minde, to know the promise of Christ . . . [for] this understanding is requisite to faith."[44] He later elaborated on this less prosaically by adding that "Christ doth make love to us, and by many faire, sweet and precious promises doth allure and intice us to embrace him."[45] Burgess noted even more the role of "reason or judgement," saying that "although man hath lost that rectitude in his will and mind, yet he hath not lost the faculties themselves." Though one be "dead" spiritually and in need of the "potent work" of conversion, one is still sufficiently "alive" in the process "to be wrought upon by arguments."[46]

This emphasis on moral suasion is most frequently combined, however, with a declaration of God's recreating act, and mind and will are brought jointly under the renewing influence of divine love. Preston's detailed analysis of conversion presents somewhat elaborately one form of this view. Four stages are identified. First, there is God's regeneration of the will, the infusion of "a habit or qualitie of holinesse, renewing it, and making it, of evill good, of unwilling willing." Second, out of this infused holiness there arise "certaine imperfect inclinations . . . to those good workes which please God." But since they lack completeness, they may be called, "not so much willings, as wishings and wouldings." Third, these inclinations are then presented to the understanding "which weighs them, debates them . . . and at length, when it hath . . . confirmed them, propounds them to the will to be chosen," a process in which the understanding itself is "enlightened by Divine Grace." Finally, "doth the Will put forth a compleat and effectuall willingnesse, from which conversion immediately doth follow." Or rather, he added, "that very willing is the conversion of a man unto God."[47] God's

[43]Richard Baxter, *Catholick Theologie*. Quotred in Packer, *Redemption and Restoration*, p. 385.

[44]Ball, *Treatise of Faith*, p. 10.

[45]Ibid., p. 156.

[46]Burgess, *Vindiciae Legis*, p. 92.

[47]Preston, *Irresistibleness of Converting Grace*, pp. 5–6.

actions touch both mind and will, and one is first turned toward God by the gift of enlightennment as well as by the gift of a new creation.

One further factor to be noted in this Puritan interpretation of conversion is that the actions of God within it cannot be rejected. Conversion, in its divine dimension, is a work of irresistible grace. To say that such grace could be resisted, declared Ball, would be "to put grace in mans power, not to put mans will under the power of grace." It would also frustrate Gods counsell ... and make God a lyar in that which he hath sworne touching the gathering of his people."[48] So the doctrine of irresistibility became guarantor of God's sovereignty and an essential for the execution of the decrees of election. This, too, was established at Dort as one of the "five points" of Calvinism, and English and American Puritans, like Dutch Reformed, found it to be an important weapon in the continuing conflict with Arminianism.

But Puritans were careful to prevent this doctrine from destroying that liberty which exists in Christian conversion and subsequent life under God. Perkins made a philosophical distinction between two types of necessity, that of "compulsion," which does constrain, and that of "infallibility," which does not. In the exercise of the latter that which is necessitated will "immutably come to passe," but this kind of necessity retains the "contingency and liberty of second causes." So "that which is free worketh freely ... by the necessary decree of God."[49] Preston's theological position likewise portrayed freedom co-existing with irresistibility in the culminating stage of conversion's process. There the will assents to the original "physical motion proceeding from God" and also "to the perswasion of the Understanding approving of it." In so doing it partakes of the two essential characteristics of liberty, that of being active rather than passive, and that of flowing "from a reasonable perswasion." So the conclusion was reached that the irresistible grace of conversion is received in an act that is free.[50] Or somewhat more directly Baynes simply stated, "God's call is unresistible. ... It is ... an over-mastering grace. ... Not that God doth force the will, but by a habite of grace maketh it willing, and by light in the understanding maketh it determine it selfe in following Him."[51] God's sovereign grace in conversion, so these Puritans maintained, does not violate the human person, but so enhances that life as to coexist in it with its living center, human freedom.

THE AGENTS OF CONTINUING CHRISTIAN LIFE

The spiritual life begun in "calling" continues for the Christian in "justification" and "sanctification." As further components in the *ordo*

[48]Ball, *Covenant of Grace*, p. 341.
[49]Perkins, "Manner of Predestination," *Works*, 2:619.
[50]Preston, *Irresistibleness of Converting Grace,*, p. 10.
[51]Baynes, *Commentarie upon Colossians*, p. 269.

salutis, these constitute the additional major stages along life's way and, in the mutuality of the covenant relationship, are contingent upon the fulfillment of conditions. Justification is received in faith, and sanctification continues only by obedience. From the conditional perspective, covenant completion involves the presence of these two qualities of spiritual and moral life, and it is proper, therefore, to be encouraged to faith and exhorted to obedience. The meeting of these covenant expectations is a human responsibility. Yet the covenant is also absolute, and within it God gives what the covenant asks. Faith and obedience, though human acts, are then likewise to be understood as divine gifts. So the question of "agency" must be explored as well in these elements of continuing Christian life.

In general Puritan divines affirmed a dual agency in these matters, seeing a "co-working" between God's action and the renewed human will. There was clearly no disposition to remove God from further participation in the pilgrim's progress. On the contrary, life must be lived constantly in reliance upon grace. Perkins dealt with the question, "whether the will, after it is renewed, be able to cause and bring forth good workes of it selfe," and his negative response went on to elaborate further forms of God's working. There is "assisting grace" by which God continues to maintain the will's renewal, aids it in following its good inclinations, and protects it in the face of temptation. There is also "exciting grace" by which God "mooves and stirres up the will, that it may indeede will and doe the good to be done." Perkins noted that such "grace in the will is like the fire of greene wood, which hardly burnes, and continues not to burne unlesse it be continually stirred up and blowed: even so the good inclination of the wil, because it is . . . mixed with contrary corruption . . . hath need continually to be excited, stirred, and mooved."[52] And this, then, is a "doing" grace, not simply an assisting grace.[53] In the grace of continued Christian life God remains agent as well as aid. At another point Perkins analyzed divine grace in terms of operating action and envisaged three forms or phases. Preventing grace, which is the grace of conversion, gives the power for good action; working grace, which follows, gives the will for such action; and co-working grace then gives the deed.[54] In all good works God is at work, a "doer" in the faith and obedience of a renewed people.

[52]Perkins, "Gods Free-grace and Mans free-will," *Works*, 1:737–38.

[53]Richard Greaves speaks of the "difference between divine grace which effectually moves man to faith and repentance, and divine grace which enables the individual to repent and believe." Attributing the former view to Bunyan and the latter to Preston, he then sees this distinction as a further part of the contrast between the Calvinist and the Zwingli-Tyndale tradition. It is the position of this present study, however, that the "enabling" and the "doing" aspects of grace cannot really be allocated in that way. They are both part of the total configuration making up this Puritan understanding. The "doing" grace is found in "moderate" as well as in "strict" Calvinists. For Greaves' discussion see his article, "Origins and Early Development," pp. 22–23.

[54]Perkins, "Gods Free-grace and Mans free-will," *Works*, 1:736–37.

At the same time, however, there was no disposition to downgrade the human and to view Christian faithfulness as essentially the work of the divine Spirit. The human person also is worker, that is, co-worker with God. When Perkins discussed the "doing" aspects of grace, he likewise presented them in relation to the human will. In the receipt of the first grace, the grace that precedes (or "prevents"), the will is passive, though, as noted earlier, of unwilling it is made willing. This is the grace of conversion and renewal. But then, in the "working" and "co-working" graces of Christian life that follow the renewed will is a concurring partner so that, as Perkins put it, "the will to obey God, or to performe any like duty, proceedes joyntly from two causes." These are: "From grace [and] . . . from the will of man."[55] Burgess noted that when grace is received it is not "as when the seale imprints a stamp upon the wax . . . where the subject recipient doth not move." Rather, "we are the subject, who . . . enabled by grace, doe work; . . . to beleeve, and to turne unto God, are our acts."[56] So the fulfillment of the covenant conditions is also a human possibility and responsibility. The human person likewise is to be a "doer" in the bringing forth of faith and obedience.[57]

Looking now specifically at the covenant condition of faith, it is apparent that this duality of agency is very broadly affirmed. First, faith is worked in the believer by God and is granted as a gift. Indeed, even prior to the believer's act of faith by which justification is received, there is the still more basic "habit" of faith which God bestows. The act of believing must come out of a soil that can produce it, and that can exist only through the unconditioned regenerating work of God. One may be called upon in the act of faith to believe the promise of the new heart. But Rutherfurd noted that such believing is possible only if the new heart is already given, a part of which is the "habituall faith" from which "actuall faith" then flows.[58] Baynes was led to similar considerations when dealing with the question, "How can wee receive the Spirit by faith, when wee cannot believe before wee have the spirit?" The response must be that even before we believe we do have the spirit, that is, the spirit of faith as a "supernaturall habit dwelling in us" and that the receiving of the spirit through believing is its fuller reception and manifestation.[59] Thus God's renewing and restoring must lie at the very

---

[55]Ibid., p. 737.

[56]Burgess, *Vindiciae Legis*, p. 97.

[57]Stoever writes, "The relation between divine sovereignty and the liberty of second causes, as expressed in the covenant doctrine, was fraught with tension. At the same time . . . a significant dialectical balance was achieved in it between divine and human autonomy." *'A Faire and Easie Way to Heaven'*, p. 115.

[58]Rutherfurd, *Covenant of Life*, p. 233.

[59]Baynes, *Commentary Upon Ephesians*, pp.115–16. See also Baynes, *Helpe to true Happinesse*, p. 213.

root of what becomes the believer's believing. Ball wrote simply that "no man can believe, unless he be created and formed anew."[60]

It is, however, actual faith, not habitual faith, that justifies. But here, too, God works and gives. Faith comes by hearing, and hearing is of preaching, and preaching presents the Word. Yet, said John Rogers, "wee must know it is not the outward ministery of the Word only, that is able to worke Faith. . . . It is neither the Ministers gifts, nor the peoples aptnesse . . . but the worke of Gods Spirit."[61] When Ames discussed in the *Marrow* the "receiving of Christ" as the appropriation of a new relationship with God, he saw it as a "passive receiving" and an "active receiving." The former is the inner conversion of the will by grace, whereas the latter involves the believer's turning to and relying upon Christ in an act of faith. But this latter act itself, so Ames wrote, "doth depend partly upon a principle or habit of grace ingenerated, and partly upon the operation of God moving before and stirring up." It is thus, whatever else, a divine act, "wherewith the will is turned to the having of the true good."[62] Ball spoke of justifying faith as a "gift of grace . . . wrought by the Holy Ghost." "The Spirit of God," he said, "is the principall worker of faith," adding that such work is done "by his powerfull operation and omnipotent hand," as "hee produceth this gracious effect."[63] And Bulkeley expressed a similar conviction when he wrote, "There is required an almighty power to work faith in us, which is done by no lesse power then that which raised Christ from the dead."[64]

Joined with this conviction, however, was the firm assertion of the role of the renewed will in the act of believing. Faith may be divinely given, but it is likewise humanly expressed. The human person is called upon to believe. There is no final proxy relationship to God which excuses one from responding in one's personal act of trust. "It is man that beleeveth," wrote Ball, even as he also added that it is God "that enableth, stirreth up, putteth forward, and enclineth the heart to believe."[65] Bulkeley found obligation to believe in the very fact of God's gift of the habit of faith: "The habit is freely given us, and wrought in us by the Lord himselfe, to enable us to act by it, . . . and then we having received the gift, the habit, . . . the Lord requires of us that we should put forth acts of faith."[66] Such acts are necessary for the

[60]Ball, *Treatise of Faith*, p. 7.

[61]J. Rogers. *Doctrine of Faith*, pp. 60–61.

[62]Ames, *Marrow*, p 113.

[63]Ball, *Treatise of Faith*, pp. 6–9. See also Ball, *Covenant of Grace*, p. 19. Here he is speaking of justifying faith as a condition of the covenant of grace, thus as an "instrument" of the soul, and says, "It is wrought therein by the Holy Ghost, and is the free gift of God." This would be another instance of a "moderate" Calvinist affirming a "doing" grace.

[64]Bulkeley, *Gospel-Covenant*, p. 363.

[65]Ball, *Treatise of Faith*, p. 11.

[66]Bulkeley, *Gospel-Covenant*, p. 332.

fulfillment of covenant conditions even though God's grace lies behind all, for, said Harris, "when he acts us, we must move; when he opens our eyes, we must see; in fine, concurre as subjects."[67] Participation as a believer can in no way be an act that is not one's own.

Thus there is a twofold agency in the fulfillment of the covenant condition of faith. Blake spoke of it as a work in which, because of the divine-human concurrence, "neither God nor man are sole efficients," with efficiency being contributed to by each.[68] Indeed, Resbury averred, one can actually attribute the whole effect to each, finding an analogy in instruction in writing, for when "the teacher guides the learners hand, they both write the whole."[69] Sibbes' analogy, in his attempt to relate these two sources of faith, presented it as "a spiritual echo, returning that voice back again which God first speaks to the soul."[70] In varying ways, therefore, Puritan thought attempted to portray this critical element in the divine-human relationship as itself emerging from actions both human and divine.

In like manner the Christian's continued obedience was understood to be both divine and human act. The sustaining of covenant relationship with God throughout the course of the Christian's journey requires dedication and faithfulness. "Covenant making" must find its fulfillment in "covenant keeping." Incorporation through faith into the covenant of grace is no license for indifference or infidelity. The very nature of sanctification is sensitivity and commitment to God's Law. This is "evangelical repentance," a continued turning about in one's life so that evil may be resisted and good accomplished. One's faith must be a living faith. "Good works" are marks of the advancing Christian. There is a "holy conspiracy," of which one needs increasingly to be a part, to serve God, church and commonwealth. The believer's life must be "obediential." And yet, said Blake, "our dexterity in holy duties" comes from sources divine as well as human.[71] Ball noted that repentance is "the gift of God, but the act of man."[72]

"When the Lampe is once lighted," wrote Preston, "you know you may feede it with Oyle, and if you put more Oyle to it, you shall have greater flame." Thus with one's life, God "kindles the first fire … But now, when thou hast it, learne to use it … use the Talent of Faith."[73] Such exhortation urges diligence in devotion to Christian duty. The presupposition, of course, is regeneration. This is not an appeal to natural ability. The lamp has been lighted. Reflected here particularly is what Perkins designated the third liberty of the renewed will. The first two are shared by all, the "liberty of

[67]Harris, *New Covenant*, 1:48.
[68]Blake, *Vindicae Foederis*, p. 127.
[69]Resbury, *Lightless-Starre*, p. 180.
[70]Sibbes, "Soul's Conflict," *Works*, 1:263.
[71]Blake, *Vindiciae Foederis*, p. 145.
[72]Ball, *Covenant of Grace*, pp. 344, 350.
[73]Preston, *Breast-Plate of Faith and Love*, 2:139.

nature" which is the capacity to will or nill and the "liberty of sinne" which is the choosing of sin freely. The third, however, the "liberty of grace," is the gift to those whom God has renewed and constitutes the capacity to will well.[74] Preston called it "a certaine free will to do good," and as a capacity for new life it must be so stirred up and employed that "in time it is quickened unto every Christian duty."[75] So the obligation rests upon the "gifted" to exercise the gift. God and neighbor must be served, the Law of God obeyed. This is to be voluntary action, for the will has been freed to act without constraint. Here is a genuine human agency at work in the Christian's life of sanctification. When Perkins discussed this obedience under the heading of "evangelical repentance" he noted that it is found when we, having been turned by God, "doe turne our selves and doe good workes."[76]

But such working cannot be effective without continued divine aid. The "reliques" of corruption remain, and beyond that the tasks are so immense and the obstacles so great. For even the "natural" actions of life the sustaining power of God is needed, so how much more is God's special help required for these "supernatural" duties. Perkins found an analogy: "A childe that can goe up and downe in an even floore, being staid by the mothers hand, for al this cannot go up a paire of staires, unlesse it be lifted up at every steppe. Like is the case of the children of God in things which concern the Kingdome of heaven."[77] Three stages of Christian experience were identified by Plaifere. In the first, one is a "meere Patient." In the second, one is a "willing Patient." And in the third, one is a "helped Agent," saying "lift me and I will rise; stay me and I will stand; draw me and I will come to you."[78] So though there is preventing grace with which conversion occurs and one's Christian journey begins, the continued aid of a concurring grace is likewise essential and also given. Caryl observed, "Conversion doth not begin at us, nor is it ended by us. They who have a stock of grace, cannot trade with it, or improve it without Christs co-partnership."[79]

Yet Puritan depiction of the divine role in human obedience showed a still further dimension. The language of assistance was supplanted by one of more complete action, the vocabulary of cooperation by one suggesting greater divine initiative and preeminence in the act of human faithfulness. As is the case generally in Puritan understanding of the nature of God's relation to Christian experience, so also here, God is agent as well as aid. "God works" is the common phrase, and it reflects the belief that beyond being "helper" God is also "doer." "God works all things in us," wrote

[74]Perkins, "Gods Free-grace and Mans free-will," *Works*, 1:736.
[75]Preston, *Saints Qualification*, 2:20.
[76]Perkins, "Reformed Catholike," *Works*, 1:614.
[77]Perkins, "Gods Free-grace and Mans free-will," *Works*, 1:738.
[78]Plaifere, *Appello Evangelium*, p. 256.
[79]Caryl, *Heaven and Earth Embracing*, pp. 2–3.

Harris.[80] "God workes in us ... and uses us in the worke," said Preston.[81] "God worketh our deeds," declared Baynes.[82] And when he discussed perseverance in human obedience and faithfulness, Jenison wrote that God "works it; beginning and perfecting his owne worke."[83] The divine agency in the works of human obedience is also one of "doing the deed." Harris defended this affirmation on the ground that such final decisiveness is essential if truly the deed is to be done. If there is no such finality of divine action, then it still is that "mans will is the principall cause of his good, not grace." Under such a conception grace "onely sets the scales upright, the will swayes them." One must affirm that "the covenant is for act too." God's covenant promising is not only based upon conditions, but also carries a guarantee of completion. Thus, Harris wrote, "not onely the power, but the act too is from God."[84] Rutherfurd, who was reluctant in general to approve anything that would diminish divine sovereignty, found that even in this balance of human and divine act in sanctification's obedience the larger weight should go to the latter. "We are more (as it were) patients," he wrote, "in obeying Gospel-Commands." Yet this did not mean "meer patients," but still "in Gospel-obedience we offer more of the Lords own, and lesse of our own."[85]

On the whole, however, when God's doing was emphasized, it was recognized that the divine agency worked through the human agency and that their working was therefore one of concurrence. God's actions are in no way pictured as disregardful of the human subjects, with their capacities and characteristics of personal life, through whom these actions occur. If one emphasis is that "God works in us," a second immediately follows: "God works by us." What this means, Harris noted, is that God "workes not in us as brute instruments." Rather, as God works by us, "he acts us and then we worke under God." Moreover, to be aware of this fact of God's working does not lessen incentives for co-working, but "quickens our care and endeavor, ... therefore we must worke out all, because we depend upon God for all."[86]

Consequently even the languages of divine gift and human labor are easily combined. The two agencies being in concert means that the two vocabularies can also merge into one another as they jointly identify this common work. When Cole discussed sanctification, for instance, he portrayed it as "the renewing of man ... by which he being purged and cleansed ... doth cleanse himself more and more ... [It is] the committing

---

[80]Harris, *New Covenant*, 2:116.
[81]Preston, *Saints Qualification*, p. 459.
[82]Baynes, *Commentarie upon Colossians*, 2:216.
[83]Jenison, *Concerning Gods Certaine Performance*, p. 76.
[84]Harris, *New Covenant*, 2:114.
[85]Rutherfurd, *Covenant of Life*, pp. 198–99.
[86]Harris, *New Covenant*, 2:116–17

of our waies to God … [which] no man can do of himselfe, but it is the speciall worke of God."[87] And Sibbes more explicitly explained, "This is grace, when thy will is made active and able to do things that now the things done by God's grace are attributed to men."[88] God's work and human work go together in the Christian's obedience. Perkins summarized by saying, "there is no vertue or gift of God in us, without our wills: and in every good act, Gods grace and mans will, concurre: Gods grace as the principall cause; mans will renewed, as the instrument of God."[89]

[87]Cole, *Godly Mans Assurance*, p. 33.
[88]Sibbes, "Pattern of Purity," *Works*, 7:510.
[89]Perkins, "Gods Free-grace and Mans free-will," *Works*, 1:738.

Chapter 7

COVENANT AND ASSURANCE

One interpreter of Puritan spirituality, in comparing it to the Wesleyan revival of a century later, has written, "Election to the Puritan Preachers was what assurance was to the Methodist Preachers," an affirmation in support of his basic claim that the Puritan preachers "do not use the word 'assurance' overmuch."[1] This statement can be seriously questioned on two grounds. First, election and assurance are not so easily separated from one another. Election is God's act, an objective occurrence in divine, and ultimately human, history. Assurance is a psychological state, a subjective awareness of that which relates to human experience and destiny. Thus election is not a substitute for assurance, for in the optimum sense assurance is of one's election. Second, the Puritan preachers did use the term "assurance" a good deal, and a primary concern of their pastoral ministry was the generation of this confidence in the mind of the believer. Theological analysis was also extensively employed to provide ground on which practical certainty could be based. When one approaches the subject of assurance, therefore, one is dealing with a portion of the Puritan outlook central to both the psychology and the theology of these divines. Thomas Blake said, "To gather up assurance from the conditions of the covenant is ... the highest pitch of Christianity."[2]

THE GOAL OF ASSURANCE

A first matter to be noted is the Puritan conviction that assurance of salvation is possible, a claim often made in explicit contrast to Roman Catholic tentativeness on this issue. The Council of Trent declared:

> Let no one promise himself anything as certain as absolute certainty. . . . let those who think they stand, take heed lest they fall, and with fear and trembling work out their salvation, in labours, in watchings, in almsgiving, in prayers and oblations, in fastings and in chastity.[3]

---

[1]I. Morgan, *Puritan Spirituality*, p. 26.

[2]Blake, *Vindiciae Foederis*, p. 197.

[3]Buckley, Theodore Alios, trans., *Canons and Decrees of the Council of Trent* (London: G. Routledge and Co., 1851), pp. 38–39. The reference is to Session 6, Chapter 13.

The certainty of salvation, Roman thought had maintained, could come therefore only as result of a special revelation to a given individual that the necessary virtues would indeed prevail. But Puritan divines would not put assurance into such a special category, or condition it upon a life of merit. Salvation is not based upon almsgiving, fasting or chastity. Rather, it is a sheer gift of God, and as such it can be known. This assurance is as much a part of the spiritual life as are other types of certainty a part of the life of nature. Baynes noted that "the young know their dams, as every Lambe knoweth its owne Ewe" and then went on to ask if God should "beget children which in ordinary course cannot know and acknowledge him who hath begotten them."[4] His answer was that they can and do so acknowledge and that assurance of God's parental and loving favor is thus possible. Perkins expressed this supreme confidence when, in a dialogue between Christian and Satan, he had the former saying, "Methinks I am as certaine of my salvation, as though my name were registred in the scriptures (as Davids and Pauls are) to be an elect vessell of God."[5]

In short, the Christian believer is to seek after assurance. If there are some, said John Rogers, who think that it is impossible to be assured of salvation and never go about seeking it, this is simply because of "their owne wretched lazinesse."[6] In the life of the secular world there is much effort expended to gain security and certainty. The "children of the world," for example, will not allow ambiguity with respect to "their possession of lands and leases." They will have all of this "under seal" and recorded "in white and blacke." So, asked Dent, "Shall not wee bee as wise in matters of tenne thousand times more importance? Shall wee hold the state of an immortal inheritance by hope well; and have no ... evidences, no seal?" That, he said, would be a "weake Tenure" indeed.[7] Thus the Christian ought earnestly to seek assurance. Sibbes felt that "we [should] ... never rest therefore till we can prove ourselves to be in the covenant of grace, till we can say, God is my God."[8]

It is not that this assurance is absolutely necessary for the life of the believer. The faith of assurance must never be confused with the faith of adherence. Participation in the covenant and sharing in its gifts of new relationship and new life are not dependent upon psychological certainty. There may well be faith and God's acceptance without an overpowering sense of it. Also assurance, when it is obtained, need not be complete. Harris said, "There be Christians of all ages and of all sizes in Gods family," meaning that "all Gods children have some assurance, though all have not

---

[4]Baynes, *Commentarie upon Colossians*, 2:70.
[5]Perkins, "Estate of Damnation," *Works*, 1:406.
[6]J. Rogers, *Doctrine of Faith*, p. 388.
[7]Dent, *Plaine Mans Path-way*, p. 238.
[8]Sibbes, "Faithful Covenanter," *Works*, 6:15.

alike."[9] Variety can exist in the strength of assurance as known and experienced by different Christians, a matter of degree in which "doubting is more or lesse excluded."[10] But if assurance is not necessary for the being, it is valuable for the well being, of a believer.[11] Assurance provides the anxious heart with the confidence of one's truly being granted the grace of God.

At least a mild demurrer was heard from Richard Baxter. It is not that he rejected the value of assurance, for he recognized this and the importance of the self-examination by which it might be gained. The question, rather, was one of balance, for, he said, "be sure that the first, and far greater part of your time, pains, and care, and inquiries, be for the getting and increasing of your grace, than for the discerning it; to perform your duty rightly, than to discern your right performance. And when you confer with ministers . . . see that you ask ten times at least, How should I get or increase my faith, my love to Christ, and to his people? for once that you ask, How shall I know that I believe or love?"[12]

An extension of the question, as also posed by others, was whether assurance itself might not lead to moral indifference and carelessness, even to presumption. But the divines had their reply. It is not presumption to be persuaded of one's salvation, for "the ground of this perswasion is not laid in our selves," but only in the righteousness of Christ and the promises of God.[13] Assurance actually, rather than discouraging moral obedience, is an incentive to it. George Downame believed that "the more a man is perswaded or assured of Gods eternall love towards him, the more fervently he will love the Lord, and carefully obey him, . . . the more readily, when he hath offended, will he returne unto him."[14] And Ball declared that "he who is best assured hath most power of Gods Spirit, and the stronger the Spirit of God is within, the more holinesse and fruits and grace without."[15] Thus, on the whole, it was held that "the doctrine of assurance . . . is no dangerous doctrine to make men secure and presumptious in sinning."[16]

The seeking of assurance, therefore, is not only possible, but desirable, and is strongly to be encouraged for the believer. As the Scripture enjoins the making of one's calling and election sure, the Christian pilgrim should be urged to seek out this support and stay for the progress of life's spiritual journey. William Whately even suggested that resistance to any such effort could itself have alarming implications, for "the unwillingnesse to enter into

[9]Harris, *Way to True Happinesse*, 2:51.

[10]Baynes, *Helpe to true Happinesse*, pp. 191–92.

[11]Downe, *Definition of Justifying Faith*, p. 69.

[12]Richard Baxter, *Catholick Theologie*, 9:138–39. Quoted in Packer, *Redemption and Restoration*, p.401.

[13]Dent, *Plaine Mans Path-way*, p. 244.

[14]G. Downame, *Certainty of Perseverance*, p. 410.

[15]Ball, *Treatise of Faith*, p. 278.

[16]Thomas Goodwin, *Works*, 3:417. Quoted in McKee, *Idea of Covenant*, p. 141.

this inquisition giveth occasion of vehement suspition that one is not regenerated."[17] But whether such conclusion might be justified or not, here was both opportunity and obligation. The results of the seeking will vary, for cirucmstances are many and spiritual conditions are diverse. But for every Christian the search should be for the faith of assurance, as well as for the faith of adherence. Perkins wrote, "We doe not teach that all and every man living within the precincts of the Church, professing the name of Christ, is certain of his salvation, . . . but that he ought to be, and must indeavour to ataine thereto."[18]

We enter here into the more introspective world of the Puritan. "Assurance" had been a matter of concern from the outset of the Reformed tradition, and consistently its possibility had been declared. With Calvin, however, the basis was more objective and external. "We have a sufficiently clear and firm testimony that we have been inscribed in the book of life," he wrote, "if we are in communion with Christ."[19] Self-examination is to be eschewed in determining that state of communion. Rather, it is to be found in one's incorporation into the Christian community, particularly in one's confessing its faith and receiving its sacraments. With Calvin's Puritan successors, however, the subjective and the introspective occupy a larger place. Here the soul is to be searched and experience is to be examined. If God's grace has been received and one stands in God's favor, there will be evidence for that in one's heart and in one's life. Thus a theology of salvation availed itself generously of the realm of private experience in order to mark out the way to certainty and comfort. Such probing might at times seem excessive. When John Owen, dean of Christ Church, Oxford in the mid-seventeenth century, held sessions exploring the testimonies of the conscience, his meetings were irreverently referred to by students as the "scruple shop."[20] But careful and penetrating self-examination was to be utilized to determine the state of one's soul.

Nathanael Cole put this somewhat graphically by writing that there are two ways to seek assurance. The first is *ascendendo*, that is, "by climbing up to heaven, there to whisper God, as it were, in the eare, and to ask his secret counsell." But it is "a vaine and dangerous curiositie" so to explore that which is hidden in God. The second and more profitable way is *descendendo*, that is, "by [one's] descending into his own hart, . . . trying and examining himself how he standeth in the grace and favor of God, . . . how hee hath used the meanes of salvation."[21] There were other ways also. The Puritan divines never relinquished the comfort that could come simply

[17]Whately, *New Birth*, p. 101.
[18]Perkins, "Reformed Catholike," *Works*, 1:606.
[19]Calvin, *Institutes*, 2:970.
[20]Sprunger, *Learned Doctor William Ames*, p. 163.
[21]Cole, *Godly Mans Assurance*, "To the Christian Reader."

through reliance on the promises of the Word. Ezekiel Culverwell's "two-fold certaintie" recognized this in advocating the "certainty which comes by Faith alone, the onely stay whereof is Gods word." But there is further the "certaintie of Sense,"[22] and by and large this occupied a preeminent position in Puritan psychology. Forbes knew the Word to be an experienced Word. In portraying his understanding of "the order of God's working," he noted that (1) God "speakes the word of trueth to the heart," (2) makes the heart "to beleeve that which it hath heard and receyved," and (3) adds "his spirit: and by the testimonie thereof . . . makes Adoption and eternall life, most certaine and sure to the soule."[23] So it is not only proper, but needful, to probe penetratingly within. Perkins found "the power and pith of true religion" to be present "when a man by observation and experience in himself, knowes the love of God in Christ towards him."[24]

ASSURANCE THROUGH EVIDENCES

The examination of one's life for evidences of God's favor must, first of all, be properly directed. Even as true grounds are to be searched into, false grounds are to be avoided, not the least of which is the outward character of one's personal estate. There are such matters as health, long life, and material prosperity, and it would be easy for the established and the prosperous to argue for the presence of God's favor on the basis of these blessings. Centuries later, it is worthy of note, that very effort was attributed to Puritanism, and indeed to all of Calvinism, in a widely held theory seeing prosperity affirmed as the evidence of election and such effort stimulated thereby toward the gaining of prosperity as to lead in the economic order to the establishment of capitalism.[25] Such a view, however, was in no way characteristic of Calvin, nor of the Puritan divines we are examining. Though this pragmatism eventually emerged to some degree in the interpretation of providence, it is not the outlook of Puritanism in its prime. Robert Bolton saw one's "arguing Gods speciall love and saving favor, from his outward prosperous state" to be one of those false approaches to assurance which cast one "into a pleasing golden dreame of imaginary spirituall safetie, and Self-deceit."[26] And Harris noted of life's material possessions that "these are things that God gives many times to his enemies," as well as to those who are specially loved, and besides, "heaven is not made up of gold and silver, and

---

[22]Culverwell, *Treatise of Faith*, p. 161.

[23]Forbes, *A Letter*, p. 37.

[24]Perkins, "Christs Sermon in the Mount," *Works*, 3:149.

[25]This is the so-called Weber-Tawney thesis. It was first developed in Max Weber, *The Protestant Ethic and the Spirit of Capitalism* (1904) and then was revised and elaborated in Richard H. Tawney, *Religion and the Rise of Capitalism* (1926).

[26]R. Bolton, *Comfortable Walking with God*, p. 299.

such like gawdes."[27] Not the goods of the world, but the goods of the spirit, reveal God's grace and favor.

Yet one must also be probing and perceptive in that realm of the spirit, searching beneath the surface for the signs of God's gracious working. Although avoidance of gross sin is a Christian's expectation, it is inadequate to identify one's moral condition simply by comparing oneself "with others who are Satans outragious revellers,"[28] nor is it sufficient to claim "God blesseth me . . . with good life; for I am neither whore nor theefe."[29] Rather, the search must be more substantial and the evidences more profound. One place to look is within the *ordo salutis* itself. The Christian pilgrimage in spiritual and moral life is under the direction, yes even under the agency, of God. Therefore its stages can be explored, its gifts searched out. And within the journey the blessings from God are so joined one with another that evidence of one is evidence for all. Perkins characterized "election, vocation, faith, adoption, justification, sanctification, and eternall glorification" as "inseparable companions," which "goe hand in hand," claiming that "he that can be assured on one of them may infallibly conclude in his owne heart, that he hath and shall have interest in all the others."[30]

Among them, however, the most readily accessible would seem to be the power and the actions of a Christian's new life. Thus, though sanctification "be the last in nature and next unto salvation itself, . . . yet when we are to gather assurance of our election, we are . . . to begin where the Lord endeth, and so ascend from the lowest degree till wee come to the highest."[31] One argument, it is true, turned this significance of sanctification into an opposite, and negative, direction, pointing out that, though for some it can be a false evidence since the power of godliness may at times seem to be present when in fact it is not, yet its absence would be indication of God's rejection. The author of the modern *Marrow* found his analogy: "though all be not Gold that glistereth, yet all Gold doth glister."[32] But the power to distinguish between true and false glister was more generally acknowledged, and sanctification could therefore be truly identified as a sign of God's favor. So one can climb "Jacob's ladder" by beginning with the bottom rung of sanctification, moving then upward to the assurance of other benefits.[33] Bulkeley wrote, "Sanctification is a blessing of the Covenant of grace, even as forgiveness is, therefore it is a warrantable and safe way for a man by and from his sanctification to take an evidence of his justification, and

[27]Harris, *Way to True Happinesse*, 2:59.
[28]R. Bolton, *Comfortable Walking with God*, p. 300.
[29]Harris, *Way to True Happinesse*, 2:59.
[30]Perkins, "Whole Treatise," *Works*, 2:18.
[31]J. Downame, *Christian Warfare*, p. 231.
[32]E. F. *Marrow*, p. 169
[33]G. Downame, *Covenant of Grace*, p. 39.

of his estate in Grace before God."[34] It was the conviction of Thomas Gouge that Christians must "prove their Mystical Union with Christ by their Moral Union."[35]

The moral union was at its heart internal. The sanctified life was the power of a new spirit, the strength of new affections, the guidance of a new direction. It was the reality of being caught up in a new compulsion, of being inwardly motivated by a new law and love. Thus the evidences of sanctification must themselves in part be found within. Sibbes said that "if we make God our God, we may know it by our obedience, specially by the obedience of the inward man." Particularly, he noted, the Christian "can performe the first and last commandments, which are the most spiritual commandments. He can make God his God in his affections . . . and he can be content not to have his lusts range and rage."[36] But in the whole sweep of inward attitudes and qualities, if they are conformed to Christ, the grace of God may be seen. The renewed life of the Christian is like a print or an impression which reveals the nature of the original, "for all Gods actions to us imprint their stamp in us." So it is, for example, with respect to the evidential value of our attitude of forgiveness: "wee feeling our selves readie to forgive, do come to know this more surely, that God's forgivenesse hath been applyed."[37]

One further important sign of this internal growth in grace was the presence of humility. It can be seen, said Harris, "especially if we grow downward, if wee grow in the roote, if we become more humble and low in our owne eyes . . . the more one growes in grace, the more hee growes out of himselfe."[38] It is not clear that the Puritan divines ever really faced up to the tension, if not conflict, between this type of declaration and their dutiful determination to search out such humility and other inner graces in order to make their calling and election sure. John Coolidge notes well the dilemma:

> The preacher appeals to an anxious self-interest to motivate an intense self-scrutiny, to which he promises the reward of assurance if it reveals a motive that is not self-centered. . . . It is like straining every nerve in an effort to relax—'labour to get humiliation,' Preston urges.[39]

But assurance was uncritically the goal, and the evidences of God's gracious, even humbling, presence must be sought out.

The inner attitudes of sanctification expressed themselves, however, in outer action. Thus the visible behavior itself of the Christian can likewise be

---

[34]Bulkeley, *Gospel-Covenant*, p. 252.

[35]Thomas Gouge, *The Principles of Christian Religion*, p. 110. Quoted in Kevan, *Grace of Law*, p. 208.

[36]Sibbes, "Faithful Covenanter," *Works*, 6:12.

[37]Baynes, *Treatise upon the Lords Prayer*, p. 113.

[38]Harris, *Way to True Happinesse*, 2:91.

[39]Coolidge, *Pauline Renaissance in England*, p. 132.

of evidential significance. There is the "practice of workes of justice, mercy and truth" which, Robert Bolton affirmed, "doth soundly comfort the heart of a man . . . about assurance of his happie state to Godward."[40] In a cataloging developed by Dent one of eight signs of salvation is "honest, just, and conscionable dealing in all our actions among men."[41] And when Ezekiel Culverwell reflected on human love being a proof of the presence of God's love, for "we love because he first loved us," he included in the former not only our love for God and for Christ, but also "our love we beare to one another, as brethren and members of the bodie of Christ"—and then he added, "Yea more, our Saviour teacheth that our love of our enemies is a good proofe that wee are children of God."[42] So, as Pemble said, "even as life is knowne by breathing, or beating of the Pulse, the trueth of an invisible Grace hath its demonstration in visible works."[43]

It is here, however, that the evidencing of grace by sanctification appeared most fallible and vulnerable. Must not one recognize the possibility of non-regenerate virtue and also the possibilities of hypocrisy which that would entail? Moral rectitude is not limited solely to Christian believers, and those who do not truly believe may therefore advance their virtue as a sign of God's favor. Since "all be not Gold that glistereth," the elect and the reprobate appear in many ways to be alike. But the Puritan divines were convinced that the distinction could be made. In broad terms it was held that the works of the hypocrite "are without the soule, life and spirit; which is in the work of a true beleever."[44] In more specific terms there was emphasis upon the presence of genuine and God-directed love as constituting the difference. So the hypocrite can do many things—in one listing there are even suffering martyrdom, giving all to the poor, and being "a very diligent Preacher of the Gospell"—yet "if these great workes be done, without love, they are nothing." And on the other side it is declared that "if you doe but the least worke, if it be but to give a cup of cold water, and doe it out of love," then "thou art on a sure ground, now thou maiest know thou art with the Covenant."[45]

But this drives the question still deeper: can one adequately identify the acts of love which are "Godward" and have their source in grace? The divines, once again, were convinced that this could be done. Baynes boldly claimed that "the love of a meer natural man to God, is as like Christian love, as an Apple is like an Oister,"[46] thus certainly suggesting a discernible basis for differentiation! Thomas Goodwin proposed somewhat more explicitly

[40]R. Bolton, *Comfortable Walking with God*, pp. 307–8.
[41]Dent, *Plaine Mans Path-way*, p. 30.
[42]Culverwell, *Treatise of Faith*, pp. 240–43.
[43]Pemble, *Vindiciae fidei*, p. 199.
[44]R. Bolton, *Comfortable Walking with God*, p. 326.
[45]Preston, *New Covenant*, 2:145–46.
[46]Baynes, *Commentarie Upon Ephesians*, p. 121.

the need for internal and subjective criteria by saying that the difference is to be found "more by tasting, and by feeling of it, than it is by setting of it forth; as it is in Wines."[47] Richard Baxter, who found genuine Christian love in much sustained and continued effort, was concerned that the distinction be maintained in pastoral practice, actually for the sake of the unregenerate, admonishing, "I would desire every Divine to beware that he tell not the unsanctified, that whoever hath the least degree of Love to God for himself . . . shall certainly be saved." This would be "to deceive many thousand miserable souls" who might be so persuaded.[48] There is a Christian love that can be identified and a sanctification that can be known. Other works, coming from an unbroken or an unregenerate heart, are like "glow-wormes" which "glister greatly in the darke, but when once the Sunne comes, their light is nothing."[49] The divines were confident that the true light could be recognized and the reality of one's sanctification discerned. And this would be certification of God's grace and favor.

As well might be expected, Antinomians protested this ground for the Christian's assurance. It is not that God's grace fails to provide the believer with new life. On the contrary, the presence of the Spirit was a central claim. But sanctification has a human locus, and any suggested reliance upon the finite cannot be endorsed. Saltmarsh was concerned that sanctification is never pure enough to be relied upon for assurance. "Like Noahs Dove" one can find no rest there.[50] Moreover, in the tempests of life the vision of God's renewing work is often obscured. Saltmarsh again observed that "clouds may hinder the beams from enlightning a room, but the Sun is still where he was; the Tree you know is there where it was, when the Apples or Grapes may be blown down." So "the glory of sanctification may be often darkened, and the fruits of it blown down by the winde of temptation,"[51] and one ought therefore rely for assurance upon the internal power and presence of Christ rather than upon any transient external manifestation. Crisp said that though a Christian may walk by the rule of the commandments "for his conversation," one cannot walk by such a rule "for his Peace."[52]

On the American scene John Cotton advanced a position close to this view. The evidences of sanctification, he maintained, were dubious and not discernible until one first discern one's justifying faith. "If my justification lyeth prostrate, that is, altogether dark and hidden from me," he wrote, "I cannot prove my self in a state of grace by my sanctification: For whilst I cannot beleeve that my person is accepted . . . I cannot beleeve that my

[47]Thomas Goodwin, *Works*, vol. I, pt. 2, p. 154. Quoted in Greaves, *John Bunyan*, p. 32.
[48]Baxter, *Of Saving Faith*, p. 93.
[49]Preston, *Liveles Life*, p. 39.
[50]Saltmarsh, *Free-Grace*, p. 88.
[51]Ibid., p. 89.
[52]Tobias Crisp, *Works*, 2:465. Quoted in Kevan, *Grace of Law*, p. 211.

works are accepted of God."[53] Consciousness of sanctification requires a prior awareness of one's faith and the way in which it derives strength and grace from Christ. It is true that ultimately for the Christian sanctification can be an evidence for justification, but justification itself "must be first evident."[54] A further complication, so he felt, was that in dealing with matters of works the difference between Law-obedience and Gospel-obedience is very difficult to determine. At one point he declared that this distinguishing is "so narrow, that the Angels in Heaven have much ado to discern who differ."[55]

Within this same American circle, however, Peter Bulkeley spoke in contrary fashion. To deny sanctification as an evidence, he urged, would be to derogate the work of the Holy Spirit and leave it uncertain at the point where it is intended to be clear. Within the work of the Trinity the Father elects "in his own bosom" and the Son saves, but in such general and hidden manner as not yet to be specifically disclosed. Then, however, the Spirit sanctifies those who are so chosen, and the importance of this work for personal assurance must be maintained.[56] Moreover, "our sanctification," said Bulkeley, "is more manifest to us then our justification. It is easier discerned."[57] So sanctification can witness to salvation. This was the prevailing view in American Puritanism, as it had been in that of England, a major feature of their rejection of Antinomianism.

From sanctification, however, one can climb Jacob's ladder to other evidences of one's calling and election, though actually the ascent is a descent into the still more intimate and secret life of the soul. The need here is to search out still more fully the "experimental knowledge" which can reveal the presence and power of God's working. It is to enter into the depths of personal experience, to probe the hidden recesses of the spirit, and to read carefully the signs of inner attitude, feeling, and life. It is to be sensitive to both the shoutings and the whispers of grace, as God works with varying intensities and the soul receives with varying degrees of responsiveness. But the confidence is that if the working of God is there, it can be known. "Can a man carry fire in his hand and not feele it?" asked Thomas Draxe. Or "Can a woman be wedded to an husband and not know it?" Nor indeed can the elect "erre and be ignorant in the knowledge and certaintie of their owne justification and salvation."[58] When Ames spoke of this experimental knowledge, he said it was that "which we come to have both

[53]Cotton, *Severall Questions*, p. 4.
[54]Cotton, *Covenant of Grace*, pp. 50–51.
[55]Ibid., p. 39.
[56]Bulkeley, *Gospel-Covenant*, p. 262.
[57]Ibid., p. 263.
[58]Draxe, *Churches securitie*, p. 40.

of God's purpose towards us, and the effectuall and saving operation thereof in our hearts."[59]

This awareness can be of the very presence of the "new heart" itself. It is, declared Preston, to have a "present sense" of being "turned up-side downe," to feel the course of one's life so changed that one can truly say, "I know such a thing as I hated, now I love it, I know such a duty that was tedious, now it is delightfull; such a thing I could not do, now I can performe it." It is for one to know that "the order and frame of his soule is altered, there are the same strings, as it were, but there is a new tune put to them." It is to be aware of looking upon everything "with a new eye," so that sin is seen more clearly, grace is seen more appreciatively, and the world is seen more critically than before. And when "a man looks upon God with another eye, now he sees his beauty, and his excellency, he sees there is nothing in the world to be desired in comparison of him."[60]

Harris likewise put before his hearers the importance of this experiential awareness. The "new heart," he said, is promised in the words of the Scripture, but the believer in covenant with God "finds this onenesse, this newnesse, this softnesse of spirit, in himselfe as well as in the text," seeing there that "hee hath the minde of God, . . . he is conformed to the will of God, made a partaker of the divine nature, he hath a divine stamp set upon him." Or again, as he urged this looking within for the new heart, he pressed the central questions for all such self-searching, "hath [God] put his loves, his fear into thy inward parts? . . . hath he given thee a new nature? art thou become another man then thou wast, cast into a new mould? hast thou new thoughts, new desires, new designes to set up God alone?"[61] Culverwell added that "one especiall marke of a sound heart" is the very desire of believers to ask these probing questions, a willingness to examine themselves and "to be tryed by others; yea they bee earnest with God to try them, to discover to them the false-hood or weaknesse of their hearts," that they be not "deceived with false Faith, Joy, and Love."[62]

As one so searches the soul, finding evidences of God's gracious work, one is aided by the testimony of God's own Spirit. This is a persuasion that can be recognized, a "voice" that can be heard. Baynes said it is a heresy that "maketh the spirit play all-hid in us, so that we cannot know what wee have, what wee do, what things abide in us through God's mercy."[63] The Spirit is promised in the Word, and that promise is fulfilled in experience. On the one hand, it is a Spirit that enables the believer more adequately to speak with God, to express sorrow for sin and longing for Christ. It is a Spirit that makes

[59] Ames, *Analytical Exposition of Peter*, p. 162.
[60] Preston, *Saints Qualification*, pp. 322–28.
[61] Harris, *New Covenant*, 2:175–76; 1:46.
[62] Culverwell, *Treatise of Faith*, pp. 59–60.
[63] Baynes, *Commentary Upon Ephesians*, p. 122.

possible more fervent and effective prayer. "He that hath it," said Preston, "is able to pray. . . . You will say, Is this such a matter? every man can pray. Beloved, it is another thing then the world imagines it to be; he that hath this spirit is mighty in prayer, he is able to wrestle with God . . . and he is able to prevaile with the Lord."[64] No longer will prayer for such a person be simply "lip labour."[65] Rather, it will become a powerful means toward the very assurance being sought. Francis Taylor saw this kind of prayer as "our fuell to make the perswasion of Gods love flame in us"—and added, "The more we seek Gods favour by fervent prayer, the more will he assure us of it."[66]

On the other hand, the Spirit also speaks directly to the believer, bringing an inner testimony of God's grace and love. This may come at special times, such as those of meditation or exercises of humiliation when, as Robert Bolton affirmed, "the Spirit may suggest and testifie to the sanctified conscience, with a secret, still, heart-ravishing voyce . . . thou art the childe of God."[67] Or it may come, said Preston, when other testimonies are not enough, but one is still willing to trust, for "then the Lord goes a step further with him, and seales the same things to him, with the spirit of promise . . . that is, he doth by his owne Spirit say to a man's soule, that he is his salvation. . . . [This is] a certaine expression of the Holy Ghost to the soule of a man that we know not how to expresse to you . . . the hidden Mannah . . . that no man knowes but he that hath it."[68]

Yet the testimony of God's Spirit was not limited in Puritan understanding to such specialized divine usage, or to such mystifying mode of operation. There was also a more "regular" role attributed to the Spirit, not only in the process of salvation itself, where the Spirit was the agent of God's working, but likewise in the believer's coming to that added assurance of being under God's favor. When Perkins, for example, spoke of the testimony of God's Spirit—to him a matter of great importance for the progress of the believer's assurance—he saw it occurring "by the certainty of faith, declaring and applying the promises of God."[69] It was, moreover, not a matter of "feeling," for it could come even by means of a "practical syllogism," in which one applies the general promise of salvation to all believers to one's own person as one who believes. The work of God's Spirit is an inner testimony, but it is also tied to the work of the Word. There is here no mysticism divorced from God's ordinary order of doing. The work of God is one, and the Spirit that secretly assures likewise utilizes the presence of faith to confirm fulfillment of the promises of the Gospel.

[64]Preston, *New Covenant*, 2:157.
[65]Preston, *Breast-Plate of Faith and Love*, 2:104.
[66]F. Taylor, *Gods Choise and Mans Diligence*, p. 199.
[67]R. Bolton, *Comfortable Walking with God*, p. 326.
[68]Preston, *New Covenant*, 2:172.
[69]Perkins, "Golden Chaine," *Works*, 1:102.

Thus a further evidence to be sought, in the gaining of assurance, is the presence of faith itself. Certainty of justification can be immensely aided by certainty of faith. "How may I be sure that I believe?" is the further question posed by Puritan introspection. Firm and true believing can be ground for confidence concerning receiving that which God has promised, but how can one be sure that one's believing is true and firm? Bulkeley, who like many others found it easier to recognize the outer works of sanctification, noted the difficulty in seeking to discern one's faith, for "faith being the root of all other graces, is more hidden then they are, as the root of the tree is more hidden in the earth then the body or branches."[70]

One answer provided by the divines was simply that faith was self-evidencing. Caspar Olevianus, continental Reformed theologian of the sixteenth century, had written, "The certainty of faith is its essential property,"[71] and Puritan successors in the Reformed tradition agreed. Ball said simply, "Such as truely believe, may know they believe, as he that hath a jewell in his hand, may know that he hath it."[72] There is no rational basis to be asserted for faith and thus no criterion of reason to be used for its authentication. Since it is more fiducial than intellectual in basic character, it cannot be evidenced by simply the affirmation of approved dogmatic positions. Faith is a personal act, the act of trust in another, and therefore cannot really be assessed by standards external to itself. Karl Reuter says of William Ames, "Faith and its certainty was to him something thoroughly inward, personal, experienced."[73] When the author of the modern *Marrow* wrote in his dialogue to a person raising the question, "How may I be sure that I am in the faith?" he gave a significant reply. "I would have you to close with Christ in the promise," he said, "without making any question whether you are in the faith or no, for there is an assurance which ariseth from the exercise of faith, by a direct act."[74] So there is most fundamentally an existential awareness involved in faith's perception, and the knowing is in the doing. "We ought to beleeve, till we be perswaded that we doe beleeve," wrote Saltmarsh. Then he added his analogy: "The way to bee warme, is not onely to ask for a fire, or whether there be a fire or no, or to hold out the hands towards it, and away, and wish for a greater; but to stand close to that fire there is, and to gether heat."[75] Though these words came from an Antinomian pen, the main body of Puritan divines would strongly agree.

Yet there are also signs which give evidence of faith's presence. One is the good works of the renewed life, for Puritans insisted that some measure of faith's reality is the vitality of its working. Preston wrote:

[70]Bulkeley, *Gospel-Covenant*, p. 264.

[71]Quoted in Citron, *New Birth*, p. 181.

[72]Ball, *Treatise of Faith*, p. 99.

[73]Reuter, "William Ames." Douglas Horton, ed., *William Ames*, p. 192.

[74]E. F. *Marrow*, p. 218.

[75]Saltmarsh, *Free-Grace*, pp. 94–95.

A woman many times thinkes she is with childe, but if she finde no motion or stirring, it is an argument she was deceived: So, when a man thinkes he hath faith in his heart, but yet he finds no life, no motion, no stirring, there is no work proceeding from his faith, it is an argument he was mistaken, hee was deceived in it: for if it be a right faith, it will worke, there will be life and motion in it. As Abrahams faith, you see, it enabled him to doe whatsoever GOD appointed.[76]

But more, another sign is faith's fidelity, especially in the face of difficulty. Although in the struggles with temptation faith may be driven from its hold, its return to former allegiance and trust is indication of its authenticity. Culverwell wrote, "when there is ... resting on Gods word after temptation, there is true faith; but where there is nothing but hanging in suspense, and uncertainty, that is wavering."[77] Again, a sign of true faith is peace. But Preston asked, "Is it a peace that comes after Warre? ... If not, this is a "blind peace," experienced by one "not because he hath escaped the danger, but because he never saw the danger."[78] True faith wears its battle scars from the struggles with temptation, and these can point to its presence.

But most of all there was the word of Puritan practicality: in the search for one's faith, one may be assured that it need not be perfect, but rather, the least spark of faith, even weak faith, can lay hold of God's promises and be the instrument for justification and salvation. Indeed, the strongest faith itself is imperfect, but it is not the strength of faith that saves. "Neyther are we saved by the worth or quantitie of our Faith," wrote John Rogers, "but by Christ, which is laid hold of by a weake Faith, as well as a strong."[79] So "the least dramme of Affiance ... doth justifie as perfectly as the greatest quantity."[80] "A weak hand receiving a gift, makes the gift our own, as well as if it were received with more strength."[81] If strong faith be required, "none should be justified and saved but the strong beleever, whereas Christ died for the weak in the faith."[82]

It may be that one's weak faith will grow strong in time, as is true in many believers' experience. John Rogers saw the progression mirrored in several ways:

the learnedst Clerke was in his horne-booke, the greatest Giant was in swaddling clothes, the tallest Oake was a twigge, and Faith groweth from a graine of mustard-seede to a tall tree.[83]

[76]Preston, *New Covenant*, 2:145.
[77]Culverwell, *Treatise of Faith*, pp. 50–51.
[78]Preston, *Breast-Plate of Faith and Love*, 2:109.
[79]J. Rogers, *Doctrine of Faith*, p. 201.
[80]Downe, *Definition of justifying faith*, p. 13.
[81]Bulkeley, *Gospel-Covenant*, p. 365.
[82]Rutherfurd, *Covenant of Life*, p. 155.
[83]J. Rogers, *Doctrine of Faith*, p. 200.

Yet if one's faith is still but as the mustard seed, one must not be dismayed. The feeble life of a child "is life as truely, as that life which a man attaineth."[84] So in the infancy of faith one can have confidence in the presence of that which in others is known in greater maturity, and "the weakest Believer is a lively member of Christ, as truly, as they that are strong."[85] All that is needed is "as much as will bring thee within the doore. . . . a little faith is enough to put a man within the Covenant . . . therefore labour to know that though you be but as smoking Flax, yet there is fire there, as well as if it were all on a flame."[86] So the message was: take heart, even though faith is weak and small.[87] Burgess noted that "Mary Magdalan was as much justified before God as the Virgin Mary."[88]

Yet further, the weakest of weak faith, but still enough to open the door, may be defined simply in terms of desire, that is, desire for mercy, desire for salvation, desire for reconciliation with God. There is positive value in yearning for Christ even if this is not yet consummated in yielding. Robert Bolton wrote that Christ "doth not say, Blessed are the strong in Faith, the fully assured . . . but, Blessed are they which doe hunger and thirst after righteousnesse."[89] In the greatness of divine mercy God "accepteth the will for the deed and our affections for the actions." "Our desire of grace, faith and repentance, are the graces themselves which wee desire."[90]

Care was exercised to provide certain qualifications. Perkins, whose concern for the condition of the conscience led him to be an early and strong proponent of this relaxation, sought nevertheless to keep it in touch with Puritan earnestness. This is not sanction for the "fleeting desires" of "carnall men," but is "the desire for reconciliation with God, that comes from a bruised heart, and brings alwaies with it reformation of life."[91] Moreover, there should be no final contentment in simply this desire. One must labor constantly to improve it and go on from faith to faith.[92] Thus "he which

---

[84]Baynes, *Commentary Upon Ephesians*, pp. 122–23.

[85]Ball, *Treatise of Faith*, p. 142.

[86]Preston, *Breast-Plate of Faith and Love*, 1:131.

[87]This idea appeared early. Peter Lake writes of the practical divinity of the 1580s and 1590s: "Since all true faith and knowledge was seen as a direct gift of God, even the smallest impulse toward true belief could be interpreted as a sign of elect status and hence be elevated at once from the level of subjective impulse to objective proof." Lake, *Moderate puritans*, p. 157.

[88]Burgess, *True Doctrine of Justification*, 2:231.

[89]R. Bolton, *Comfortable Walking with God*, pp. 380–81.

[90]R. Bolton, *Comforting Afflicted Consciences*, p. 375.

[91]Perkins, "Exposition of the Creed," *Works*, 1:128.

[92]Although weak faith can save, stronger faith can obviously be more certain. So Peter Lake writes: "It was the need to reach that certainty that provided the internal spiritual dynamic of puritan religion. For in such a situation no true believer could rest content with those initial stirrings of faith. He was compelled to push on up the path of spiritual development. . . . Indeed, the very fact that his faith must in this life remain imperfect provided a further incentive as the individual strove to distinguish his profession from that of the . . . hypocritical believer." Lake, *Moderate puritans*, p. 159.

thinkes hee hath a desire to beleeve, and contents himself therewith; hath indeede no true desire to beleeve."[93] But still the embryonic turning is of the same nature as the final embracing, and confidence can emerge from the detection of its presence in the soul's life. Preston spoke of this beginning of faith in terms of "willingness" and declared passionately to his hearers, "If thou bee but willing, Christ desires no more. . . . Put the case thou wert able to get the victory over thy lust, wouldst thou be content to part with it, and to take CHRIST? . . . God requires no more but a willingnesse to come."[94] Robert Bolton summarized for the anxious spirit. "Take it in short from me thus," he wrote, "A true desire of grace argues a saving and comfortable estate."[95]

DEALING WITH DOUBT

The life of the Christian, however, is a wayfaring and a warfaring, and the search for evidences, even in their minimal form, can be plagued by problems and disturbed by doubt. The pilgrim may make progress, but obstacles also obstruct the way. First among these is the continuation of temptation, and also of sin. "The grace of regeneration," wrote Burgess, "cut the hair of sin, as Delilah did Samsons, yet it groweth again, as long as the root is there."[96] There is a "spiritual war" in the life of every believer. Guilt may be removed and new life engendered, but the vestiges of corruption remain to lead the soul into continued trial and tribulation. So sin exists in the believer, and the sensitive conscience can be led to doubt and despair.

It is not that God's forgiveness and healing make no difference. Sin has been delivered a "wound" by Christ's redemptive work and, translated into the life of the believer, this means that, though sin is real, it does not reign. "The godly man . . . doth not sin wittingly, and willingly . . . he maketh not a trade of sinne . . . he doth never sinne with full consent and swinge of will."[97] So "the Saints in their worst state have a tincture of holinesse, a thread of Skarlet runs through their whole lives, after they are once changed, they never fall in that [former] degree."[98] In a dialogue written by Perkins we find "Christian" saying of his sin, "my heart is against it, and I hate it. . . . afterward, when it is committed, I am grieved and displeased at my self, and doe earnestly . . . aske at Gods hand forgivenesse."[99] But sin is still there, and ever recurringly the temptations that lead to its increase. Perkins felt that as God "hath made a covenant with his people, so Satan joynes in league

[93]Perkins, "Reformed Catholike," *Works*, 1:605–6.
[94]Preston, *Breast-Plate of Faith and Love*, 1:92–93.
[95]R. Bolton, *Comforting Afflicted Consciences*, p. 377.
[96]Burgess, *True Doctrine of Justification*, 1:239.
[97]Cole, *Godly Mans Assurance*, pp. 48–49.
[98]Preston, *Saints Qualification*, pp. 394, 396.
[99]Perkins, "Estate of Damnation," *Works*, 1:418.

with the world, labouring to binde some men unto him, that so, if it were possible, he might draw them from the covenant of God and disgrace the same."[100] The enticements of the tempter are everywhere. "Seeme the place never so secret," wrote Thomas Taylor, "the greenest grasse may harbor a serpent."[101]

In the content of the pilgrim's consciousness the counterpart to the presence of Satan could be the absence of God. Perkins has Christian saying to his minister, "I oftentimes find my selfe like a very timberlog, void of all grace and goodness." And Minister replies, "As it is in the strait seas, the water ebs and flowes, so it is in the godly."[102] Here is a further aspect of the doubt that plagues the way. Assurance relies upon sense for its support, but feeling fluctuates. There can be a dryness in the spirit, a deadness in experience, even a dark night of the soul. If God's graces are real, they can still be hidden from perception. It is like trees in the winter, "beaten with winde and weather, bearing neither leafe nor fruit, but looke as though they were rotten and dead, because the sap doth not spread it selfe, but lies hid in the roote."[103] Similarly, the sun may be hidden under a cloud, the child hidden in the womb, the fire hidden in the ashes. So "the graces of the Spirit may lie hid in the hearts of the regenerate, and worke insensibly to the feeling and discerning."[104] There are times when Christian faith may "faint" and "a slouthfull kind of Sleepinesse ... seize upon it, and unfit it and disable it,"[105] times when faith "lyeth flat ... in a swoone."[106] God, who should be present to the Christian's feeling, can seem absent. Where there should be vitality in Christian experience, there is a void. Perkins recognized this heaviness of heart by noting that though some "members of Christ ... feele and shew forth the power of Christ," there are others, equally ingrafted, who have "no feeling of the power and efficacie of the quickening spirit."[107] And then the sense of abandonment by God can easily be temptation to one's own abandoning of God. Doubt can lead to despair and to denial. At any rate, it destroys assurance. Culverwell noted that persons who doubt excessively "rob God of his honor and themselves of their comfort."[108]

But the pilgrim must not remain in the slough of despond. The responsibilities of both theologian and pastor are to deal with doubt. Puritan divines therefore found many responses to those of anxious mind and spirit.

[100]Perkins, "Discourse of Witchcraft," *Works*, 3:615.
[101]T. Taylor, *Christs combate*, p. 20.
[102]Perkins, "Estate of Damnation," *Works*, 1:413.
[103]Ibid., p. 418.
[104]Ball, *Treatise of Faith*, pp. 173–74.
[105]Dyke, *Commentary upon Philemon*, pp. 133–34.
[106]Perkins, "Manner of Predestination," *Works*, 2:635–36.
[107]Perkins, "Graine of Musterd-seede," *Works*, 1:79.
[108]Culverwell, *Treatise of Faith*, p. 238.

One beginning place was simply the urging that doubt is more normal than the doubter normally thinks. One stands in good historical company if one is anxious of spirit and disturbed by doubt. "Thinke it not strange," said Robert Bolton, "that thou art fallen into this kinde of spirituall affliction. . . . For herein thou becomest conformable to as holy Men as ever the world had: Job, David, Luther . . . Nay, to the Sonne of God himselfe."[109] Their struggles, recorded in Scripture and history, reflect the intensity that can characterize a sense of God-forsakenness. Their anguish was profound, their desperation real. Yet in the midst of their trials there was triumph. Perkins noted that David cried out, "My God, my God, why hast thou forsaken me?" which surely "may seeme to be the complaint of a desperate man, not having so much as one sparke of faith." But one should observe that the complaint began with the words, "My God, my God," words which "containe a confession proceeding from true faith."[110] Job likewise found his peace after protest. And Christ who suffered temptation even on the cross, using the very words of David, also triumphed with affirmation of faith.

Then, asked Baynes, "wherefore did our Saviour overcome that fearefull conflict of temptation, but that it should be our medicine when we are overcome of it?"[111] One indeed can find a conformity with Christ in afflictions and a sense of his partnership in them, so that, as Ball noted, "the sorrowes which we beare, are not so much ours as Christs. In all our troubles he is troubled with us."[112] So perhaps it is better, Thomas Hooker maintained, "sometimes to goe downe into the pit with him, who beholding darknes, and bewailing the losse of inward joy and consolation crieth from the bottome of lowest hell . . . then continually to walke arme in arme with Angels, to sit, as it were, in Abrahams bosome."[113] Perkins declared, "Hee which never doubted of his salvation, never beleeved."[114]

If even these best of saints have had their anguish, and thousands upon thousands of common Christians with them, it is not because God's graces are truly absent, but rather because they are sometimes hidden. Puritan divines therefore went on to remind the doubter that faith and fear are not mutually exclusive, for under the fearing there may be the genuineness of faith. These two "may well stand together," said Harris, "as a man may be surely ancred, and yet be waved and tossed with the billowes and surges of the sea."[115]

---

[109]R. Bolton, *Comforting Afflicted Consciences*, p. 527.

[110]Perkins, "Estate of Damnation," *Works*, 1:377.

[111]Baynes, *Christian Letters*, p. 28.

[112]Ball, *Treatise of Faith*, p. 326.

[113]Quoted in R. Bolton, *Comforting Afflicted Consciences*, p. 518. No source in Hooker is given. And Bolton, who describes "Master Hooker" as "very sound in this point," also adds concerning his quotation, "I varie the words, but keepe the sense entire."

[114]Perkins, "Estate of Damnation," *Works*, 1:410.

[115]Harris, *Way to True Happinesse*, 2:50.

Thus we come in this pastoral perspective to the insistence, for all of its stress upon evidences, that sense cannot be relied upon as having full evidential validity. There can be discrepancy between the hidden graces of God and their appearance or their apprehending.[116] In repentance "there may be true humiliation, though with drie cheeks."[117] As to faith, that "may sinke as a Corke"—but then it will rise again.[118] The important thing, however, is that in time of doubt the Christian remember that not all God's working is revealed and that a sense of desertion is not therefore to be taken as necessary sign that one is deserted. "It is one thing to have a thing surely," said Baynes, "another thing to know, I have it surely."[119] The faith of adherence is not the faith of assurance, and whereas in Christian life the former is sure in reality, the latter may be unsure in experience. "The life of the faithfull," said Perkins, "is hid in Christ, . . . their life is not in sense and feeling, but in hoping and beleeving."[120] Indeed, "faith without feeling," Timothy Rogers affirmed, "is stronger and more precious, than faith with feeling."[121] And this type of faith can transcend the contrary appearances of outward experience, recognizing in its trusting that there are hidden graces of God.

Though these trials of the spiritual life may conceal God's hidden graces, they may also be understood to be more direct instruments of God's working. Thus the troubled Christian should be aware that, within the providence of God, both temptation to sin and seeming absence of grace may be God's means of furthering one's own good. When "ordinary meanes of humiliation . . . will not prevaile; it pleaseth God sometimes by meanes extraordinary . . . to draw men unto him, as it were, by a strong hand, adding to the ministry of the word afflictions and crosses."[122] God works in many and mysterious ways, and even by the use of tribulation God can minister in mercy. Rather than being a further plaguing of the spirit, afflictions can be "a restorative against many a quame and swoune of spirit."[123] They can be "as pangs of child birth, to deliver . . . souls into the world of the sons of God."[124]

Thus afflictions can be seen as sent by God to help one feel the bitterness of sin, to keep one more watchful with respect to its temptation, to show the limits of one's strength and, above all, to lead to firmer reliance upon God. Often these are necessary for growth. "Thou hast neede of strong afflictions," said Preston. "Some Colts are so untamed, they must needs be

---

[116]Bacon, *Spirit of Prelacie Working*, p. 16.

[117]Perkins, "Whole Treatise," *Works*, 2:15.

[118]Preston, *Breast-Plate of Faith and Love*, 2:28.

[119]Baynes, *Helpe to True Happinesse*, p. 195.

[120]Perkins, "Estate of Damnation," *Works*, 1:358.

[121]T. Rogers, *Righteous Mans Evidence*, p. 204.

[122]G. Downame, *Covenant of Grace*, p. 85.

[123]Perkins, "Estate of Damnation," *Works*, 1:420.

[124]Twisse, *Riches of Gods Love*, p. 287.

broken. So some corruptions are so unruly, that they will not be wrought out without great affliction."[125] As to the significance of these trials for faith, Ball wrote, "by affliction and trouble, by distrusts and fearefull doubts, [God] whetteth and sharpeneth our faith and assurance; which by fighting increaseth, and the longer it wrastleth, the stronger it waxeth."[126] Afflictions can also vary in nature and be many and diverse. Ball further noted that "If one medicine fit not a sore, will we not seeke anouther. . . . our heavenly Father keepes us in a daily course of physicke, now with one thing, now with another, because we profit not with any one alone."[127] This is the wonderful providence of God at work, perceptive, though in strange and hidden ways, to one's every need.

Afflictions therefore, rather than be resisted, need to be appreciated for the healing they can bring. If afflictions are so accepted, they can be recognized as occasions of God's grace, stimulating the believer to new commitment and faith.[128] This is what they were, said Sutton, for the prodigal son and Jonah: "The prodigal sonne concludes not to returne till he was brought low by afflictions. . . . Jonah sleeps in the ship, but watcheth and prayes in the whale's belly."[129] So "the believer must not looke to walke on smoothly without any rubs, or to enjoy perfect assurance without doubting and assaults." These can, however, enhance the striving after assurance, which is a "wrestling and combatting" and "lookes not to come to perfection but by temptation."[130]

If one can find help in the conviction that spiritual afflictions are a part of the medicine of God, employed by divine providence for human healing, one must also know that the healing process itself is frequently slow under the same providence, so that enlarged perception of its benefits is only gradual. This, too, said the divines, is often the manner of God's working. When God "doth a cure, he beginnes at the bottome, and so heals it upward, and this must have time." Moreover, the healing is invisible, a work in the life of the spirit, and, like the healing of an internal wound in the body, is not easily accessible to perception. "A man seeth himselfe cured, but how and when it healeth, he sees not."[131] One can be confident that God works "no

---

[125]Preston, *Breast-Plate of Faith and Love*, 2:206.

[126]Ball, *Treatise of Faith*, p. 111.

[127]Ibid., p. 337.

[128]Perkins' mentor, Laurence Chaderton, made a distinction between a "judiciary" and a "castigatory" affliction from God, the former looked upon as punishment and the latter as warning to amend one's life accordingly. Peter Lake writes that if one chose to amend, the affliction "was presumably castigatory and there was a presumption that he was elect," but if one did not, "there was an equal presumption that it was judiciary and he was reprobate." Lake, *Moderate puritans*, p. 156.

[129]Sutton, *Lectures on Romans*, p. 211.

[130]Ball, *Treatise of Faith*, p. 257.

[131]Harris, *New Covenant*, 1:44.

half-cures upon any diseased persons," but heals perfectly. Yet "he works by degrees."[132]

That deliberate divine working reminds us again of the evolutionary character of assurance. Even as there is moral progress in the Christian's life, there is psychological progress, and "assurance comes not at first when we believe, but little by little as God seeth it requisite, according to the triall he hath appointed to make of us."[133] Christians can move through different stages in the growth of assurance. "Some are incipients, some proficients, some perfect or growne men in Christ ... [yet] none are so perfect, but that their assurance may be increased."[134] It is unrealistic to think that one can have full assurance at the very outset, "as if ... the Sun at his first peeping were in the height of heaven; or that a Schollar must be placed in the upper forme as soone as he enters the Schoole."[135] Throughout the pilgrim's journey there is only a gradual reception of increased confidence. Said Harris, one drinks a "cup of spirits" differently than a "cup of beere," that is, slowly, by degrees![136] Or perhaps more appropriately, in Perkins' words, "A vessell with a narrow necke, which being cast into the sea, ... receiveth water drop by drop." So it is with Christians "when God giveth unto us in Christ, even a sea of mercie."[137] Those in doubt should be patient with the gradual nature of God's consoling.

Yet there was also another dimension to what might be called the Puritan *ordo persuasionis*, as anxiety was faced and certainty sought. The search for "evidences," we have seen, turned the searcher in an inward direction, moving from stage to stage in introspection. This brought a probing of feeling, an exploration of spiritual sense, an examination of private experience for signs of God's working and favor. And when afflictions came and doubt assailed, much of the counsel given was itself related to this internal form of evidencing: absence of evidence has been the experience even of the saints; God sometimes hides clear evidences; God uses the lack of such evidences for positive purpose; the growth of evidence is by degrees. The focus of both seeking and reflection in these Puritan efforts to attain to the persuasion of assurance, was largely subjective. Not neglected in the Puritan mind, however, despite at times appearing to be a court of last resort, was also an objective consideration: the testimonies of God as given in Word and sacraments must likewise be relied upon for comfort by the troubled soul.

This comfort, then, is of a different order than that of experiential evidencing. It rests not on personal experiencing, but simply on believing.

---

[132]Burgess, *True Doctrine of Justification*, 1:152.
[133]Ball, *Treatise of Faith*, p. 96.
[134]G. Downame, *Covenant of Grace*, p. 109.
[135]O. Sedgwick, *Doubting Beleever*, p. 60.
[136]Harris, *New Covenant*, 2:195.
[137]Perkins, "Reformed Catholike," *Works*, 1:564.

Or better, since one does not here examine one's belief, it is a confidence resting on the object of one's believing, namely, Christ. In developing an analysis of this matter, Obadiah Sedgwick posed the question to a doubter, "Why dost thou not beleeve?" The doubter's answer was, "If I had assurance that God were my God, and Christ were my Christ, and the Promises were mine, I would." But Sedgwick responded, "Is the Word or thy Assurance the ground of faith? And would thou have the fruit before the tree? . . . The sweetnesse of assurance flowes from that faith which by beleeving feeds on Christ." And then he added, "Experiences are good encouragements to the future acts of faith, but the Word of God is still the ground of faith."[138]

In a way, therefore, the Word can be considered both alpha and omega for the Christian's journeying. The Word is alpha as it provides the promises with which the believer's life begins. Shackled by sin, one knows new life to be possible as proclaimed by those promises, and one is then led into that order of salvation offered and committed in the Word. But in Puritan practice one is equally led into an order of persuasion to search for assurance that the offer has been accepted and the commitment truly applies. Conscience needs to be satisfied and evidence obtained. Yet the attaining of evidence has its own difficulties—and in some respects the labyrinth entered by introspection seems no less complex than the labyrinth entered by probing one's election. If the search for certainty *ascendendo*, by climbing into the secret mysteries of the eternal counsels, leads one to further uncertainty, the same might often be said of the search *descendendo*, by descending into the depths of one's own heart. Thus beyond all self-searching there is the Word as omega, the final resting place for commitment and further ground for security, more certain than any transient feeling. So, said the author of the modern *Marrow*, "When all other things fail, . . . look to Christ; that is, go to the word and promise, and leave off, and cease a while to reason about the truth of your faith, and set your heart on work to believe."[139] Robert Bolton saw this need explicitly within the framework of affliction:

> When in time of temptation thou art terrified . . . with renewed scruples about thy spirituall well-being . . . [go] to the Word, and to the Testimony; let thy trembling heart cleave to the impregnable truth of those sweetest promises . . . and thou art safe for ever.[140]

Harris added, "Thou must deny thine owne sense and feeling; rest upon the word, if thou would'st be on sure ground."[141]

Resting on the Word is also achieved through resting on the sacraments, for the sacraments are "signes representing to the eyes that which the word

---

[138]O. Sedgwick, *Doubting Beleever*, pp. 125–27.
[139]E. F. *Marrow*, p. 226.
[140]R. Bolton, *Comfortable Walking with God*, p. 320.
[141]Harris, *Way to True Happinesse*, 2:50–53.

doth to the eares."[142] The sacraments are never to be divorced from the Word, but are to be seen as servants of it in the sense that they testify in this visible manner to the promises which the Word audibly proclaims. The sacraments are "seals" in the standard definition of Puritanism and of the Reformed tradition as a whole. They seal and confirm, in formal manner which God has established, the commitments God has given, and certify, therefore, that the believer shall partake of that which is signified. They also seal or signify the response of the believer in faith and faithfulness, a matter essential to the receiving of that which is promised. There is no independent significance for the sacraments apart from the Word and faith. George Downame wrote, "Sacraments are as seales annexed to the letters patent of Gods evangelicall promises, which assure or conveigh nothing, but what is contained in the promise, and upon the same condition. And it is absurd to extend the benefit of the sacrament beyond the covenant."[143] So the sacraments were established by God for the better assurance of the believer, who was called upon to respond in faith to the Word. "To all the promises of God," said Sutton, "are added the seales in the true use of the Sacraments, that if any of the faithfull should doubt of the generall promises, he might there have it sealed to his particular person."[144]

This particularization of God's promise is first to be found in baptism, and its power of assurance can continue far beyond the time of its actual act. The promises sacramentally sealed in the event of baptism can be extended throughout the course of the believer's life, so long as there is believing and repentance. Thus one can rely for comfort, in continuing times of tribulation, upon those promises sealed personally to one in earlier days. Ball's statement is characteristic:

> Baptisme is of great force to strengthen faith, and ease the heart in distresse. For when the repentant sinner feeles himselfe heavie laden with the burden of his sinnes; when Sathan temptes him to doubt or despaire . . . when his own corruption moveth him to sinne, and he is even now in the combate, the Spirit lusting against the flesh, . . . and when he is deeply perplexed with feare of falling away: then the consideration and remembrance of what was promised, and sealed in Baptisme, will serve to stay, support, and comfort the soule. For there he shall finde . . . that God hath promised . . . to wash away all his sinnes . . . and having such a faithfull promise confirmed by seale, wherefore should he be dismayed? In Baptisme also God hath sealed unto him the mortification of his sinne . . . which is ground of confidence that God will enable him to overcome the rebellious lusts of his heart, and crucifie the old man more and more.[145]

[142]Perkins, "Reformed Catholike," *Works*, 1:610.
[143]G. Downame, *Certainty of Perseverance*, pp. 395–96.
[144]Sutton, *Lectures on Romans*, p. 25.
[145]Ball, *Treatise of Faith*, p. 413.

There is solace to be found in recalling, and again relying upon, the objective fact of one's baptism. Perkins said, "When a man is in danger of the shipwreck of his soul," baptism is "a plank on which to swim to safety."[146] Baptism thus makes visible, continuous, and personal the promises of the Word.

Similarly, the sacrament of the Lord's Supper is a "visible Gospell," for the material elements in its celebration are themselves preachers of the Word. In its visibility it is a sign of that which is promised, but it is more than a "bare sign" or "naked sign" merely pointing to that which it signifies. Rather, it also "gives interest into the thing . . . gives Title to the thing . . . conveys the thing to us" to which it points.[147] And that which is both represented and presented in the Sacrament is Christ and his redemptive work. As in baptism, the Supper needs to be received in faith, and indeed each new receiving becomes occasion for new commitment and trusting, but the very nature of the Sacrament, as a form of the Gospel, likewise aids in faith's increase. So this, said Ames, is a "Sacrament of the nourishing and growth of the faithfull in Christ" and one in which Christ is "spiritually present with them who receive in Faith."[148] Preston could urge that in such receiving "We should doe . . . as Joab did, lay hold upon the hornes of the Altar; that is, take hold upon CHRIST, and remember that sure word of promise."[149]

The sacraments, therefore, accompany the Word and can make it more explicit and also more particular in the experience of the believer. As outward and visible signs, they have an objectivity which can be relied upon in their mediation of the promises. Even as in secular life "the sight of his evidences confirmes a man in the hope of the quiet possession of his Lands," so "the right use of the Sacraments assures us of Gods favour."[150]

But there is a still more special way in which the sacraments, in Puritan thought, aid in encouraging assurance. They are seals, but even more explicitly, they are seals of the covenant. God's promises are covenant promises, divine offers and pledges within the covenant of grace, and the sacraments can be instruments in God's hands to make those more plain and clear, as well as occasions in human life for covenant commitment. Because the theology of the Puritan divines was a covenant theology, the sacraments were most basically interpreted in relation to covenant promise and response. Ames wrote, "The primary end of a Sacrament is to seale the covenant, and that not on God's part onely, but consequently also on ours,

[146]Perkins, *Cases of Conscience*, 2:80. Quoted in Breward, *Life and Theology of William Perkins*, p. 222.

[147]Preston, *Saints Qualification*, pp. 485, 488.

[148]Ames, *Marrow*, pp. 183–84.

[149]Preston, *Breast-Plate of Faith and Love*, 1:88.

[150]F. Taylor, *God Choise and Mans Diligence*, p. 199.

that is, not onely the grace of God, and promises are sealed to us, but also our thankfulnesse and obedience to God."[151]

Thus baptism is a sign and pledge of God's covenant favor, promising forgiveness and salvation. But it also the occasion of "a reall passing over of our selves to God," for, as Harris told his hearers, "Baptisme was the seale of the Covenant given on God's part and taken on your part."[152] "As we covenant one by one at our Baptisme with him, to be obedient and faithfull," said Nehemiah Rogers, "so also he with us to be a God All-Sufficient unto us, and our God for ever."[153] In baptism, therefore, covenant assurance and covenant obligation are brought together.[154] In the Lord's Supper this double significance for covenant likewise prevails. "God is pleased in that Sacrament," wrote Bulkeley, "to renue the Seale of his Covenant towards us for the settling of our faith, and the establishment of us in the assurance of grace."[155] But the occasion must also be one, the divines urged, in which there is renewal of the believer's covenant consent. Preston said of the Lord's Supper: "As this is the Covenant on God's part that is sealed, so you must ... put to your seale likewise, to confirme the condition of the Covenant on your part ... for all Covenants must be mutuall."[156] Charles Hambrick-Stowe points out that in New England Puritanism "popular eucharistic manuals and Sacrament day sermons encouraged the understanding that 'in receiving the Lord's Supper, we renew covenant with God.'"[157]

Thus in the struggle with doubt and in the search for assurance the objective realities of Word and sacraments played an important role. And they must be understood in relation to the covenant, God's chosen means of relating to a called and gathered people. William Strong wrote that all of God's promises spring from the "mother-root," which is the covenant of grace.[158]

COVENANT CERTAINTY

The covenant of grace, said John Cotton, is "a soveraign and sufficient medicine to heal all our disorders, and remove all our impediments."[159] It is "a port of refuge," declared Peter Bulkeley.[160] It is "the first and most firm

[151]Ames, *Marrow*, p. 165.
[152]Harris, *New Covenant*, 2:171.
[153]N. Rogers, *True Convert*, p. 160.
[154]For discussion of this see Holifield, *Covenant Sealed*, pp. 42–45.
[155]Bulkeley, *Gospel-Covenant*, p. 416.
[156]Preston, *New Covenant*, 1:180.
[157]Hambrick-Stowe, *Practice of Piety*, p. 130.
[158]Strong, *Discourse of Two Covenants*, p. a2.
[159]Cotton, *Covenant of Gods free Grace*, p. 16.
[160]Bulkeley, *Gospel-Covenant*, p. A2.

foundation of a Christians comfort," said Simeon Ash.[161] Without question a recurring theme in the writings of the covenant theologians was the power of the covenant for consolation as mediator of assurance of salvation. "Rebels and traitors as we are," it is a "sign of God's great love, that he will stoop so low as to make a covenant with us, to be our God."[162] Thus it is no presumption for believers to assure themselves of God's favor. When God entered into covenant with Abraham, all Abraham's seed were likewise included; so all who share in Abraham's faith become heirs of the covenant promises. Here in God's commitment in covenant is a giving of "such security to the creature, as he cannot tell how to demand greater."[163] Obadiah Sedgwick defined that security in comprehensive fashion for the believer: "I assure thee, O Christian, if this were once out of doubt, that thou and God were entred into Covenant, thou wouldst not so much doubt thy title, or question thy right to apply any particular promise to any condition or exigence wherein thou lyest."[164] Perkins asked, "What better ground of true comfort?"[165]

One aspect of this covenant certainty was the conviction that the covenant cannot be broken by sin. It is true that one's sins call for repentance and renewed faith. It is also true that they can destroy one's sense of assurance, like David's sins that "did exceedingly weaken his spiritual condition, and wiped off all his comfortables."[166] Yet, though one can sin away the evidence, one cannot sin away the grace. And the evidence can be restored through repentance. So, counselled Sutton, "if thou sinne with David, repent with David; if thou sinne with Peter, repent with Peter; if thou be drunke with Noah, repent with Noah; God will be entreated, and his mercie shall appeare."[167] The covenant is stronger than one's sin, and one within the covenant "does not fall on all four" by sinning.[168]

From a pastoral perspective, however, there is a qualification. Though all sin is to be avoided, there is an ultimate sin which is destructive of the covenant and is above all to be avoided, and that is the willful and deliberate rejection of God. This is the sin against the Holy Ghost, and the favorite analogy was that of marriage broken by adultery. In the covenant one is "married to Christ," and the marriage can stand the impact of many peccadilloes and even more serious offenses. "God taketh not advantage against us for every petty breach." The significance of the covenant is that such "breaches" are really not breaches at all. Rather, "it must be some great

[161]Simeon Ash, "To the Reader." Ball, *Covenant of Grace.*
[162]Sibbes, "Faithful Covenanter," *Works*, 6:6.
[163]Harris, *New Covenant*, 1:33.
[164]O. Sedgwick, *Doubting Beleever*, p. 237.
[165]Perkins, *Commentarie upon Galatians*, p. 186.
[166]O. Sedgwick, *Doubting Beleever*, p. 42.
[167]Sutton, *Lectures on Romans*, p. 17.
[168]Sibbes, "Life of Faith," *Works*, 5:366.

breach of Covenant, as when we runne awhoring from under him."[169] Here is the "spiritual adultery" most to be feared. Preston could say that if one is in the covenant, one should not be anxious that "a sinne or two or daily failings shall breake the Covenant," for that is impossible. But the covenant indeed would be shattered if one were to "forsake GOD, . . . leave GOD, and chuse thee a new Master."[170]

The detecting of such apostasy is again a matter of introspection. Preston urged self-examination to see "if thy heart is stolne away with anything in the world . . . so that thou commest indeed to performe holy duties from day to day, but they have no taste, no relish." One should also ask if sin has dominion, if it runs as a thread throughout one's whole life.[171] Ball saw those sinning against the Holy Ghost as those who have "maliciously set themselves against the truth and Gospell of God,"[172] and Bulkeley spoke of the covenant being voided "when men turne back from the grace which they have received, and grow weary of it . . . doe take hold of the Covenant, as it were with one hand, but not with all our heart."[173] However defined and detected, there is a sin by which the covenant presumably can be broken.

And yet, though pastoral and pragmatic inclinations might lead to warnings against such destructive apostasy, the theological convictions of Puritanism led to the accompanying assertion that this could not really happen for those who are truly or "effectually" within the covenant of grace. Prynne wrote that for "those whom God hath chosen for to be his people, and hath like wise caused them to choose him for their God, and to joyne themselves unto him in an everlasting Covenant . . . it is impossible that they should ever finally or totally fall from grace."[174] And Cotton said of the covenant of grace, "though on our parts it may be broken, yet because Christ hath it in keeping, it shall never be so broken. . . . God will put his feare in our hearts, which shall work in us holy care of keeping covenant with him." This meant to him that "if we be hemm'd in within this Covenant, wee cannot break out."[175]

The distinction underlying this affirmation was between those who are effectually in the covenant and those who are merely externally in the covenant. It is not that the distinction could be empirically enforced, though in New England there was attempt to do so, but it did allow for the urging of piety seeking to move persons from the latter to the former, along with the convictions of predestination that the former could not be moved. Bulkeley wrote of this distinction: "the Covenant . . . is everlasting and without end:

[169]Harris, *New Covenant*, 1:47.
[170]Preston, *Breast-Plate of Faith and Love*, 2:152.
[171]Preston, *New Covenant*, 2:215–21.
[172]Ball, *Treatise of Faith*, p. 184.
[173]Bulkeley, *Gospel-Covenant*, p. 105.
[174]Prynne, *Regenerate Mans Estate*, p. 111.
[175]Cotton, *Covenant of Gods free Grace*, pp. 13, 18.

Its never to be broken, if once made in truth; men may seem to be in Covenant with God, and . . . such a Covenant may break and come to an end. . . . But where we truly give up our selves unto God . . . his Covenant with us is for ever."[176]

The proclamation of such solid security within the covenant, however, could not but raise again, though now under slightly different form, the earlier subjective questions. If the assurance of the covenant's unbrokenness is for those who are effectually called to be within it, the query now for the individual could be, "How do I know that I am truly within the covenant as one of the effectually called?" Though certainty through the covenant could extricate Puritan soul-searching from the labyrinthine complexities of analysis of spiritual sense and feeling, the personal element in the equation continued to persist. Puritanism, therefore, even as it moved to stress the importance for assurance of the objective Word, sacraments, and covenant, found itself tied again to the definition of subjective criteria and the search for qualification. Perhaps this is unavoidable when final focus is not on a reality, but on a relationship. Within the relationship Puritanism honored highly the saving power of the divine Reality, a power so great that even the establishment of the relationship was held to be its sovereign act. But for personal assurance the prior matter was confidence of one's personal inclusion. Benefit of the almost indescribable and totally indefectible gifts of the covenant relationship with God required one's own participation as a genuine partner. Thus Puritan divines were once again involved in clarifying the subjective criteria upon which confidence could rest.

The main conclusion reached was in effect an extension of that which had been offered in the discussion of the final ground for the evidencing of faith. Indeed, the two go together, for we are dealing here more with logical than chronological sequence. With respect to the faith which brings one into the covenant, it is minimally sufficient for there to be present simply an earnest desire. The beginnings of faith are in a yearning for Christ and a willingness to place one's trust in him. Though this in no way approximates the maturity of faith which should be sought as the Christian's life advances, it is sufficient, for God accepts the will for the deed. When thought focused upon the criteria for continued covenant inclusion, a matter broadly involving both faith and faithfulness, a generally similar minimization was voiced. The key concept in this instance was "sincerity," though it also had many variant designations. Despite the imperfections in one's covenant obedience and the breaches in one's covenant faithfulness, the covenant holds if in one's covenant participation one is sincere. This once more is because of God's acceptance of the will for the deed. Ball wrote that "in the Covenant of grace obedience is required, repentance is admitted, and sincerity

---

[176]Bulkeley, *Gospel-Covenant*, p. 415.

accepted."[177] And in somewhat more comprehensive fashion Dyke declared, "We must remember, that God accepts affecting for effecting; willing for working; desires for deeds; purposes for performances; pence for pounds; and unto such as doe their endeavour, hath promised His grace enabling them every day to doe more and more."[178] Perkins said explicitly, "God will accept our imperfect obedience if it be sincere."[179]

The nature of "sincerity" was variably expressed. Basically it related to the "condition of the heart" and was designated by such terms as "purity," "simplicity," "wholeness," "uprightness," "soundness," "integrity," and "perfection." The focus was upon an inner attitude, rather than upon an outer performance, and even more particularly upon the attitude lying at the very center of one's loyalties and loves. If this attitude is sincere the heart may be said to be sound, "as an Apple . . . is said to be sound, when it is not rotten at the core, though there be many specks in it; and a Ship is said to be sound, when there is no leaks in it, though it may have other flawes, and defects; and a Vessell is said to be sound, when there is no clift in the bottom, though it may otherwise be brused and battered."[180] This is "integrity of the heart" and includes a purity of heart that rejects all sin, a wholeness of heart that respects all the commandments, an uprightness of heart that aims at God's glory and one's own salvation, and a simplicity or singleness of heart that cleaves only to God.[181]

To such an attitude the term "perfection" was also applied, though it was an "evangelical perfection" rather than a "legal perfection," one of its characteristics being the feeling and confession of one's imperfections. Indeed, Perkins added the note that if such grief is difficult and not present, but "if thou be truly and unfainedly greeved for this, that thou canst not be greeved, thy humiliation shall be accepted."[182] Thus, said Preston, "to have a heart and spirit ready to cleanse it selfe, this is to have a perfect heart. So that a Godly man . . . may have it clouded and overcast with passions and unruly affections, but yet it cleeres up againe, and hee comes out of them . . . with more cleerenesse and pureness of heart."[183]

Negatively portrayed, this sincerity of heart is seen as one's being "voyd of hipocrisie."[184] If the heart is sound, it is free from all false pretense. George Downname said that "those who are sincere and upright" are "purified from the leaven of hypocrisy," adding that "to walke uprightly is to

---

[177]Ball, *Covenant of Grace*. p. 26.

[178]Daniel Dyke, *Of Self-deceiving*, chap. 19. Quoted in R. Bolton, *Comforting Afflicted Consciences*, p. 377.

[179]Quoted in Kevan, *Grace of Law*, p. 212

[180]Preston, *New Covenant*, 1:223.

[181]Ibid., pp. 218–35.

[182]Perkins, "Whole Treatise," *Works*, 2:14.

[183]Preston, *New Covenant*, 2:2.

[184]Cole, *Godly Mans Assurance*, p. 38.

goe with a right foote neither treading awry by dissimulation nor halting . . .
to walke with God or before God without hypocrisie, in sincerity and truth,
with perfect, with pure, with whole harts."[185] So the ultimate criterion for
covenant continuation is to be found deep within. God, in accepting the will
for the deed, looks beyond one's actions and honors the "bent of the heart,"
as "the Goldsmith, who hath a skilfull eye to finde out the smaller, and
neglected wayes of gold, though covered with much drosse."[186] Without this
uprightness, said George Downame, there is no steadfastness in the covenant, for "our faith be dead, our love fained, our wisdome divelish, our
repentance unsound, our obedience counterfeit."[187] But "a sincere heart and
walke" holds one in covenant communion, for "Faith gives access to God in
grace and through sincerity we walk with God in grace, to glory."[188] When
Shepard responded to the question, "How shall I know whether I have these
[covenant] conditions truly in me?" he commented simply, "Sincerity is a
very witnessing grace."[189]

   Only rarely did Puritans raise the still further question whether, in the
light of the pervasiveness of human corruption, there can in fact be such an
unassailed inner citadel of sincerity, uprightness and purity. Might not it also
be invaded by insincerity, considering the magnitude of sin's attack even on
the regenerated will and heart? Perhaps there are no motives fully immune.
Burgess took note of this possibility, but did not really explore its implications, when, in commenting on a reference in Psalm 19 to the "errors of the
heart," he said, "there is hypocrisie in the heart of the most upright man for
which God might justly condemn him."[190]

   More extended probing of the issue came from outside Puritan orthodoxy. John Goodwin wrote that the discerning of the "uprightness and
simplicity" of one's heart is a very difficult and uncertain matter. Seldom is
such discernment built on foundations sufficient really to warrant it, so that
"the testimony which Consciences give concerning these" is liable to many
Disputes and Questions about the certainty and truth of it." Goodwin then
added, "There is not one true Believer of an hundred (I might say of many
thousands) who hath any such assurance as this of the truth and soundnesse
of their Faith."[191] Even more serious questioning came from Tobias Crisp,
an Antinomian. One cannot finally rely, he believed, on anything within our
humanity, for all partakes of frailty and corruption. This is true of such a
matter as the presumed "constant purpose of the heart." "Let me tell you,"
he declared, "there is no person under Heaven, is able to say truly . . . that

[185]G. Downame, *Covenant of Grace*, pp. 122–27.
[186]O. Sedgwick, *Doubting Beleever*, p. 162.
[187]G. Downame, *Covenant of Grace*, p. 133.
[188]Blake, *Vindiciae Foederis*, p. 158.
[189]Shepard, "Certain Select Cases Resolved," *Works*, 1:322.
[190]Burgess, *True Doctrine of Jusitification*, 2:152.
[191]J. Goodwin, *Redemption Redeemed*, p. 159.

he hath a constant purpose of heart, a constant inclination to the whole will of God." And as to "sincerity," one should know that all motives are mixed, and self-seeking is a part of the mixture for all of them. "No man," he concluded, "can find that sincerity in his heart that may comfort him." In anything we do "our hearts have by-ends in them," and "there is a defect of sincerity and singleness of heart."[192]

Whenever the orthodox considered this issue, however, it seems to have led to defense of the unassailable citadel, at least semantically if not in fact. Burgess prefaced his comment on the prevalence of hypocrisy by saying, "God doth accept of believers as sincere, that they are not hypocrites, but they are not justified by this," implying a sort of imputed sincerity despite its absence in reality. A more extended treatment, with similar conclusion, is found in George Downame. He noted that there are indeed "reliques" of corruption in the regenerate and that these include not only infidelity, pride, and self-love, but also hypocrisy. But then he added his evaluation:

> so long as a man seeth, and detesteth this corruption and laboureth to mortifie it ... though there be some matter of hypocrisie remayning in him, yet he is not formally an hypocrite, but is reputed upright.

The only hypocrites, he added, are those "in whom this corruption reigneth without resistance."[193] One may perhaps conclude from both this silence and this defense that Puritan commitment to the subjective factor in the search for assurance led to the retention of this point of final incorruptibility in the human soul. There was a sanctity of sincerity which for the saints could not be debased. Shepard had said that sincerity was "a very witnessing grace," and Puritan theology, in searching for a final subjective ground for the security of being in the covenant, was not disposed to qualify the possibility of that witness.

For a sense of continuation in the covenant sincerity of purpose must have the support, however, of dedicated endeavor. If faith without works is dead, sincerity without striving also lacks life. Inner sincerity itself is expressed and sustained by outer act. A primary way of such continued commitment was that of covenant renewal. It is wholesome, if not imperative, for the believer frequently to "own" the covenant and renew the allegiance to God which it entails. This rests back in part upon a long tradition in Elizabethan Puritanism of the private vow which the dedicated individual makes frequently to God. Sometimes these vows were general in character, sometimes very specific, making precise commitments concerning particular problems or temptations in one's life. Puritan diaries often recorded these acts of dedication as, for example, the diary of Richard Rogers

---

[192]Crisp, *Christ Alone Exalted*, pp. 449–53.
[193]G. Downame, *Covenant of Grace*, pp. 146–47.

for 1587/88 in which he noted that he, along with other ministerial colleagues, decided "to renue our covenant more firmly with the lorde, then we
had done, to come neerer to the practize of godlines and oftener to have our
conversation in heaven, our mindes seldomer and more lightly uppon the
thinges of this life."[194] Greenham looked upon these private vows as offered
"either to pricke us to good, or to stay us from some evill . . . in a desire of
Gods glorie, and in craving of Gods grace."[195] Perkins saw their value as a
binding of oneself to increase one's zeal and to make one "more forward in
duties of love to men, and the worship of God."[196] These acts of private piety
were thus encouraged as a form of private covenant.

Perhaps more commonly, however, the renewal of covenant was seen as
the reaffirmation of the broad covenant tendered in one's baptism, and thus
the committing of oneself anew to fulfillment of all the conditions of the
covenant of grace. "Sometimes God's children may be in covenant," wrote
Sibbes, "yet because they renew not their covenant, especially after some
breaches, God is not with them so comfortably as he would."[197] Thus
frequent, even daily, renewal was recommended. This can occur in private
meditation or in public worship, but especially should it occur at the
sacrament of the Lord's Supper, an ordinance instituted by God to serve this
very end. Sibbes asked concerning the sacrament, "Do we come only to
receive his love to us?" And he replied, "No; we make a covenant with God
in the sacrament that he shall be our God, and we promise by his grace to
lead new lives henceforth. We have made a covenant with God at first in
baptism, now we renew it in the taking of the sacrament."[198] Inclusion in the
covenant is strengthened by these repeated acts of commitment.

But even here the subjective concern continued to be present. The
question can be raised by the scrupulous as to whether one's act of covenant
renewal is itself purely motivated and sound. Even in the commitment made
at the Lord's table one can be tempted to question, and perhaps even despair
of, one's performance. Out of this very consideration some were hesitant to
receive the communion. Sibbes gave pastoral counsel, but it really left the
matter where it was before: God's performance in the covenant can be
counted on if in the renewal in the sacrament "we come in sincerity of
heart."[199] Yet, practically, there can be urging to this. Harris said to his
hearers, "Every time you come to the Lord's Table, you renue this Covenant

---

[194]Knappen, *Two Elizabethan Diaries*, p. 64.
[195]Richard Greenham, *Works*, 5:480. Quoted in Møller, "Beginnings of Puritan Covenant
Theology," p. 66.
[196]Perkins, "Reformed Catholike," *Works*, 1:584.
[197]Sibbes, "St. Paul's Challenge," *Works*, 7:396.
[198]Sibbes, "Faithful Covenanter," *Works*, 6:24.
[199]Ibid., p. 25.

. . . you seale to it that you wil be Gods people . . . Now therefore, see that ye be men of your words, and keepe the covenant you have made with God."[200]

If believers keep the covenant made with God, God will keep the covenant made with them. This is a further, and crucial, element in covenant certainty. Ames declared one is to understand "by the covenant that God will mightily preserve those that believe and repent."[201] This, said Bulkeley, is a source of great comfort for those who "endeavour to walk uprightly and faithfully in covenant with God," for "God cannot break with them, if they breake not with him. . . . he cannot be a covenant breaker."[202] So the very act of divine covenanting is itself understood to be an act of the self-binding of God. Ball wrote that in the covenant of grace God "is content to undertake and indent with us, and by Indenture to bind himselfe to bestow great things and incomprehensible upon us,"[203] and this is a recurrent theme in Puritan covenant theology. The very nature of covenanting involves this type of committing. In the mutuality of the covenant there is also the human commitment which is equally "binding." But human frailty prevents this from being steadily fulfilled. On the human side of the covenant there are "covenant breakers." On the divine side, however, the commitment holds, for God is God, and God is unchangeable. When God so "ties himselfe,"[204] there is certainty. Sutton wrote, "Whatsoever God hath promised or bound himselfe by covenant to performe . . . it shall come to passe at last."[205] It may not come to pass immediately, for the manner of the covenant's fulfillment rests ultimately in the working of God. However, said Preston, "though the Lord may deferre long, yet he will doe it, he cannot chuse; for it is a part of his covenant."[206]

This confidence in the bound character of the covenanting God led to still further practical reliance upon the covenant for the purpose of assurance. It was often urged that those seeking such comfort can indeed plead with God to fulfill the covenanted divine promises. It is not enough simply to await in hope the ultimate consummation of what has been committed. Rather, the covenanter can now take the initiative and press for divine performance. Bulkeley called upon such believers to "beg, intreat, require, . . . sue and plead . . . and say, Lord here is thine own Covenant and promise," holding that "such importunities the Lord will not take ill, he delights thus to be overcome by the pleas of his people."[207] In similar vein

---

[200]Harris, *New Covenant*, 2:171.

[201]Ames, *Marrow*, p. 132.

[202]Bulkeley, *Gospel-Covenant*, pp. 52–53.

[203]Ball, *Covenant of Grace*, p. 199.

[204]Bacon, *Spirit of Prelacie Working*, p. 18.

[205]Sutton, *Lectures on Romans*, p. 401.

[206]Preston, *New Covenant*, 2:231.

[207]Bulkeley, *Gospel-Covenant*, p. 237.

Harris affirmed that God "takes it wel, if we mind him of his covenant, and presse him with his promise," adding the conviction that "the more wee urge him with his covenant, and hold him to it, the better hee likes it and the sooner he inclines to us."[208] God will then surely "stand to his word, and be as good as his bargaine."[209]

The importunities, moreover, can be comprehensive in scope, reaching out toward all that God has promised the faithful as covenant blessing. Harris did note that "temporall things indeed you must seeke and aske of God with reservation, if God sees it good for you," but with regard to spiritual mercies "you may aske them absolutely."[210] If one's conscience is distressed by a sense of guilt, said Preston, one should "goe to the Lord and say, "Lord, notwithstanding this, I know I am in covenant with thee, and Lord, this is one part of thy covenant, that thou wilt remember our sinnes no more." One must "tell him it is a part of his Covenant, and ... hee cannot be a Covenant-breaker." Similarly, one can plead for other covenant gifts which God has promised, as the overcoming of "some strong lust, some violent temptation," or deliverance from "any calamity, any crosse, and disease, any affliction."[211] Wherever there is a covenant promise one can plead with God for its fulfillment. Cotton spoke of this entreating of the Lord by those in covenant as a way to "make use of" the covenant for "the perfecting of their salvation."[212] In the conditional covenant one can be confident that God will be faithful to those who comply with the stated conditions. Covenant certainty rests strongly upon the bound nature of the covenanting God.

And yet, in the last analysis, there is also that still further dimension contributed by the conviction that the covenant promises of God are not only conditional, but likewise absolute. If God's promise in the evangelical covenant is to be faithful in mercy to those who themselves live in covenant faith and faithfulness, the very fulfillment of that condition rests upon the further, and even prior, promise of God to give such compliance itself as divine gift. Said Sibbes, God "works ... our part and his own too. In effect, he makes a testament, and not a covenant."[213] Here, again, evangel and election go together. The promises of God revealed as part of the economy of the Gospel cannot be separated from those that reflect the sovereign decrees of eternity. The divine promises are given both to piety and from predestination. Thus a final comment must be made concerning the inter-relationship of the conditional and the absolute in the Puritan search for covenant certainty.

From a general theological perspective the ultimate theoretical ground

[208]Harris, *New Covenant*, 2:163.
[209]Ibid., p. 195.
[210]Ibid., 1:42.
[211]Preston, *New Covenant*, 2:224–30.
[212]Cotton, *Covenant of Gods free Grace*, pp. 23–24.
[213]Sibbes, "Bride's Longing," *Works*, 6:542.

for certainty is located in the absolute covenant and its promises. Here is the comfort that all Calvinism found in the doctrine of predestination. Salvation is in sovereign hands, and for those for whom it is destined it cannot be subverted by human weakness or sin. God "effects what he hath decreed, and as he decreed,"[214] wrote Ames, and this "doth make this inheritance firme and sure unto us . . . because all the whole businesse of our salvation depends upon the omnipotency of God."[215] Or, from another perspective, Perkins noted that if the decree of God is mutable, then uncertainty will result, "whereby that notable stay and onely sure ground of our full assurance to bee saved, is utterly shaken and overturned."[216] The absolute promise, therefore, must underlie all covenant certainty, at least in the sense of assuring that what is eternally decreed will truly come to pass. One does not need to fear a human impeding of the divine plan.

Certainty, however, must be more personally appropriated, and it is here that the conditional promises play their important role. Bulkeley's observation was that "the absolute promises are laid before us as the foundation of our salvation . . . and the conditionall as the foundation of our assurance." The former, he affirmed, were the ground for the "faith of adherence," whereas it was basically on the latter that "faith of assurance" must rest,[217] a conviction maintaining that distinction of long and important standing in Puritan thought. And two matters, as we have indeed seen, are involved in this form of assurance. On the one hand, there is the subjective search for "evidences" and the confidence that can come from such "tryall of our estates" as may reveal one's fulfillment of the covenant's conditions. And on the other hand, there is the confidence resting upon the reliability of God as one who makes the conditional promises and, in being self-bound by them, will be faithful in carrying them out. All told, then, covenant certainty is more personally approprated through this use of the conditional covenant.

And yet, the absolute promises are not abandoned even in this latter Puritan search. Personal appropriation can continue to look to them as well, for evangel and election cannot really be separated even here, as the one covenant remains both conditional and absolute. Even Peter Bulkeley, whose reliance upon evidences of the fulfillment of conditions figured so large in his understanding of assurance, felt that there were times from a pastoral perspective when it was more profitable to stress reliance upon the absolute promises of God. When carelessness and a sense of security prevail among Christians, he declared, it is important to look to the conditional promises and the qualifications they prescribe, "not giving rest unto our selves untill we finde them in our selves." But contrariwise, he added,

[214]Ames, *Marrow*, p. 23.
[215]Ames, *Analytical Exposition of Peter*, pp. 10–11.
[216]Perkins, "Golden Chaine," *Works*, 1:99.
[217]Bulkeley, *Gospel-Covenant*, pp. 323–24.

"when the soule lyes under feare, pressed downe with a sense of our own vile unworthinesse, then is a time to looke unto the absolute promises, considering . . . the Lord hath promised for his owne sake to succour us, and to doe us good."[218]

Even as the fulfillment of the conditions was essential, therefore, it was by God's absolute promise that they were to be fulfilled. God's saving act rested upon God's sovereign act, the supplying of the conditions requisite for salvation. So in the search for personal certainty Thomas Shepard could ask the question as to how one might "seek for the good of the absolute promises, as therein to find (oneself) within the compass of some conditionall one." Though grounds for assurance are in the conditional covenant, they are not removed from the covenant as absolute. Reliance must somehow be upon the promises of the latter in order that it may also be on the conditions of the former. Shepard counselled that one may even "sue for the good of the absolute promise until . . . he perceives himself adorned and dignified with the qualifications of some conditional promise; and then . . . he may conclude that the conditional promise belongs to him."[219] Thus covenant certainty may involve a pleading with God to fulfill not only the promises of the evangel, but also those of election! Sibbes likewise encouraged this importuning. One can appropriately cry out, "Lord . . . thou knowest I cannot perform . . . the condition thou requirest, of myself. But in the covenant of grace thou hast said thou wilt make good the condition"[220]— and so one can implore God to fulfill the absolute promise itself.

But will God fulfill in one's own life the absolute promise? Subjective evidences must be searched out as testimony *ex post facto*, but assurance also rests upon the fact of the absolute promise itself. Shepard, who urged that one "sue" for that promise's fulfillment, also urged that in the process of expectation one be "humbly contented . . . seeing the Lord hath absolutely promised to work and do all for the soul he intends for to save."[221] And Ames added another significant dimension when he spoke of this in the more traditional language of God's decree, for "in the Decree of God," he wrote, "there appeareth his . . . faithfulnesse."[222] Not only the God of the evangel is faithful, but also the God of election. Even here, in the mysterious realm of predestination, the emphasis is not upon divine arbitrariness, but upon divine fidelity.

This linkage, then, between the guarantee of the promises of the conditional covenant and that of the promises of the absolute covenant can likewise witness to the duality in the grounds for one's hope. Without question the major emphasis in Puritan theology and practice was upon the

[218]Ibid., pp. 405–6.
[219]Shepard, "Certain Select Cases Resolved," *Works*, 1:320.
[220]Sibbes, "Faithful Covenanter," *Works*, 6:24.
[221]Shepard, "Certain Select Cases Resolved," *Works*, 1:320.
[222]Ames, *Marrow*, p. 23.

conditional. This was the direction of Gospel piety, leading to the introspective search for evidence of covenant partnership with a faithfully responding
God. But as the doctrinal heritage of predestination was united with these
concerns of piety, the search for certainty needed to recognize another kind
of faithfulness, that which carried out the promise actually to supply the
conditions upon which one's covenant partnership was based. Like the
Puritan doctrine of the covenant, the Puritan view of assurance held together
both the conditional and the absolute.[223] When Perkins discussed the
certainty of one's election at the conclusion of "A Golden Chaine," he
portrayed this duality found within Puritan thought. He wrote that such
assurance must come especially from "the testimonie of God's spirit, and the
workes of Sanctification." And yet, he also added, since our salvation
"neither dependeth upon workes, nor faith, but upon Gods decree . . . this
teacheth that the anker of hope must be fixed in that truth and stability of the
immutable good pleasure of God."[224]

[223]For a parallel statement to this concluding observation see Stoever, 'A Faire and Easie Way',
pp. 147–48.
[224]Perkins, "Golden Chaine," Works, 1:114.

APPENDIX

The Continental Beginnings of Covenant Theology

Since Luther made almost no mention of the covenant concept, the sixteenth century beginnings of covenant theology are found in the Swiss Reformed tradition, with its two originating centers of Zurich and Geneva. Although Huldreich Zwingli (1484–1531) introduced the use of the covenant idea in Zurich, its fuller blossoming and larger influence came through the work of his successor, Heinrich Bullinger (1504–1575). Both reformers interpreted the covenant as a unifying element throughout the entirety of biblical history, the way of God's salvation in times of both Old and New Testament. But whereas Zwingli emphasized somewhat more the gift character of the covenant and its blessings, Bullinger stressed strongly the covenant's bilateral nature and the fullness of responsible human participation required.

Thus the covenant of grace for Bullinger was a conditional covenant. In his understanding the covenant's conditions were expressed throughout the biblical literature: God's requiring of faith and a blameless walk in the covenant with Abraham, the moral mandates of the Law and the prophets, the teachings of Christ concerning the duties of love for God and neighbor, and the still further reiterations of these obligations in the apostolic church. And yet, though this element of conditionality was central, the covenant was not understood by Bullinger in terms reminiscent of the "pact" of late medieval nominalism with its semi-Pelagian optimism and its tendency toward a purely legalistic *quid pro quo*. For Bullinger the conditional covenant resided within the context of the Reformation doctrine of justification by faith and a doctrine of single predestination, God's election of some for salvation. However, Bullinger does not appear to have sought to resolve the tensions which such juxtaposition of ideas would produce. The freedom of God's election is maintained, but also the fact of human responsibility for fulfillment of covenant conditions. Despite the fact that salvation was *sola gratia*, the covenant remained bilateral, contingent upon human response. One could affirm that those who had faith were the elect, but faith was a human condition to be exercised. So tensions remained between the grace of predestination and a bilateral covenant of grace. For a presentation of this aspect of Bullinger's views see J. Wayne Baker, *Heinrich Bullinger and the Covenant: The Other Reformation*, Prologue and Chapters 1 and 2.

The second center of early Reformed thought was Geneva, and there under John Calvin (1509–1564) the idea of covenant took a different form, tending in the direction of being God's unilateral action for saving the elect. Calvin affirmed a doctrine of double predestination, but it is doubtful that the doubling of God's decree affected perceptibly his covenant thought. The covenant was strictly a covenant of grace and God's action within it was saving. But Calvin's idea of predestination took a more explicitly operative form than did Bullinger's, becoming the basis for inclusion in the covenant. In the exercise of divine sovereignty God brings the elect into the covenant of grace. This means that the conditional element is considerably minimized in Calvin's understanding. His language here was not always clear or consistent, and some interpreters see in his thinking a contingency factor. Yet basically faith is not a human condition to be fulfilled, but a gift of God through the Holy Spirit resting on a promise of free mercy. The character of faith may appear human, but the source is divine. Thus at this point the covenant is announced, rather than urged. There was for Calvin, however, a conditional factor for those within the covenant itself, for covenant inclusion mandates responsibility for faithfulness, that is, obedience to the requirements of God's law. For Calvin, as for Bullinger, the covenant was the way of God's salvation throughout the whole of history, but dissimilarity in emphasis existed between the two with regard to the roles of both human and divine action.

Beyond these beginnings in Zurich and Geneva use of the covenant theme soon developed in Swiss and German Rhineland cities, especially through the work of Johannes Oecolampadius (1482–1531) and Martin Cellarius (1499–1564) in Basel and of Martin Bucer (1491–1551) and Wolfgang Capito (1478–1541) in Strassburg. Leonard Trinterud associates each of these early Reformed theologians with the Bullinger emphasis, even seeing in Rhineland covenant theology as a whole a "law-covenant" pattern in which God's covenant is a conditional promise, so relying on human response as to create, in effect, a mutual pact or treaty. Wayne Baker, however, disputes this characterization of the other Rhineland leaders with the exception of Bucer. Rather, he sees in the work of Oecolampadius, Cellarius, and Capito, as likewise in that of the other early Reformed theologians, a view portraying the covenant as God's unilateral action in saving the elect. Only Bucer among them, in Baker's judgment, adopted a bilateral view, following in 1527 the path which Bullinger had established. It is also to be noted that within the Lutheran tradition Philip Melanchthon (1497–1560) developed in the 1550s a view affirming human cooperation with God's grace in the process of salvation, leading to the concept of a mutual covenant in which the divine-human condition was faith.

Further employment of covenant thought occurred on the continent throughout the late sixteenth and early seventeenth centuries, with a new and important Reformed center being developed in Holland. On the whole, within Reformed theology, tensions continued between the Bullinger and Calvin emphases, and out of this came even more contrasting and extreme views. The Bullinger tradition was initially continued in Switzerland by Wolfgang Musculus (1497–1563) of Bern, but soon found an expanded expression among increasingly liberal Reformed leaders in Holland. Johannes Veluanus and Gellius Snecanus were early representatives there, followed later by Cornelius Wiggertsz. Among these theologians the conditional character of the covenant was strongly emphasized, with faith and love as its conditions, and this view, then, led them more and more toward an Arminian universalism with respect to the divine offering of salvation and likewise toward an interpretation of predestination which saw it as conditional in nature. Indeed, Wiggertsz (d. 1624) explicitly expounded these views at the end of the sixteenth century and for this was excommunicated in 1598 by the Dutch Reformed church.

Within the Calvin tradition, on the contrary, there developed a growing rigidity concerning divine sovereignty, shaped by an emerging scholasticism. And prominent among Holland's extreme Calvinists, then, were covenant theologians who viewed God's covenanting in a quite different light than did their liberal contemporaries. Franciscus Junius (1545–1602), professor at Leyden for the last decade of his life, combined covenant thought with a supralapsarian double predestinarianism, as did his younger Leyden colleague, Franciscus Gomarus (1557–1644), who also later taught at Groningen. It was Gomarus who led the struggle against Arminianism in the succeeding decades and there portrayed the covenant of grace as fulfilled entirely by God's sovereign working in the elect. Probably the most important Dutch covenant theologian, however, fitted neither the Arminian nor Calvinist extreme position. This was Johannes Cocceius (1603–1669), who taught at Bremen, Franeker, and Leyden, but entered the scene well after the heat of the condemnation of Arminianism at the Synod of Dort (1619). Though a follower of Calvin, his struggle was with scholastic Calvinism, and his effort involved replacing a theology based on decrees with one more faithful to the reality of God's saving actions through the course of biblical and subsequent history. To that end human participation in history's succession of covenants was of utmost importance, and the covenantal relationship with God was seen by Cocceius under the categories of both divine sovereignty and human act.

Another significant development in continental covenant theology occurred in Germany through the work of Zacharius Ursinus (1534–1583) and Caspar Olevianus (1535–1587), the authors of the Heidelberg Catechism. This was the development of the idea of a yet earlier covenant than the covenant of grace in God's relationship with humanity. If the covenant of grace was given to a fallen people, then prior to the fall another had prevailed defining God's original expectations and promises. Other theologians had anticipated this idea, but now in Heidelberg in the 1560s it was made explicit. Ursinus spoke of it as the "natural covenant." Olevianus added the terms "covenant of creation" and "legal covenant." Not long thereafter this Edenic covenant came to be know in federal theology as the "covenant of works." Thus by the 1580s covenant theology spoke of God's two covenants with humanity, the one pristine and soon broken by human act, the second subsequent and established by divine redemptive mercy. Both Ursinus and Olevianus placed the covenant of grace itself within the framework of a double predestinarian Calvinism, seeing it as a gift of God to the elect and the consequence of unconditional election. Ursinus, however, as a former student of Melanchthon, also viewed the covenant as a mutual pact, thus bringing together seemingly without resolution the contrasting themes in Reformed covenant understanding.

One further significant expression of continental covenant thought appeared in the writings of Moses Amyraut (1596–1664), French Huguenot theologian and leading figure in the academy at Saumur where additional effort was made to overcome the growing scholasticism of Calvinist theology. Actually, Amyraut had been influenced by a Scottish Puritan predecessor at Saumur, John Cameron (1580–1625), and so there is a not insignificant connection between his outlook and that of British Puritanism itself. Like the Puritans, Amyraut spoke of the covenant of grace as both conditional and absolute, but made knowledge of the latter dependent upon awareness of the former. Predestination is affirmed, but not because of the decrees. Rather, it is permissible in theology only as explanation of why some have fulfilled covenant conditions and others have not. Thus by attention to the conditional covenant both the mystery and the mercy of the absolute covenant can be known.

BIBLIOGRAPHY

PRIMARY SOURCES

Ainsworth, Henry. *A Seasonable Discourse, or a Censure upon a Dialogue of the Anabaptists, Intitled, A Description of what God hath Predestined concerning Man.* 1623. Reprint, London, 1644.

Allen, William. *A Discourse of the Nature, Ends, and Differences of the Two Covenants.* London, 1673.

Ames, William. *An Analytical Exposition of both Epistles of the Apostle Peter . . . and applyed by their uses, for a further progress in holinesse.* London, 1641.

————. *The Marrow of Sacred Divinity, Drawne out of the Holy Scriptures and the Interpreters thereof, and brought into Method.* London, 1642.

Bacon, Robert. *The Spirit of Prelacie Yet Working. Or, Truth From Under a Cloud.* London, 1646.

Ball, John. *A Treatise of the Covenant of Grace: wherein the graduall breakings out of Gospel-grace from Adam to Christ are clearly discovered . . . diverse errours of Arminians and others are confuted.* London, 1645.

————. *A Treatise of Faith, Divided into Two Parts, The first shewing the Nature, The second, the Life of Faith.* Second edition. London, 1632.

Baxter, Richard. *Aphorismes of Justification with their Explication Annexed, wherein also is opened the nature of the covenants, satisfaction, Righteousnesse, Faith, Works, etc.* Hague, 1655.

————. *Of Saving Faith: That it is not only gradually, but specifically distinct from all Common FAITH.* London, 1658.

————. "A Christian Directory." *The Practical Works of the Rev. Richard Baxter.* 23 vols. London, 1830.

————. *A Treatise of Justifying Righteousness.* London, 1676.

Baynes, Paul. *Briefe Directions unto a Godly Life.* London, 1637.

————. *Christian Letters of Mr. Paul Baynes.* London, 1637.

————. *A Commentarie upon the First and Second Chapters of Saint Paul to the Colossians.* 2 pts. London, 1634.

————. *A Commentary upon the whole Epistle of the Apostle Paul to the Ephesians . . . opened, with a logical analysis, spiritual and holy observations, confutation of Arminianisme and Popery.* Fifth edition. London, 1658.

————. *A Helpe to true Happinesse: or, a briefe and learned exposition of the maine and fundamental points of Christian religion.* Third edition. London, 1635.

————. *Holy Soliloquies: or a Holy Helper in God's building.* Second edition. London, 1618.

————. *The Trial of a Christian Estate: Or a Discoverie of the Causes, degrees, signes and differences of the Apostasie both of true Christians and false.* London, 1618.

————. *Two Godly and Fruitfull Treatises: The one, Upon the Lords Prayer: The other, Upon the sixe Principles.* London, 1619.

Blake, Thomas. *Vindiciae Foederis: Or, A Treatise of the Covenant of God Entered with Man-kinde.* London, 1658.

Bolton, Robert. *Instructions for a Right Comforting Afflicted Consciences, with special Antidotes against some grievous temptations.* London, 1631.

————. *Some Generall Directions for a Comfortable Walking with God.* Fifth edition. London, 1638.

Bolton, Samuel. *The Sinfulness of Sin: held forth in a sermon preached ... at Margarets Westminster.* London, 1646.

————. *The True Bounds of Christian Freedome: Or a Treatise wherein the Rights of the Law are vindicated, the Liberties of Grace maintained, And the severall late Opinions against the Law are examined and confuted.* London, 1645.

Bulkeley, Peter. *The Gospel-Covenant; or The Covenant of Grace Opened.* Second edition. London, 1651.

Bunyan, John. *A Defence of the Doctrine of Justification by Faith.* London, 1672.

————. *The Doctrine of the Law and Grace Unfolded.* London, 1659.

————. *Grace Abounding to the Chief of Sinners.* London, 1666.

Burgess, Anthony. *The True Doctrine of Justification Asserted and Vindicated, From the errours of Papists, Arminians, Socinians, and more especially Antinomians.* 2 pts. London, 1655.

————. *Vindiciae Legis: Or, A Vindication of the Morall Law and the Covenants, From the Errours of Papists, Arminians, Socinians, and more especially Antinomians.* London, 1646.

————. "A Treatise of Grace and Assurance." *Spiritual Refining,* pt. 1. London, 1652.

Calamy, Edmund. *The Great Danger of Covenant-refusing, and Covenant-breaking.* London, 1646.

————. *Two solemne Covenants made Between God and Man: viz. The Covenant of Workes, and the Covenant of Grace.* London, 1647.

Calvin, John. *Institutes of the Christian Religion.* Edited by• John T. McNeill, translated by Ford Lewis Battles. 2 vols. Philadelphia: Westminster Press, 1970.

Cameron, John. *Certain Theses, or Positions of the Learned John Cameron, Concerning the three-fold Covenant of God with Man.* Printed in Samuel

Bolton, *The True Bounds of Christian Freedome*. London, 1645. pp. 353–401.

Capel, Richard. *Tentations: their nature, danger, cure*. London, 1633.

Caryl, Joseph. *Heaven and Earth Embracing; or, God and Man Approaching*. London, 1646.

Cochrane, Arthur C. *Reformed Confessions of the 16th Century*. Philadelphia: Westminster Press, 1966.

Cole, Nathanael. *The Godly Mans Assurance: Or A Christians Certaine Resolution of his owne Salvation*. Fourth edition. London, 1633.

Cotton, John. *The Covenant of Gods free Grace, Most sweetly unfolded, and comfortably applied to a disquieted Soul*. London, 1645.

———. *Severall Questions of Serious and necessary Consequence*. London, 1647.

———. *A Treatise of the Covenant of Grace, As it is dispensed to the Elect Seed, effectually unto Salvation*. Third edition. London, 1671.

The Covenant of Grace not Absolute, but Conditional, Modestly Asserted. London, 1692.

Crisp, Tobias. *Christ Alone Exalted*. 1642. Reprint, London, 1690.

Crooke, Samuel. *The Guide unto True Blessednesse*. London, 1613.

Culverwell, Ezekiel. *A Treatise of Faith: Wherein is declared, how a man may live by Faith, and finde reliefe in all his necessities*. Seventh edition. London, 1633.

Davenport, John. *The knowledge of Christ indispensably required of all men that would be saved*. London, 1653.

———. *The Saint's Anchor-hold in all storms and tempests*. London, 1661.

Dent, Arthur. *The Opening of Heavens gates, Or The ready way to everlasting life*. London, 1610.

———. *The Plaine Mans Path-way to Heaven. Wherein every man may cleerly see whether he shall be saved or damned*. 1601. Twelfth edition. London, 1610.

———. *A sermon on God's Providence*. London, 1609.

Downame, George. *The Covenant of Grace*. Dublin, 1631.

———. *A Treatise of the Certainty of Perseverance*. Dublin, 1631.

———. *A Treatise of Justification*. London, 1633.

Downame, John. *The Christian Warfare*. 1604. Third edition. London, 1612–19.

———. *A Guide to Godlynesse, Or a Treatise of a Christian Life shewing the duties wherein it consisteth*. London, 1622.

Downe, John. *Of the Faith of Infants, and How they are Justified and Saved*. Oxford, 1635.

———. *A Treatise of the True Nature and Definition of justifying faith*. Oxford, 1635.

Draxe, Thomas. *The churches securitie. Togither with the antidote or preservative of ever waking faith*. London, 1608.

Durham, James. *The Law Unsealed: Or, A Practical Exposition of the Ten Commandments*. Edinburgh, 1676.

Dyke, Daniel. *A Commentary Upon the Epistle of Saint Paul to Philemon*. London, 1618.

Eaton, John. *The Honey-Combe of Free Justification by Christ alone*. London, 1642.

E. F. *The Marrow of Modern Divinity, Touching both the Covenant of Works, and the Covenant of Grace*. London, 1646.

Fenner, William. *The riches of grace: A treatise shewing the value and excellency of a gracious spirit*. London, 1641.

———. *A treatise of the affections: or the soules pulse. Whereby a Christian may know whether he be living or dying*. London, 1642.

Flavel, John. *The Reasonableness of Personal Reformation and the Necessity of Conversion*. London, 1691.

Forbes, John. *A Letter . . . for resolving this Question: How a Christian man may discerne the testimonie of Gods spirit, from the testimonie of his owne spirit, in witnessing his Adoption*. Middelburgh, 1616.

———. *A Treatise Tending to Cleare the Doctrine of Justification*. Middelburgh, 1616.

Ford, Simon. *The Spirit of Bondage and Adoption*. London, 1655.

Geree, Stephen. *The doctrine of the Antinomians by evidence of Gods truth, plainely confuted*. London, 1644.

Goad, Thomas. *A Disputation concerning the Necessity and Contingency of Events, in respect of God's Eternal Decrees*. Published in *A Collection of Tracts Concerning Predestination and Providence*. Cambridge, 1719.

Goodwin, John. *The Agreement and Distance of Brethren*. London, 1652.

———. *Imputatio Fidei. Or A Treatise of Justification wherein ye imputation of faith for righteousness . . . is explained*. London, 1642.

———. *Redemption Redeemed*. London, 1651.

Goodwin, Thomas. "Of Christ the Mediator." *Works*, vol. 3. London, 1692.

Greenham, Richard. *Works . . . collected . . . by H. H.* Third edition. London, 1601.

Harris, Robert. *A Treatise of the New Covenant*. 2 pts. London, 1632.

———. *The Way to True Happinesse*. 2 pts. London, 1632.

Harsnet, Samuel. *A Sermon Preached at S. Pauls Cross in London (1584)*. Published in Richard Stuart, *Three Sermons*. London, 1656.

Heppe, Heinrich. *Reformed Dogmatics*. Edited by Ernst Bizer, translated by G. T. Thomson. London: Allen & Unwin, 1950.

Hoard, Samuel. *Gods Love to Mankind, manifested by disproving his absolute decree for their damnation*. London, 1633.

Hooker, Thomas. *The Application of Redemption by the effectual Work of the Word, and Spirit of Christ, for the bringing home of lost Sinners to God*. London, 1656.

———. *The Covenant of Grace, opened*. London, 1649.

———. *An Exposition of the Principles of Religion.* London, 1645.

———. *The Faithful Covenanter.* London, 1644.

———. *The Soules Exaltation. A Treatise containing The Soules Union with Christ, The Soules Benefit from Union with Christ, The Soules Justification.* London, 1638.

———. *The Soules Vocation, or Effectual Calling to Christ.* London, 1637.

The Iudgement of the Synode holden at Dort, concerning the five Articles. London, 1619.

Jacob, Henry. *A Treatise of the Sufferings and Victory of Christ, in the work of our redemption.* London, 1598.

Jeanes, Henry. *A Vindication of Dr. Twisse from the Exceptions of Mr. John Goodwin in his Redemption Redeemed.* Printed in William Twisse, *The Riches of Gods Love.* Oxford, 1653.

Jenison, Robert. *Concerning Gods Certaine Performance of his conditional Promises, as touching the Elect.* Printed in Robert Jenison, *Two Treatises.* London, 1642.

———. *Concerning the extent of Christs death and love.* Printed in Robert Jenison, *Two Treatises.* London, 1642.

Knappen, M. M., ed. *Two Elizabethan Puritan Diaries. By Richard Rogers and Samuel Ward.* Chicago: American Society of Church History, 1933.

Leigh, Edward. *A System or Body of Divinity.* London, 1662.

———. *The Treatise of the Divine Promises.* London, 1633.

———. *A Treatise of Religion and Learning.* London, 1656.

Lightfoote, John. *Miscellanies Christian and Judiciall.* London, 1629.

Marshal, Walter. *Gospel Mystery of Sanctification.* London, 1692.

Mather, Cotton. *Magnalia Christi Americana.* Hartford: Silas Andrus, 1820.

Milbourne, William. *Wisdome Crying out to Sinners to returne from their evill wayes.* London, 1639.

Nichols, Josias. *Abraham's Faith.* London, 1602.

Norton, John. *The Answer.* Translated by Douglas Horton. Cambridge, Mass.: Harvard University Press, Belknap Press, 1958.

Owen, John. *The Doctrine of Justification by Faith through the Imputation of the Righteousness of Christ.* London, 1677.

Pemble, William. *Vindiciae fidei, or a treatise of Justification by faith.* Oxford, 1625.

Perkins, William. "A Brief Discourse Taken out of the Writings of H. Zanchius." *Works.* London, 1631. 1:429–38

———. "A Case of Conscience, the Greatest that ever was: how a man may know whether he be the childe of God or no." *Works.* London, 1631. 1:421–28.

———. "A Christian and Plaine Treatise of the Manner and Order of Predestination, and of the largenesse of Gods Grace." *Works.* London, 1631. 2:603–41.

————. *A Commentarie, Or, Exposition upon the five first Chapters of the Epistle to the Galatians*. Cambridge, 1617.

————. "A Discourse of Conscience. Wherein is set down the nature, properties, and differences thereof: as also the way to get and keepe a good Conscience." *Works*. London, 1631. 1:515–54.

————. "A Discourse of Witchcraft." *Works*. London, 1631. 3:607–52.

————. "An Exposition of the Symbole or Creed of the Apostles." *Works*. Cambridge, 1608. 1:123–329.

————. "A faithfull and plaine Exposition Upon the Two First Verses of the second Chapter of Zephaniah." *Works*. London, 1631. 3:411–27.

————. "A Godly and Learned Exposition upon Christs Sermon in the Mount." *Works*. London, 1631. 3:1–264.

————. "A Golden Chaine: Or, The Description of Theologie: Containing the Order of the Causes of Salvation and Damnation." *Works*. London, 1631. 1:9–116.

————. "A Graine of Musterd-seede: Or, the Least Measure of Grace that is or can be effectuall to salvation." *Works*. Cambridge, 1608. 1:627–34.

————. "A Reformed Catholike." *Works*. Cambridge, 1608. 1:549–618.

————. *Ten Letters (1586–1602)*. Printed in H. C. Porter, *Puritanism in Tudor England*. Columbia, S. C.: University of South Carolina Press, 1971.

————. "A Treatise of Gods Free-grace and Mans free-will." *Works*. London, 1631. 1:717–46.

————. "A Treatise of Mans Imaginations. Shewing His naturall evill thoughts, His want of good thoughts: The way to reforme them." *Works*. London, 1631. 2:453–83.

————. "A Treatise Tending unto a Declaration, Whether a Man be in the Estate of Damnation or in the Estate of Grace." Works. London, 1631. 1:353–420.

————. "The Whole Treatise of the Cases of Conscience." *Works*. London, 1631. 2:1–152.

Plaifere, John. *Appello Evangelium for the True Doctrine of the Divine Predestination, Concorded with the Orthodox Doctrine of Gods Free-Grace, and Mans Free-Will*. London, 1652.

Powell, Vavasor. *Christ and Moses Excellency, or Sion and Sinai's Glory . . . distinguishing and explaining the Two Covenants*. London, 1650.

Preston, John. *The Breast-Plate of Faith and Love*. 3 pts. Second edition. London, 1630.

————. *The Golden Scepter Held Forth to the Humble*. 2 pts. Edited by Thomas Goodwin and Thomas Ball. London, 1638.

————. *Life Eternall or, A Treatise Of the knowledge of the Divine Essence and Attributes*. 2 pts. Edited by Thomas Goodwin and Thomas Ball. London, 1631.

————. *A Liveles Life: Or, Mans Spirituall death in Sinne*. 2 pts. Third edition. London, 1635.

———. *The New Covenant, or the Saints Portion. A Treatise Unfolding the All-sufficiencie of God, and Mans uprightnes, and the Covenant of grace.* 3 pts. Edited by Richard Sibbes and John Davenport. London, 1629.

———. *The Position of John Preston . . . Concerning the Irresistibleness of Converting Grace.* London, 1654.

———. *The Saints Qualification: or, A Treatise I. Of Humiliation . . . II. Of Sanctification.* Third edition. London, 1637.

———. *Sermons: New Life.* London, 1631.

———. *Sinnes Overthrow: or, A Godly and Learned Treatise of Mortification.* Third edition. London, 1635.

Prynne, William. *Anti-Arminianisme.* London, 1630.

———. *The Perpetuitie of a Regenerate Mans Estate.* London, 1626.

Resbury, Richard. *The Lightless-Starre: Or, Mr. John Goodwin discovered a Pelagio-Socinian.* London, 1652.

———. *Some stop to the Gangrene of Arminianism, Lately promoted by M. John Goodwin in his Book entituled, Redemption Redeemed.* London, 1651.

Roberts, Francis. *Mysterium & Medulla Bibliorum. The Mystery and Marrow of the Bible: viz. God's Covenants with Man.* London, 1657.

Rogers, John. *The Doctrine of Faith.* Second edition. London, 1627.

Rogers, Nehemiah. *The True Convert.* 3 pts. London, 1632.

Rogers, Richard. *Seven Treatises.* London, 1603.

Rogers, Timothy. *The Righteous Mans Evidences for Heaven.* Fourth edition. London, 1621.

Rutherfurd, Samuel. *The Covenant of Life Opened: Or, A Treatise of the Covenant of Grace.* Edinburgh, 1655.

———. *A Survey of the Spirituall Antichrist.* London, 1648.

The Sacred Doctrine of Divinitie. London, 1599.

Saltmarsh, John. *Dawnings of Light.* London, 1646.

———. *Free-Grace: Or, The Flowings of Christs Blood freely to Sinners.* Sixth edition. London, 1649.

———. *Sparkles of Glory: Or, some Beams of the Morning-Star.* London, 1648.

Sedgwick, John. *Antinomianisme Anatomized. Or, A Glasse for the Lawlesse: Who deny the Ruling use of the Morall Law unto Christians under the Gospel.* London, 1643.

Sedgwick, Obadiah. *The Bowels of Tender Mercy sealed in the Everlasting Covenant.* London, 1661.

———. *The Doubting Beleever: Or, A Treatise Containing The Nature, The Kinds, The Springs, The Remedies of Doubtings, incident to weak Beleevers.* London, 1653.

Schaff, Philip, ed. *The Creeds of Christendom.* 3 vols. New York: Harper and Brothers, 1877.

Shepard, Thomas. "To the Reader." Printed in Peter Bulkeley, *The Gospel-Covenant*. London, 1651.

———. *Works*. 3 vols. Edited by John A. Albro. Boston: Doctrinal Tract and Book Society, 1853.

Sibbes, Richard. "The Art of Contentment." *Works*. 5:175–93. Edinburgh, 1863.

———. "Bowels Opened: or, Expository Sermons on Canticles." *Works*. 2:1–195. Edinburgh, 1862.

———. "The Bride's Longing for her Bridegroom's Second Coming." *Works*. 6:553–60. Edinburgh, 1863.

———. "The Christian's End." *Works*. 5:287–322. Edinburgh, 1863.

———. "Commentary upon the First Chapter of the Second Epistle of St. Paul to the Corinthians." *Works*. 3:1–537. Edinburgh, 1862.

———. "The Demand of a Good Conscience." *Works*. 7:478–91. Edinburgh, 1864.

———. "Divine Meditations and Holy Contemplations." *Works*. 7:179–228. Edinburgh, 1864.

———. "The Faithful Covenanter." *Works*. 6:1–25. Edinburgh, 1863.

———. "The Fountain Opened: or, The Mystery of Godliness Revealed." *Works*. 5:457–540. Edinburgh, 1863.

———. "A Glance of Heaven: or, A Precious Taste of a Glorious Feast." *Works*. 4:152–200. Edinburgh, 1862.

———. "The Life of Faith." *Works*. 5:357–84. Edinburgh, 1863.

———. "Lydia's Conversion." *Works*. 6:519–534. Edinbrugh, 1863.

———. "The Pattern of Purity." *Works*. 7:505–16. Edinburgh, 1864.

———. "The Privileges of the Faithful." *Works*. 5:249–85. Edinburgh, 1863.

———. "St. Paul's Challenge." *Works*. 7:386–97. Edinburgh, 1864.

———. "Salvation Applied." *Works*. 5:385–408. Edinburgh, 1863.

———. "The Soul's Conflict With Itself, And Victory Over Itself By Faith." *Works*. 1:119–294. Edinburgh, 1862.

Strong, William. *A Discourse of the Two Covenants: Wherein The Nature, Differences, and Effects of the Covenant of Works and of Grace are ... discussed*. Edited by Th. Gale. London, 1678.

———. *A Treatise Shewing the Subordination of the Will of Man unto the Will of God*. London, 1657.

Sutton, Thomas. *Lectures on the 11th Chapter of Romans*. Edited by John Downame. London, 1632.

Taylor, Francis. *Gods Choise and Mans Diligence: in which is explained the Doctrine of free Election, and Vocation answerable to it*. London, 1654.

———. *Gods Glory in Mans Happiness: With The freeness of his Grace in Electing us*. London, 1654.

———. *Justification Cleared*. London, 1654.

Taylor, Thomas. *Christs combate and conquest*. London, 1618.

Twisse, William. *An Answer to a Discourse of D. H. about Predestination.* Oxford, 1653.

———. *The Riches of Gods Love unto the Vessells of Mercy, Consistent with His Absolute Hatred or Reprobation Of the Vessells of Wrath.* 2 pts. Oxford, 1653.

———. *A Treatise of Mr. Cottons, Clearing certaine Doubts Concerning Predestination. Together with an Examination Thereof.* London, 1646.

Walker, Williston. *The Creeds and Platforms of Congregationalism.* Boston: Pilgrim Press, 1960.

Welde, Thomas. *A Short Story of the Rise, reigne, and ruine of the Antinomians.* London, 1644.

Whately, William. *The New Birth.* London, 1619.

Womock, Laurence. *The Examination of Tilenus Before the Triers in order to his intended Settlement in the Office of a Public Preacher, in the Common-wealth of Utopia.* Published in *A Collection of Tracts Concerning Predestination and Providence.* Cambridge, 1719.

SECONDARY SOURCES

Allison, C. F. *The Rise of Moralism: The Proclamation of the Gospel from Hooker to Baxter.* New York: Seabury Press, 1966.

Althaus, Paul. *Der Prinzipien der deutschen reformierten Dogmatik im Zeitalter der aristotelischen Scholastik.* Darmstadt: Wissenschaftliche Buchgesellschaft, 1967.

Armstrong, Brian G. *Calvinism and the Amyraut Heresy: Protestant Scholasticism and Humanism in Seventeenth-Century France.* Madison: University of Wisconsin Press, 1969.

Babbage, Stuart Barton. *Puritanism and Richard Bancroft.* London: SPCK, 1962.

Baker, J. Wayne. *Heinrich Bullinger and the Covenant: The Other Reformation.* Athens, Ohio: Ohio University Press, 1980.

Bangs, Carl. "Arminius and the Reformation." *Church History* 30 (1961):155–70.

———. *Arminius, A Study in the Dutch Reformation.* Nashville: Abingdon Press, 1971.

Battis, Emery. *Saints and Sectaries: Anne Hutchison and the Antinomian Controversy in Massachusetts Bay Colony.* Chapel Hill, N. C., 1963.

Baur, Jörg. *Salus Christiana. Die Rechtfertigungslehre in der Geschichte des christlichen Heilsverständnisses.* Gütersloh: Gütersloher Verlaghaus Gerd Mohn, 1968.

Beebe, David Lewis. "The Seals of the Covenant." Th.D. dissertation, Pacific School of Religion, 1966.

Berkhof, Louis. *Reformed Dogmatics.* 2 vols. Grand Rapids: Wm. B. Eerdmanns, 1932.

Bizer, Ernst. *Frühorthodoxie und Rationalismus*. Theologische Studien, vol. 71. Edited by Karl Barth and Max Geiger. Zurich, 1963.

————. "Reformed Orthodoxy and Cartesianism." Translated by C. Mac-Cormick. *Journal for Theology and the Church* 2 (1965): 20–82.

Boettner, Loraine. *The Reformed Doctrine of Predestination*. The Presbyterian and Reformed Publishing Co., 1932.

Bogue, Carl W. *Jonathan Edwards and the Covenant of Grace*. Cherry Hill, N. J.: Mack Publishing Co., 1975.

Brauer, Jerald C. "Puritan Mysticism and the Development of Liberalism." *Church History* 19 (1950):151–70.

————. "Reflections on the Nature of English Puritanism." *Church History* 23 (1954):99–108.

Breward, Ian. "The Life and Theology of William Perkins." Ph.D. Dissertation, University of Manchester, 1963.

————. "The Significance of William Perkins." *Journal of Religious History* 4 (1966–67):113–28.

————. *The Work of William Perkins*. Abingdon, Berkshire: Sutton Courtenay Press, 1970.

Bronkema, Ralph. *The Essence of Puritanism*. Goes, Holland: Oosterbaan and Le Cointre, 1929.

Brown, William Adams. "Covenant Theology." *Encylopedia of Religion and Ethics*. Edited by James Hastings. 12 vols. New York: C. Scribner's Sons, 1908–22. 4:216–24.

Brumm, Ursula. *Puritanismus und Literatur in Amerika*. Darmstadt: Wissenschaftliche Buchgesellschaft, 1973.

Bush, Sargent, Jr. *The Writings of Thomas Hooker: Spiritual Adventure in Two Worlds*. Madison: University of Wisconsin Press, 1980.

Caldwell, Patricia. *The Puritan Conversion Narrative: The Beginnings of American Expression*. Cambridge: Cambridge University Press, 1983.

Cherry, C. Conrad. "The Puritan Notion of Covenant in Jonathan Edwards' Doctrine of Faith." *Church History* 34 (1965): 328–41.

————. *The Theology of Jonathan Edwards: A Reappraisal*. Garden City, N. Y.: Doubleday & Co., 1966.

Citron, Bernhard. *New Birth: A Study of the Evangelical Doctrine of Conversion in the Protestant Fathers*. Edinburgh: University Press, Clarke, Irwin, 1951.

Clark, Henry W. *History of English Nonconformity*. London: Chapman and Hall, 1911.

Clebsch, William A. *England's Earliest Protestants, 1520–1535*. New Haven: Yale University Press, 1964.

Cohen, Alfred. "Two Roads to the Puritan Millenium: William Enbury and Vavasor Powell." *Church History* 32 (1963):322–38.

Collinson, Patrick. *The Elizabethan Puritan Movement*. London: Jonathan Cape, 1967.

Coolidge, John. *The Pauline Renaissance in England*. Oxford: Clarendon Press, 1970.

Cremeans, Charles Davis. *The Reception of Calvinistic Thought in England*. Urbana: University of Illinois Press, 1949.

Davies, Godfrey. *Arminianism versus Puritanism in England, ca. 1620–1640*. Huntington Library Bulletin No. 5 (1934).

Davies, Horton. *Worship and Theology in England: From Cranmer to Hooker, 1534–1603*. Princeton: Princeton University Press, 1970.

———. *Worship and Theology in England: From Andrewes to Baxter and Fox, 1603–1690*. Princeton: Princeton University Press, 1975.

———. *The Worship of the English Puritans*. London: Dacre Press, 1948.

de Jong, Peter Y. *The Covenant Idea in New England Theology, 1620–1847*. Grand Rapids: Wm. B. Eerdmanns Publishing Co., 1945.

Dorner, J. A. *History of Protestant Theology*. Translated by George Robson and Sophia Taylor. 2 vols. Edinburgh: T. & T. Clark, 1871.

Emerson, Everett H. "Calvin and Covenant Theology." *Church History* 25 (1956):136–44.

———. "Thomas Hooker: The Puritan as Theologian." *Anglican Theological Review* 49 (1967):190–203.

Eusden, John D. "Introduction." William Ames, *The Marrow of Theology*. Translated by John Eusden. Boston: Pilgrim Press, 1968.

———. "Natural Law and Covenant Theology in New England, 1620–1670." *Natural Law Forum* 5 (1960):1–30.

———. *Puritans, Lawyers, and Politics in Early Seventeenth Century England*. New Haven: Yale University Press, 1958.

Fiering, Norman. *Jonathan Edwards's Moral Thought and Its British Context*. Chapel Hill: University of North Carolina Press, 1981.

———. *Moral Philosophy at Seventeenth-Century Harvard*. Chapel Hill: University of North Carolina Press, 1981.

Fisher, George P. *History of Christian Doctrine*. New York: C. Scribner's Sons, 1888.

Foster, Frank Hugh. *A Genetic History of the New England Theology*. Chicago: University of Chicago Press, 1907.

Foster, Herbert Darling. "Liberal Calvinism; the Remonstrants at the Synod of Dort in 1618." *Harvard Theological Review* 16 (1923):1–37.

Foster, Stephen. *Their Solitary Way: The Puritan Social Ethic in the First Century of Settlement in New England*. New Haven: Yale University Press, 1971.

Frere, W. H. *The English Church in the Reigns of Elizabeth and James I*. London: Macmillan, 1904.

Fulcher, J. R. "Puritan Piety in Early New England." Ph.D. dissertation, Princeton University, 1963.

George, Charles H. and George, Katherine. *The Protestant Mind of the*

English Reformation, 1590–1640. Princeton: Princeton University Press, 1961.

George, Timothy. *John Robinson and the English Separatist Tradition.* Macon, Georgia: Mercer University Press, 1982.

Greaves, Richard L. *John Bunyan.* Courtenay Studies in Reformation Theology. vol. 2. Grand Rapids: Wm. B. Eerdmanns Publishing Co., 1969.

————. "John Bunyan and Covenant Thought in the Seventeenth Century." *Church History* 36 (1967):151–69.

————. "The Origins and Early Development of English Covenant Thought." *The Historian* 31 (1968):21–35.

————. *Theology and Revolution in the Scottish Reformation.* Grand Rapids: Christian University Press, 1980.

Gründler, Otto. *Die Gotteslehre Girolami Zanchis und ihre Bedeutung für seine Lehre von der Prädestination.* Neukirchener Verlag des Erziehungsverein, Gmb H, 1965.

Hagen, Kenneth. "From Testament to Covenant in the Early Sixteenth Century." *Sixteenth Century Journal* 3 (1972):1–24.

————. *A Theology of Testament in the Young Luther: the Lectures on Hebrews.* Studies in Medieval and Reformation Thought. vol. 12. Leiden: E. J. Brill, 1974.

Hall, Basil. "Puritanism: the Problem of Definition." *Studies in Church History.* Edited by G. J. Crummey. London, 1965. 2:283–96.

Hall, David D., ed. *The Antinomian Controversy, 1636–1638: A Documentary History.* Middletown, Conn.: Wesleyan University Press, 1968.

————. *The Faithful Shepherd: A History of the New England Ministry in the Seventeenth Century.* Chapel Hill: University of North Carolina Press for the Institute of Early American History and Culture, 1972.

————. ed. *Puritanism in Seventeenth-Century Massachusetts.* New York: Holt, Rinehart and Winston, 1968.

————. "Understanding the Puritans." Stanley N. Katz, ed. *Colonial America: Essays in Political and Social Development.* Boston: Little, Brown and Co., 1971. pp. 31–50.

Haller, William. *Liberty and Reformation in the Puritan Revolution.* New York: Columbia University Press, 1955.

————. *The Rise of Puritanism.* New York: Harper & Bros., 1938.

————. "The Word of God in the New Model Army." *Church History* 19 (1950):15–33.

————. "The Word of God in the Westminster Assembly." *Church History* 18 (1949):199–219.

Hambrick-Stowe, Charles. *The Practice of Piety: Puritan Devotional Disciplines in Seventeenth-Century New England.* Chapel Hill: University of North Carolina Press, 1982.

Hargrave, O. T. "The Freewillers in the English Reformation." *Church History* 37 (1968):271–80.

Harrison, A. W. *Arminianism*. London: Duckworth, 1937.

————. *The Beginnings of Arminianism*. London, 1926.

Heppe, Heinrich. *Geschichte des Pietismus und der Mystik in der Reformierten Kirche*. Leiden: E. J. Brill, 1879.

Hill, Christopher. *Puritanism and Revolution. The English Revolution of the 17th Century*. New York: Schocken, 1958.

Hoekema, Anthony. "The Covenant of Grace in Calvin's Teaching." *Calvin Theological Journal* 2 (1967):133–61.

Holifield, E. Brooks. *The Covenant Sealed: The Development of Puritan Sacramental Theology in Old and New England*. New Haven: Yale University Press, 1974.

Hollinger, David A. "Perry Miller and Philosophical History." *History and Theory* 7 (1968):189–202.

Huehns, G. *Antinomianism in English History*. London: Cresset Press, 1951.

Jackson, Thomas. *The Life of John Goodwin*. London: Longman, Hurst, Rees, Orme and Brown, 1822.

Johnson, George A. "From Seeker to Finder: a Study in Seventeenth Century English Spiritualism Before the Quakers." *Church History* 17 (1948):299–315.

Jones, James W. *The Shattered Synthesis: New England Puritanism Before the Great Awakening*. New Haven: Yale University Press, 1973.

Kendall, R. T. *Calvin and English Calvinism to 1649*. Oxford: Oxford University Press, 1977.

Kevan, Ernest F. *The Grace of Law: A Study in Puritan Theology*. London: The Carey Kingsgate Press, 1964.

Knappen, M. M. *Tudor Puritanism*. Chicago: University of Chicago Press, 1939.

Knox, D. B. *The Doctrine of Faith in the Reign of Henry VIII*. London: James Clarke and Co., 1961.

Lake, Peter. *Moderate Puritans and the Elizabethan Church*. Cambridge: University of Cambridge Press, 1982.

Lang, August. *Puritanismus und Pietismus: Studien zu ihrer Entwicklung von M. Butzer bis zum Methodismus*. Buchhandlung des Erziehungsvereins Neukirchen Kreis Moers, 1941.

Levy, Babette May. *Preaching in the First Half Century of New England History*. Hartford: American Society of Church History, 1945.

Lewis, Peter. *The Genius of Puritanism*. Haywards Heath Sussex: Carey Publications, 1975.

Little, David. *Religion, Order, and Law: A Study of Pre-Revolutionary England*. New York: Harper & Row, 1969.

Lowrie, Ernest Benson. *The Shape of the Puritan Mind: The Theology of Samuel Willard*. New Haven: Yale University Press, 1974.

MacKenzie, J. A. Ross. "The Covenant Theology—A Review Article." *Journal of Presbyterian History* 44 (1966):198–204.

Maclear, James Fulton. " 'The heart of New England rent': The Mystical Element in Early Puritan History." *Mississippi Valley Historical Review* 42 (1956):621–52.

———. "The Puritan Party, 1603–1643: A Study in the Lost Reformation." Ph.D. dissertation, University of Chicago, 1947.

Marsden, George M. "Perry Miller's Rehabilitation of the Puritans: A Critique." *Church History* 39 (1970):91–105.

Martin, Hugh. *Puritanism and Richard Baxter*. London: SCM Press, 1954.

Martin, J. W. "English Protestant Separation at Its Beginnings: Henry Hart and the Free-will Men." *Sixteenth Century Journal* 7 (1976):55–74.

McCoy, Charles S. "The Covenant Theology of Johannes Coccceius, 1603–69." Ph.D. dissertation. Yale University, 1956.

———. "Johannes Coccceius: Federal Theologian." *Scottish Journal of Theology* 16 (1963):352–70.

McGiffert, Michael. "American Puritan Studies in the 1960s." *William and Mary Quarterly*, 3rd series 27 (1970):36–67.

———. "Covenant, Crown, and Commons in Elizabethan Puritanism." *Journal of British Studies* 20 (1981):32–52.

———. ed. *God's Plot: The Paradoxes of Puritan Piety, Being the Autobiography and Journal of Thomas Shepard*. Amherst, Mass.: University of Massachusetts Press, 1972.

———. "Grace and Works: The Rise and Division of Covenant Divinity in Elizabethan Puritanism." *Harvard Theological Review* 75 (1982):463–505.

———. "The Problem of the Covenant in Puritan Thought: Peter Bulkeley's Gospel-Covenant." *New England Historical Genealogical Register* 130 (1976):107–29.

———. "William Tyndale's Conception of Covenant." *Journal of Ecclesiastical History* 32 (1981):167–84.

McKee, William W. "The Idea of Covenant in Early English Puritanism, 1580–1643." Ph.D. dissertation, Yale University, 1948.

McLelland, Joseph C. "The Reformed Doctrine of Predestination according to Peter Martyr." *Scottish Journal of Theology* 8 (1955):257–71.

McNeill, John T. *Modern Christian Movements*. New York: Harper & Row, 1968.

Middlekauf, Robert. *The Mathers: Three Generations of Puritan Intellectuals, 1596–1728*. New York: Oxford University Press, 1971.

Miller, Perry. *Errand into the Wilderness*. Cambridge: Harvard University Press, 1956.

———. *The New England Mind: The Seventeenth Century*. Cambridge: Harvard University Press, 1939.

————. " 'Preparation for Salvation' in Seventeenth Century New England." *Journal of the History of Ideas* 4 (1943): 253–86.

Møller, Jens G. "The Beginnings of Puritan Covenant Theology." *Journal of Ecclesiastical History* 14 (1963):46–67.

Moltmann, Jürgen. "Prädestination und Heilsgeschichte bei Moyse Amyraut." *Zeitschrift für Kirchengeschichte* 65 (1954): 270–303.

————. *Prädestination und Perseveranz.* Neukirchener Verlag, 1961.

Morgan, Edmund S. *The Puritan Dilemma: The Story of John Winthrop.* Boston: Little, Brown, 1958.

————. *Visible Saints: The History of a Puritan Idea.* New York: New York University Press, 1963.

Morgan, Irvonwy. *The Godly Preachers of the Elizabethan Church.* London: Epworth Press, 1965.

————. *The Nonconformity of Richard Baxter.* London: Epworth Press, 1946.

————. *Puritan Spirituality.* London: Epworth Press, 1973.

Morison, Samuel Eliot. *The Intellectual Life of Colonial New England.* Ithaca, 1956.

Muller, Richard A. "Perkins' *A Golden Chaine*: Predestinarian System or Schematized *Ordo Salutis?*" *Sixteenth Century Journal* 9 (1978):69–81.

New, John F. H. *Anglican and Puritan: The Basis of Their Opposition, 1558–1640.* London: Adam & Charles Black, 1964.

Nuttall, Geoffrey F. *The Holy Spirit in Puritan Faith and Experience.* Oxford: Blackwell, 1946.

————. *Richard Baxter.* London: Thos. Nelson and Sons, 1965.

Oki, H. "Ethics in Seventeenth Century English Puritanism." Ph.D. dissertation, Union Theological Seminary, New York, 1960.

Packer, J. I. "The Redemption and Restoration of Man in the Thought of Richard Baxter." D.Phil. dissertation, Oxford University, 1954.

Parker, T. M. "Arminianism and Laudianism in Seventeenth-Century England." *Studies in Church History.* Edited by C. W. Dugmore and Charles Duggan. London: Thos. Nelson and Sons, 1964. 1:20–34.

Perry, Ralph Barton. *Puritanism and Democracy.* New York: Vanguard Press, 1944.

Pettit, Norman. *The Heart Prepared: Grace and Conversion in Puritan Spiritual Life.* New Haven: Yale University Press, 1966.

Priebe, V. L. "The Covenant Theology of William Perkins." Ph.D. dissertation, Drew University, 1967.

Reilly, Bart M. *The Elizabethan Puritan's Conception of the Nature and Destiny of Fallen Man.* Washington, D. C.: Catholic University of America Press, 1948.

Reuter, Karl. "William Ames: The Leading Theologian in the Awakening of Reformed Pietism." Douglas Horton, *William Ames.* Cambridge: Harvard Divinity School Library, 1965. pp. 155–277.

Ritschl, Otto. "Die Entwicklung des Bundesgedankens in der reformierten Theologie des 16. und des 17. Jahrhunderts." *Dogmengeschichte des Protestantismus*. Göttingen: Vandenhoeck & Ruprecht, 1926. 3:412–58.

Rosenmeier, Jesper. "New England's Perfection: The Image of Adam and the Image of Christ in the Antinomian Crisis, 1634 to 1638." *William and Mary Quarterly* 27 (1970):435–59.

Schmidt, Martin. "Biblizismus und natürliche Theologie in der Gewissenslehre des englischen Puritanismus." *Archiv für Reformationsgeschichte* 42 (1951):198–219, 43 (1952):70–87.

Schneider, Herbert W. *The Puritan Mind*. New York: H. Holt & Co., 1930.

Schrenk, Gottlob. *Gottesreich und Bund im älteren Protestantismus vornehmlich bei Johannes Coccejus*. Gütersloh: C. Bertelsmann, 1923.

Solt, Leo F. "Anti-Intellectualism in the Puritan Revolution." *Church History* 25 (1956):306–16.

———. "John Saltmarsh: New Model Army Chaplain." *Journal of Ecclesiastical History* 2 (1951):69–80.

———. *Saints in Arms: Puritanism and Democracy in Cromwell's Army*. Stanford, 1959.

Sommerville, C. J. "Conversion Versus the Early Puritan Covenant of Grace." *Journal of Presbyterian History* 44 (1966):178–97.

Sprunger, Keith L. "Ames, Ramus and the Method of Puritan Theology." *Harvard Theological Review* 59 (1966):133–51.

———. *The Learned Doctor William Ames*. Urbana: University of Illinois Press, 1972.

Stearns, R. P. "Assessing the New England Mind." *Church History* 10 (1941):246–62.

Stoeffler, F. Ernest. *The Rise of Evangelical Pietism*. Leiden: E. J. Brill, 1965.

Stoever, William K. B. 'A Faire and Easie Way to Heaven': *Covenant Theology and Antinomianism in Early Massachusetts*. Middletown, Conn.: Wesleyan University Press, 1978.

Tipson, Baird. "The Development of a Puritan Understanding of Conversion." Ph.D. dissertation, Yale University, 1972.

Toon, Peter. *God's Statesman:The Life and Work of John Owen, Pastor, Educator,Theologian*. Exeter: Paternoster Press, 1971.

Torrance, James B. "Covenant or Contract? A Study of the Theological Background of Worship in Seventeenth-Century Scotland." *Scottish Journal of Theology* 23 (1970):51–76.

Torrance, Thomas F. "Justification: Its Radical Nature and Place in Reformed Doctrine and Life." *Scottish Journal of Theology* 13 (1960):225–46.

———. *The School of Faith: The Catechisms of the Reformed Church*. London, 1959.

Trevelyan, G. M. *England under the Stuarts*. New York: Barnes and Noble, 1965.

Trinterud, Leonard J. "The Origins of Puritanism." *Church History* 20 (1951):37–57.

———. "A Reappraisal of William Tyndale's Debt to Martin Luther." *Church History* 31 (1962):24–45.

Visscher, Hugo. "William Ames: His Life and Works." Douglas Horton, *William Ames*. Cambridge: Harvard Divinity School Library, 1965. pp. 23–154.

von Korff, Emmanuel Graf. *Die Anfänge der Föderaltheologie und ihre erste Ausgestaltung in Zurich und Holland*. Bonn: Emile Eisele, 1908.

von Rohr, John. "Covenant and Assurance in Early English Puritanism." *Church History* 34 (1965):195–203.

———. "*Extra ecclesiam nulla salus*: An Early Congregational Version." *Church History* 36 (1967):107–21.

Wakefield, Gordon S. *Puritan Devotion: Its Place in the Development of Christian Piety*. London: Epworth Press, 1957.

Wallace, Dewey D., Jr. "The Doctrine of Predestination in the Early English Reformation." *Church History* 43 (1974):201–15.

———. *Puritans and Predestination: Grace in English Protestant Theology, 1525–1695*. Chapel Hill: University of North Carolina Press, 1982.

Weir, David A. "*Foedus Naturale*: The Origins of Federal Theology in Sixteenth Century Reformed Thought." D.Phil dissertation, University of Saint Andrews, 1984.

West, W. Morris. "John Hooper and the Origins of Puritanism." *Baptist Quarterly* 15 (1954):346–68, 16 (1955):22–46, 67–88.

Wilcox, William G. "New England Covenant Theology. Its English Precursors and Early American Exponents." Ph.D. dissertation, Duke University, 1959.

Wilson, John F. *Pulpit in Parliament: Puritanism during the English Civil Wars, 1640–1648*. Princeton: Princeton University Press, 1969.

Wood, Thomas. *English Casuistical Divinity During the Seventeenth Century*. London: SPCK, 1952.

Yates, Arthur S. *The Doctrine of Assurance, with Special Reference to John Wesley*. London: Epworth Press, 1952.

Yule, George. "Theological Developments in English Puritanism." *Journal of Religious History* 1 (1960):16–25.

———. "Developments in English Puritanism in the Context of the Reformation." *Transactions* supplement (1964):8–27.

Ziff, Larzer. *The Career of John Cotton, Puritanism and the American Experience*. Princeton: Princeton University Press, 1962.

INDEX OF PERSONS

INDEX OF SUBJECTS